J. L. AUSTIN

The Arguments of
the Philosophers

EDITOR: TED HONDERICH

Grote Professor of the Philosophy of
Mind and Logic, University College, London

The purpose of this series is to provide a contemporary assessment and
history of the entire course of philosophical thought. Each book
constitutes a detailed, critical introduction to the work of a philosopher
of major influence and significance.

Already published in the series

Ayer	John Foster
Augustine	Christopher Kirwan
*Bentham	Ross Harrison
*Berkeley	George Pitcher
Bergson	A. R. Lacey
Butler	Terence Penelhum
*Descartes	Margaret Dauler Wilson
Dewey	J. E. Tiles
Gottlob Frege	Hans Sluga
Hegel	M. J. Inwood
Hobbes	Tom Sorell
*Hume	Barry Stroud
Husserl	David Bell
William James	Graham Bird
*Kant	Ralph C. S. Walker
Kierkegaard	Alastair Hannay
*Karl Marx	Allen Wood
John Stuart Mill	John Skorupski
G. E. Moore	Tom Baldwin
*Nietzsche	Richard Schacht
Peirce	Christopher Hookway
*Plato	J. C. B. Gosling
*Karl Popper	Anthony O'Hear
*The Presocratic Philosophers	Jonathan Barnes
Thomas Reid	Keith Lehrer
*Russell	R. M. Sainsbury
*Sartre	Peter Caws
*Schopenhauer	D. W. Hamlyn
Socrates	Peter Caws
*Socrates	Gerasimos Xenophon Santas
Spinoza	R. J. Delahunty
*Wittgenstein	Robert J. Fogelin

*Available in Paperback

J. L. AUSTIN

G. J. Warnock

R

Routledge
London and New York

First published 1989
by Routledge
11 New Fetter Lane, London EC4P 4EE
29 West 35th Street, New York, NY 10001

Set in Garamond 10/12pt
by Input Typesetting Ltd, London
and printed in Great Britain
by T. J. Press (Padstow) Ltd,
Padstow, Cornwall

British Library Cataloguing in Publication Data

Warnock, G. J. (Geoffrey James), *1923–*

J. L. Austin. (The arguments of the philosophers).
1. English philosophy. Austin, John Langshaw
I. Title II. Series
192

ISBN 0–415–02962–7

Library of Congress Cataloging in Publication Data

Warnock, G. J. (Geoffrey James), 1923–
J. L. Austin.
(The Arguments of the philosophers)
Bibliography: p.
Includes index.
1. Austin, J. L. (John Langshaw), 1911–1960.
I. Title. II. Series.
B1618.A84W37 1989 192 88–32338

Contents

Preface   vii

I	INTRODUCTION	1
II	PERCEPTION AND OTHER MATTERS	11
III	KNOWLEDGE AND OTHER MINDS	32
IV	TRUTH	45
V	EXCUSES AND ACCUSATIONS	65
VI	IFS AND CANS	80
VII	SOME OTHER PAPERS	98
VIII	WORDS AND DEEDS	105

Bibliographical Note   152
Notes   153
Index   163

Preface

I have conceived what follows as a book about Austin, rather than about Austin and his critics and commentators. I have accordingly aimed at plain exposition and discussion of his texts, rather than at much examination of the controversial literature to which some of them have given rise. I hope that those many people who have written about Austin will not assume, if their contributions are unmentioned here, that I have not read or do not esteem them – though the opposite assumption, I fear, may also not always be quite safe.

G. J. Warnock,
Hertford College,
Oxford
April 1988

I

Introduction

Austin died in February 1960, at the age of 48. He would have been 49 on 26 March of that year. Though comparatively young, he held at that time, and in fact had held for a good many years, a leading position among philosophers not only in Oxford – where he lived and taught – but in Britain, and to some extent in the English-speaking world as a whole. He had been elected in 1952 to one of Oxford's only three (at that time) professorships of philosophy – a noteworthy election, in that the chair in question, that of the White's Professor of Moral Philosophy, was 'officially' in a field in which he was only pretty marginally interested and had published nothing; it must have been felt that it would nevertheless have looked obviously wrong to elect anybody else, and fortunately the University had long countenanced considerable latitude in such matters. In 1955 he delivered, but by 1960 was still revising for possible publication, the William James lectures at Harvard.

His immensely high standing among philosophers was certainly not attributable, at any time, to sheer quantity of publication. At the date of his election as White's Professor he had edited H. W. B. Joseph's *Lectures on the Philosophy of Leibniz*,[1] had translated Frege's *Grundlagen der Arithmetik*,[2] and had published only three papers of his own; and of the thirteen articles now included in his *Philosophical Papers* (1961; 3rd edition 1979) only seven were actually published in his own lifetime. His two books – *Sense and Sensibilia* and *How to Do Things with Words* (the latter being the text of his William James lectures) – both appeared after his death. That his reputation owed much to his certainly formidable personality is probably, though usually said by would-be detractors, not entirely untrue; he was a natural leader, and could scarcely have been inconspicuous in any company. But of course it rested, and rests, essentially upon the quality of his writings – above all, I think, upon a quality of originality, of 'newness', that he brought to any topic – and upon the vitality of his performance, not so much in

1

lecturing (which he did not greatly enjoy) as in teaching and discussion, in every degree of formality and informality. But it is probably inevitable that in a case such as his – in which formal writing for publication played so comparatively small a part – the impression that he made as a philosopher upon those who knew him may be difficult fully to appreciate for those not included in that now diminishing number.

He had been primarily a classical scholar as a schoolboy at Shrewsbury, and in his early undergraduate years at Balliol had again achieved distinction in classical scholarship. But it was as a philosopher that he was elected to a Fellowship at All Souls in 1933, and he began regularly to teach philosophy in 1935, when he became a Fellow and tutor at Magdalen. His career, like many another, was interrupted by the war, in which he served for six years in the Intelligence Corps, eventually with the rank of lieutenant-colonel (and receiving French and American, as well as British, decorations for his notable services). After the war his principal service to his University, apart of course from his teaching and lecturing, was to the Oxford University Press. He became a 'Delegate' in 1952, and from 1957 was Chairman of its Finance Committee – the most important, and certainly by far the most responsible and laborious, non-professional office in that very large publishing business. He was by no means a reclusive, unworldly, unpractical academic. He would have made, for instance, a first-rate Cabinet Secretary – unless perhaps Ministers would have found him too formidable for their comfort, as some of his academic colleagues certainly did from time to time.[3]

Was Austin a linguistic philosopher? At one time many people would have thought this a reasonably answerable question, and many would have said without hesitation that the answer was 'Yes' – perhaps, even, that he was *the* linguistic philosopher. (I was interested to see that, as recently as 1987, Austin was described by Sir Alfred Ayer, in dialogue with Bryan Magee, as 'a linguistic philosopher in the narrowest possible sense'.) I think it may be worth considering – I hope without undue raking-over of archaic embers – first what that (actually) rather obscure question might mean, and also why the label 'linguistic philosophy' now seems to me, as applied to Austin's work, more liable to be obfuscatory than helpful.

One thing that a linguistic philosopher, usefully so called, might be would be one who held a particular view of the relation between philosophy and language – such as that the typical problems and perplexities of philosophy are in some way latent in, or generated by, or spring out of, language itself, and are therefore to be solved, or in one way or another dealt with, by the scrutiny of language. Such a view has of course been held. Gilbert Ryle, at least for a time, though he would not have liked the label 'linguistic philosopher', was inclined to the idea that philosophical troubles typically arise because in some cases current forms of expression in natural languages are, as he put it, 'systematically misleading'; linguistic-surface congruities and superficial linguistic similarities overlay and may blind us to deep conceptual differences, so that we seek, uncomfortably and sometimes even nonsensically, to represent and to discuss one 'kind of thing' as if it were some radically different 'kind of thing', just because we *seem* to speak of both in much the same way.[4] If so, then the goal of philosophy would be resistance to being thus misled: to unmask misleading forms of expression *as* misleading, to avoid the snares of false analogy and misassimilation which language lays under our feet, and so to do away with the discomfort and puzzlement of trying to squeeze our thought into forms that will not fit. Wittgenstein, too, more famously, often spoke in very much the same vein:

> We have to resist 'the bewitchment of our intelligence by means of language', superstitions 'produced by grammatical illusions', 'through a misinterpretation of our forms of language'; therefore, we must look 'into the workings of our language, and that in such a way as to make us recognize those workings: *in despite of* an urge to misunderstand them'. We must make it our aim to 'command a clear view', in spite of the fact that 'our forms of expression prevent us in all sorts of ways' from seeing clearly what lies before us.[5]

This would be linguistic philosophy in at least one comparatively good and clear sense; the thesis is that philosophical problems arise *because of* (certain features of) our language, and that it is therefore our language itself to which we must attend – resisting 'bewitchment' – if those problems are to be solved, or dissipated, or done away with. I suppose that, in a different, cruder, and more dogmatic way, Logical Positivism too could be intelligibly and defensibly said to be a species of 'linguistic' philosophy. For one thing, in that doctrine the characteristic sin of philosophers (other than Logical Positivists) was diagnosed as a linguistic one, namely the proliferation of 'meaningless' sentences, 'pseudo-propositions'; and more importantly, the legitimate role for philosophy being said to be that of 'analysis', the subject-matter of legitimate philosophy was itself held to be linguistic, namely the analysis of propositions of mathematics and the natural sciences.

It is certain that Austin was not a linguistic philosopher in any such sense. Not only did he embrace no 'theory' of philosophy assigning to language any central or primary role in the generation of typical philosophical problems, or for any other reason making language the special subject-matter of philosophical investigation; he in fact held no such general theory of philosophy at all – unless a certain purely negative view could be accounted a theory. If one had asked him 'What makes a philosophical question *philosophical?*', he would have said in effect – if, indeed, he had been willing to answer such a question at all – 'Its *not* being a question of any other recognizable kind'. In no other way – which is really to say, in no way – were the questions debated among philosophers to be seen as a *special kind* of questions, or to be usefully characterized in any single, general way. He used here several times the image of sun and planets – for example in the closing paragraph of 'Ifs and cans':

> In the history of human inquiry, philosophy has the place of the initial central sun, seminal and tumultuous: from time to time it throws off some portion of itself to take station as a science, a planet, cool and well-regulated, progressing steadily towards a distant final state. This happened long ago at the birth of mathematics, and again at the birth of physics: only in the last century we have witnessed the same process once again, slow and at the time almost imperceptible, in the birth of the science of mathematical logic, through the joint labours of philosophers and mathematicians. Is it not possible that the next century may see the birth, through the joint labours of philosophers, grammarians, and numerous other students of language, of a true and comprehensive *science of language?* Then we shall have rid ourselves of one more part of philosophy (there will still be plenty left) in the only way we ever can get rid of philosophy, by kicking it upstairs.[6]

It would no doubt be a mistake to take this sort of peroration over-seriously (did he *really* think that the sciences, once safely born, were 'progressing steadily towards a distant *final state*'?); the general point for the present purpose is that, even if a future comprehensive 'science of language' should emerge *out of* philosophy, 'there will still be plenty left'. There is in Austin's view no case for saying that philosophy just *is* – though there may well be a good case for saying that it includes – a science of language in an unformed, embryonic state. It includes a lot else as well.

But, it may be said, even if Austin was not a linguistic philosopher in *that* sense – even if he espoused no general theory about philosophy itself which presented language pre-eminently as both its cause and cure – surely he did notoriously assign to a certain kind of linguistic inquiry a central role in philosophical *method*. This deserves to be taken more seriously, and looked at in some detail. It is less obviously untrue.

In 'A plea for excuses', Austin himself refers to the 'method' of proceeding 'from "ordinary language", that is by examining *what we should say when*, and so why and what we should mean by it'. Perhaps, he goes on to say, 'this method, at least as *one* philosophical method, scarcely requires justification at present';[7] but he does offer one or two remarks by way of justification. The paragraph that follows has been

4

quoted almost *ad nauseam*, but it seems necessary to quote it once again here:

> First, words are our tools, and, as a minimum, we should use clean tools: we should know what we mean and what we do not, and we must forearm ourselves against the traps that language sets us. Secondly, words are not (except in their own little corner) facts or things: we need therefore to prise them off the world, to hold them apart from and against it, so that we can realize their inadequacies and arbitrariness, and can re-look at the world without blinkers. Thirdly, and more hopefully, our common stock of words embodies all the distinctions men have found worth drawing, and the connexions they have found worth marking, in the lifetimes of many generations: these surely are likely to be more numerous, more sound, since they have stood up to the long test of the survival of the fittest, and more subtle, at least in all ordinary and reasonably practical matters, than any that you or I are likely to think up in our arm-chairs of an afternoon – the most favoured alternative method.[8]

And again:

> Certainly ordinary language has no claim to be the last word, if there is such a thing. It embodies, indeed, something better than the metaphysics of the Stone Age, namely, as was said, the inherited experience and acumen of many generations of men. . . . [But] certainly ordinary language is *not* the last word: in principle it can everywhere be supplemented and improved upon and superseded. Only remember, it *is* the *first* word.[9]

The main thing that needs to be said, I think, about these oft-quoted passages is that we must get right way up, so to speak, the claim that Austin is putting forward here. I think it has usually been assumed that he is commending, even if in fairly cautious terms, a certain 'method' of doing philosophy – the 'method' of making a *beginning* (at any rate) by scrutinizing the resources of 'ordinary language', of examining 'what we should say when'. And of course that is right enough, in a way; no doubt he did think that that was often a good way to begin, and particularly in discussions he quite often did begin in that manner. Nevertheless, what he is actually doing in these pages of 'A plea for excuses' is *not* that way up; he is actually not commending a philosophical method, but rather commending a philosophical *topic*, *if* one chooses to proceed in that way. Examining the resources of 'ordinary language' – 'the inherited experience and acumen of many generations' – is a way (notice that he carefully and explicitly does not say *the* way) of making a start; and *if* you are going to make a start in that way, then the subject of 'excuses' is, he says, a rather specially appropriate topic for the purpose. It is 'an attractive subject methodologically, at least if we are to proceed from "ordinary language" '. Obviously this is not to say that 'proceeding from ordinary language' is *the* way even to get started on a piece of philosophical inquiry; it is to imply, quite clearly, not only that there are other ways, but also that there are areas of philosophical inquiry in which the 'ordinary language' way would not be particularly promising.

It is worth noting that Austin recommends the topic of excuses – 'a good site for *field work* in philosophy'[10] – also for the reason that we have useful material to hand here 'in the shape of the Law'. 'This will provide us with an immense miscellany of untoward cases, and also with a useful list of recognized pleas, together with a good deal of acute analysis of both.' Admittedly, this sort of material may sit rather uneasily with that supplied from 'ordinary language' – for, since law requires that an immense variety of novel and complicated questions be actually *decided* in not unmanageably complicated terms, 'it is necessary first to be careful with, but also to be brutal with, to fake and to override, ordinary language: we cannot here evade or forget the whole affair' – because we have to *decide*. 'Nevertheless, it is a perpetual and salutary surprise to discover how much is to be learned from the law.'[11] Now, very obviously, Austin is not recommending attention to the law as some sort of sovereign nostrum in philosophy; he recommends it for particular cases in which it is likely to prove helpful; and he recommends attention to 'ordinary language' for *exactly the same reason*, remarking for good measure that, if we bring law into the picture, it will be particularly evident that the niceties of ordinary language are not the 'last word'.

As if foreseeing how the (uncharacteristically) programmatic remarks in 'A plea for excuses' might be misconstrued – might be taken, as they all too often have been, to be propounding an ambitious new methodology for philosophy in general – Austin later gave, to a set of notes for an informal talk on the subject, the title 'Something about one way of possibly doing one part of philosophy'.[12] That is worth remembering. It is also quite evident, in fact, from his own writings that he was not wedded to any particular 'linguistic' method of proceeding. More usually, he just *argues* – just as anybody else might do, or try to do.

What did Austin think, then, about philosophy in general? What is there to be said? I have already mentioned one negative thing: he thought that the questions typically, recurrently, in some cases indeed perennially, debated among philosophers were *not* of any single, specific sort. But there was something else that he thought remarkable about those questions, namely the extraordinary paucity of *agreement* as to how they should be answered. Philosophy seemed to him extraordinarily, even shockingly, at times almost laughably, disorderly and inconclusive. Argument among philosophers seemed to consist in perpetual wrangling and disputation, never-ending controversy and disagreement, perpetual refutation and counter-refutation, almost pathetically unlike his (idealized!) picture of 'a science . . . cool and well regulated, progressing steadily towards a distant final state'; it was not easy to see it, in fact, as *progressing* at all. It is crucially important to understanding his general view of the subject both that he was powerfully struck by this unflattering, but scarcely unfair or unrealistic, picture of what philosophy, historically speaking, was in general like, and also that he did not believe the case to be beyond hope or cure. Inconclusive wrangling was indeed characteristic of philosophy, but not in his opinion *intrinsic* to it. It has indeed been held by some to be somehow in the nature of philosophy that it should not be 'progressive' in the manner of a natural science, that its theories and theses should be essentially, permanently, inherently, inconclusive and contestable, its questions for-ever open, and that philosophy itself should inescapably have the form of a never-ending debate. Austin's own view was simpler, less sophisticated, more austere; he thought that philosophers should simply *try much harder*. There were, he thought, failings to which philosophers were particularly prone, which were particularly liable to issue in perpetual wrangling, but which, if not perhaps completely eliminable by imperfect human beings, might at least be diminished by conscientious effort. Nor is there any mystery as to what he thought those failings were. They were carelessness; haste; a persistent tendency to invent and to rely on ill-defined and slippery technical terms; over-simplification; reckless and premature generalization; and, perhaps above all, a predilection for ambitious either-or dichotomies. (And of course these overlap: the dichotomy of 'judgments of perception' into 'sense-datum propositions' and 'material-object propositions' manages to look sustainable in so far as it relies on two, perhaps three, ill-defined technical terms.) It would not be very helpful, I think, to say much more about this in general terms. The sorts of things that, in Austin's opinion, are liable to go wrong in philosophy, and some at least of the sorts of ways in which he tried to make things go better, will, I hope, become clearer in con-sidering his particular arguments, both critical and constructive. I would wish simply to emphasize what might be called the unsophistication of Austin's general attitude. He thought that philosophy brought before us difficult, unclear questions – often difficult at least partly *because* unclear – treatment of which called for cleverness, lucidity, care, industry, and patience. It was the last four of these requisites that he found to be in short supply.

There are two things, however, that I would like to mention in con-cluding these introductory musings. In the last paragraph of the last paper published in his own lifetime, Austin says – having raised the question why the topic of that paper was 'important' – 'I am not sure importance is important: truth is'.[13] This is obviously a bit of an epigram, no doubt deliberately provocative, and needs some commentary. I have even heard it suggested that the remark must have been really disingenuous. For one thing, Austin certainly did not believe, as indeed a great many published remarks of his own make quite clear, that truth *was* 'important', just like that: one could easily, and uselessly, make sure that everything one said or wrote was true, simply by sticking firmly to uncontentious, incontestable trivialities. Nor surely did he believe – it would even be rather scandalous if he *had* believed – that philosophy itself was perhaps *un*important, or that philosophers should never bother their academic heads with the question whether what they were engaged in was or was not worth doing. I think it certain that he had two things chiefly in mind. First, on the matter of 'importance': certainly we shall wish, in general, to turn our thoughts to matters that, in one way or another, seem worth seriously thinking about; and that may well mean that our chosen topic is – as he says, for example, of his own topic of 'excuses' – 'neighbouring, analogous or germane in some way to some notorious centre of philosophical trouble'.[14] But what we should *not* do is assume that it is already known, known in advance, what are the 'important' questions to raise and to consider. To make that assumption is too likely to mean that we stick forever to 'traditional' questions and manoeuvres, and so to fields already 'trodden into bogs or tracks' by traditional philosophy. It may well be more hopeful to look at less familiar matters, matters not already well-thumbed and much-mooted in the tradition (even though 'germane' to it); we do not *know* that nothing 'important' will come of doing so. At the very least, if we can restrain our impetuosity well enough to keep away for a while from the bogs and tracks, 'we should be able to unfreeze, to loosen up and get going on agreeing about discoveries, however small, and on agreeing about how to reach agreement'.[15] Perhaps he may also have had in mind a rather different point. It is usually thought to be a merit in a creative artist, a poet, say, or a composer, to be 'original'; but one could make a strong case, I believe, for the view that it is not a good thing at all for an artist to *try* to be original, to adopt originality as a conscious aim. Perhaps it would be equally dubious in a philosopher too consciously to *try* to say 'important' things. One can see all too well how that could go badly wrong.

Then about 'truth': certainly Austin did not think that a philosophical doctrine or dictum was, necessarily, completely worthless if it was *not* true; on the contrary, 'in philosophy, there are many mistakes that it is no disgrace to have made: to make a first-water, ground-floor mistake, so far from being easy, takes one (*one*) form of philosophical genius'.[16] And of course he did not think that any dictum at all merited much respect *simply* for being true. I think he had in mind two things here. The first would be, I think, that philosophers – whose constructions

8

unfortunately, unlike those of engineers for example, do not literally have to face the relentless test of whether they will stand up – are liable, in the stress of theoretical ambition and excitement, to be extraordinarily *careless* about truth in minor matters, and often in matters that are not minor at all. The second, more importantly perhaps, would be that philosophical dicta are liable to be so vague, so obscure, so ill-formulated, so vastly general or so loftily abstract, or so much freighted and frilled with jargon and 'technical' neologism, as to offer no serious hope of its ever being decideable whether they are true or not. *One* thing that Austin thought highly desirable in philosophy was that we should aim to have on our plate, so to speak, questions of such shape and size as at least to hold out some realistic prospect of our deciding – and *agreeing* – whether or not some putative answer was true. It was 'important' to try to set up our inquiries in such a way that solid truth was, at least in principle, an attainable objective, something that could seriously be hoped for.

The other thing that I would like to mention is this. I believe one could say that the only rather special view – idiosyncratic view, perhaps – that Austin really did hold about 'method' in philosophy was the view that, ideally, it would be a *co-operative* pursuit.[17] I mentioned a moment ago that he was distressed, even scandalized, by the paucity of agreement in philosophy, its depressing appearance of perpetual dissension and wrangling about almost everything. I have cited too his highly significant words about getting going 'on agree[ment] about discoveries, however small, and on agreeing about how to reach agreement'. I am quite sure that he believed that the best way, perhaps the only way, to reach solid agreement was by way of co-operative (not competitive) discussion of (well-defined) questions among (reasonably like-minded) collaborators; and I believe that, as a matter of fact, he greatly preferred that form of philosophical activity to that of the solitary composition of lectures, articles, or books. He certainly devoted much more time to it. That is, I think, more unusual than perhaps it looks at first sight. For some reason the traditional paradigm of academic work – in 'arts' subjects at any rate, much less so in the sciences – has come to be (as it was not in classical, or at any rate Greek antiquity) that of the solitary toiler alone in his study, single-handedly at work on 'his' paper, 'his' book, his individual contribution. Austin, I think, deeply distrusted this in-dividual-centred paradigm. If your aim is – really and *seriously* is – not to make a certain individual effect, not to contribute to literature or to the general cultural stock, but to reach conclusions on some matter that are actually *so*, does it not look sensible to, as it were, try things out as you go along on other critical people – the closest, perhaps, one can get to an 'experimental' test? If, say, a dozen or so colleagues actually agree, that is at any rate better than no agreement at all, and there is at least a fair chance that what seems to them all, after patient discussion, to be

9

acceptable, may actually be true. To mention again the topic that Austin called 'excuses': he writes 'I owe it to the subject to say, that it has long afforded me what philosophy is so often thought, and made, barren of – the fun of discovery, the pleasures of co-operation, and the satisfaction of reaching agreement'.[18] That, if anything, was his view of philosophical method: discussion – careful, critical discussion – in the hope and with the intention of reaching agreement, and with the consequential hope of getting something right.

II

Perception and Other Matters

The little book *Sense and Sensibilia*, which was published in 1962, stands apart from Austin's other writings in certain respects, and I had better begin by saying something about that.

First, it is almost throughout undeviatingly negative, critical, even polemically critical. Austin usually, in the writings he published or intended to publish, took up a question because there was something that he wished to say about it; he seldom wrote with the primary purpose of showing that what somebody else had written about it was wrong. *Sense and Sensibilia* is something of an exception to that (on the whole, no doubt, admirable) policy. It is, at least primarily, simply *against* some things that Ayer had said in his book *The Foundations of Empirical Knowledge*,[1] and does not undertake much of the positive task of handling better what he claims to be badly mishandled in that book. It is not, as I shall argue later, that Austin believed that whole battery of issues to be simply bogus or unreal; but he does not say much in the book either of how the issues should be treated, or even of what he thought the issues really were.

Second, it is much the least 'finished' of his printed works, and in fact it was, literally, never finished at all, but existed at his death only in the form of successive sets of notes for lectures, which had been progressively amended and tinkered with over a number of years. There is no way of knowing whether he ever seriously intended publication. The care with which his notes were kept, and progressively revised, might suggest that he did; but it is not impossible that, recognizing the rather 'negative' quality already mentioned, he may have felt that a mere rebuttal of someone else's writing was not worth the trouble, or at any rate was not the sort of thing that he usually did.

I ought of course to mention, next, the rather curious point that the printed text we have is, in a sense, actually mine rather than Austin's; not of course that it expresses – at least I hope it does not – any

11

philosophical views of mine rather than his, but in that I put into grammatical sentences and continuous paragraphs what was, in the manuscripts, unprintably fragmentary, as an experienced lecturer's notes would very naturally be. I said in the Foreword, written in 1960, that 'the most that can be claimed – though I venture to claim this with confidence – is that in all points of substance (and in *many* points of phraseology) his *argument* was the argument which this books contains'. I say the same now: not all of the words are Austin's, but the argument is his.[2]

One prefatory word more. In what follows I have, I fear, actually exaggerated the 'negative' aspect of *Sense and Sensibilia*. In the book Austin turns aside, from time to time, from his critical hatchet-work to sketch what he takes to be right on certain matters. Thus, besides complaining that Ayer and others tend to shuffle about such words as 'looks', 'appears', and 'seems' as if they were more or less equivalent, he has things of his own to say about their uses and the differences of each from the others. Besides complaining that Ayer's account of what 'real' means is wrong or at least very inadequate, he has important suggestions of his own to make about the proper understanding of 'real' and 'really'. Again, he has interesting things to say about 'vague' and 'precise', 'accurate' and 'exact'. I have passed over these, regretfully, simply because I felt that pursuit of the main-line critical argument needed all the space I had. It is some consolation that what Austin had positively to say on these topics is – though some of it at least has been quite fiercely criticized[3] – not at all obscure, and not in need of elucidation.

The difficulty that a reader may have with *Sense and Sensibilia* is unlikely to arise, one might say, from the text itself. That text, though terse – and no doubt Austin expanded upon it to some extent, in delivering the lectures for which it constituted the basis – is on the whole perfectly clear, and in a sense not difficult; the points made are straightforward enough, and the structure of argument is not in the least convoluted or elaborate; the language is without technicalities, and as plain as could be. The possible puzzle might be expressed in various ways: how does Austin's argument fit in? To what doctrines, or whose doctrines, if to any, is it effectively fatal? What, or how much, is Austin undertaking to do? What, and how much, can he be held to have succeeded in doing? Though not an obscure text, it is certainly a rather strange one: what is it *for*? What does it *do*?

I think there are at least two reasons why this sort of puzzle is liable to arise – a puzzle not as to what is being said, but as to what, when it *has* been said, we are to make of it, how it should be taken. The first reason involves the history of (most) philosophical writing on perception. The main target of Austin's critical fire in *Sense and Sensibilia* is that venerable piece of philosophical weaponry called 'the argument from illusion'; and while it is reasonably clear, in the tradition, how that 'argument' is supposed to go, there has been a considerable diversity of opinion from time to time as to what exactly it proves. It has certainly been held by some writers to show that, in the matter of perception and everyday judgments of perception, the pre-philosophical 'plain man' holds beliefs which are simply false, untenable, and which accordingly stand in need of philosophical correction. Another view has been that while the plain man's beliefs may not be actually false, the argument shows at least that there is something defective in the plain man's plain language, a defect to be cured by a philosophically purified variant. But if there is, as there is in fact, this degree (and much more) of instability in what the 'argument from illusion' has been supposed to prove, there will be a corresponding sort of complexity in the contention that it does not work as it has been supposed to: in *which* of those supposed ways is it contended to fail? In all of them, or only in some of them? If it does not prove what has been claimed, are we to conclude perhaps that it proves nothing at all? What *are* we to conclude? The murk is deepened, in the present case, by the fact that Austin surveys the argument from illusion mainly, though not quite exclusively, as it is expounded by Ayer in *The Foundations of Empirical Knowledge;* and Ayer's exposition makes it perfectly clear that he himself does not for a moment suggest that the 'argument' proves all that has been traditionally claimed for it; he has very substantial reservations of his own. Thus Austin's critical fire is directed, one might say, at an extraordinarily wobbly, wandering, and even wispy, target; and if that is the case, there is room for understandable uncertainty as to whether he has hit it or, if he has, what damage has been done.

The other reason, of greater interest and importance, has to do with Austin's own general intentions. He believed – and it is difficult indeed not to agree with him on this – that traditional, time-hallowed modes of argumentation about perception instantiated (I put it, for brevity, rather too rudely) a characteristic tendency of philosophers, while continuing to talk, to stop thinking; the points routinely made, the jejune little list of 'examples' repetitively deployed, the conclusions drawn, had come, he felt, to be not much more than recited as a sort of formulae, professional patter, shuffled rapidly around like counters in a familiar game; philosophers had become habituated to a certain way of talking, to a certain repertoire of 'moves', and had ceased to consider, to look really closely at, what they were talking about, or really to apply their minds and their critical faculties to what they were saying about it. Accordingly an important part of what he wanted was, so to speak, to interrupt the performance, to slow things down, to put a spoke or two in the familiar revolving wheels; and he sought to do this in a way that would seem absolutely natural if it were not so acutely disconcerting: by saying 'But wait a moment – *is it true?*' I believe that the targets of his criticism felt, and it is not at all unnatural that some of his readers should feel, that there is something somehow unfair about this way of proceeding, something negative, obstructive, wilfully uncooperative. These philosophers are doing their best to attack important problems, and Austin seems merely to want to stop them, to trip them up in a thicket of pedantic over-exactitude. As Professor Pears has said, many people even found this whole manner of doing philosophy

> maddening. For consecutive thought is such a difficult achievement that it is natural to feel resentment when someone takes up the first word and questions its exact application. He is not playing the game. But of course he is not. That is his whole point.[4]

There is that reason too, then, for perplexity as to how *Sense and Sensibilia* is to be taken: if in some sense he is not playing the familiar game at all, what is to count as winning or losing? But perhaps what Austin wanted was not to win the game, but to get his readers to ask themselves whether they really wanted to go on playing it.

Let us consider the outlines of an argument which, following Ayer quite closely, one might write down like this: the plain man believes that, in perception, he is directly aware of material things. But the recurrence of 'illusions' – of refraction, reflection, mirages, double vision, hallucination – shows at least that this cannot *always* be true. For in these cases there is either no material thing at all of which he is aware, or things are not in reality as they appear to him to be. In such cases it must be something else of which the percipient is directly aware; let us call this sort of item, the object of direct awareness, by the technical term 'sense-datum'. But now these cases of 'illusion' in which the percipient is deceived by his senses are not intrinsically distinguishable from those in which he is not so deceived. This would mean there is reason to conclude that that which he directly perceives is *always* a sense-datum, never a material thing as the plain man supposes; and these sense-data will be sometimes 'veridical', sometimes 'delusive': things sometimes are as they appear, but sometimes not.

Austin contends, I believe, that a line of argument such as this, which at one time would have seemed quite routine and wholly unsurprising to many philosophers, is in fact objectionable, sometimes multiply objectionable, in every sentence. Take it step by step.

Does the plain man believe that he perceives material things – that is, that he *always* perceives material things, or that everything he perceives is a material thing? There is really no clear answer to that question straight off, since 'material thing' is not a plain man's expression: but it

14

seems that, however that so far unelucidated expression might be eluci-
dated, the answer will have to be that the plain man believes no such
thing. Among things that he sees, is the sky a material thing? Does he
believe that it is? Or a rainbow, or the beam from a searchlight, or a
reflection in water, or a flash of light, or the flame of a candle? Among
things that he hears, is a voice a material thing? Is any sound? He is said
further to believe that he perceives material things 'directly'. It is again
not in the least clear what that means; but we do at any rate have the
notion of looking directly at something; and if so, if that is the sort of
thing that 'directly' means, then surely we do sometimes see a thing
directly, and equally certainly – when looking through a periscope perhaps, or into a mirror – sometimes we do not. And in any case the
notion of directness or otherwise – of a *straight line* or otherwise – seems
not naturally to fit in any case except that of vision; what would smelling
*in*directly be, or feeling *in*directly?

Austin further objects, with reason, to this venerable argument's venerable name: the argument from 'illusion'. For most of the cases cited, he
observes, appear not really to be cases of illusion at all. It is possible,
no doubt, to produce illusions by the cunning use of mirrors; but the
argument appears to claim, surely quite wrongly, that illusion occurs
whenever one looks into a mirror. Again it is possible, by cunning use
of perspective, to give the illusion that a piazza, say, is larger than it
really is; but to some extent perspective rules, so to speak, whenever we
look at almost anything. Is it to be suggested that almost *all* vision is a
case of illusion? Further, it is clearly not the case, as the argument
suggests that it is, that even a true case of illusion – say Müller-Lyer's
parallel lines, which obstinately look of different lengths though in fact
they are equal – must raise a doubt as to *what it is* that the perceiver
sees; in that very case, for example, there is no such doubt: he sees two
parallel lines on a page, of which one looks, though it is not, longer
than the other. If a church is camouflaged to look like a barn, then that
is what we see when we look at it – a church that looks like a barn; and
that is true, whether or not we are disposed to conclude that it *is* a barn.

Again, cases differ: when, in perception, we might be inclined to say
that in some way or other something is 'wrong', there are important
differences in *what* is wrong. There is no single, cover-all diagnosis, such
as that the perceiver is not really perceiving what he incautiously believes
that he is. Sometimes what is 'wrong' is the sensory organ itself: if two
objects different in colour look indistinguishable to me, perhaps I am
colour-blind. Sometimes the conditions or attendant circumstances are
'wrong': we are looking at things under a strong red light, say, or
through a refracting medium. Sometimes it may be just that one thing
looks very like another: a woman seen against a dark background with
her head in a black bag may look (from a certain distance) just like a

headless woman. And sometimes – a very importantly different case – there may be something badly 'wrong' with the perceiver himself: he may for instance be hallucinating, seeming to see or hear (though not necessarily believing that he actually does) 'sights' or 'sounds' which are simply not there to be seen or heard at all. It seems to be no service to clarity to seek to lump all these (and other) cases together as 'illusions', as cases of perceiving 'delusive sense-data', or some such phrase. The cases differ importantly, and that fact should not be slurred over and obscured.

There is much more detail, of course, in Austin's survey of this part of the traditional 'argument', but it is already possible to sum up, I think, what he first seeks to show, and (surely) succeeds in showing. The implied allegation is (at this stage) that the 'argument from illusion' effectively undermines the plain man's *beliefs*, and shows that, in his general views about everyday perceiving, he is in some way *mistaken*. The counter-allegation is simply that it shows no such thing. The 'plain man' just does not believe that whenever he is perceptually conscious of anything, he *always* perceives a 'material thing': it is therefore not to the purpose to point out that he sometimes does not – he knows that very well. He is also perfectly aware that there are cases, sometimes very familiar indeed, in which in one way or another 'appearances' may be 'deceptive', or in which he may even seem to perceive what is not there at all; again, it is nothing to the purpose to point out to him that that is so, for he does not doubt it. Does he believe that he perceives things 'directly'? But first, it is far from clear what that question means; and second, if we take it to mean what it naturally might – does he, for instance, ever see what is plainly before him, at which he is directly looking? – then it seems both that he thinks he often (of course not always) does perceive things directly, and that he is obviously correct in so thinking. It looks, then, as if the idea that the argument from illusion undermines the plain man's *beliefs* rests partly upon very careless mis-representation of what it is that the 'plain man' does believe, and to some extent also upon careless misdescription of the phenomena which are supposed to refute him.

We have considered, then, the question whether the plain man is always mistaken in believing that the objects he directly perceives are material things; and it is clear enough that Austin, while very far from happy about the terms in which the question is put – particularly about the under-explained expressions 'directly' and 'material things' – would answer: no, it has not been shown that he is always so mistaken. We must now note – bringing Ayer's particular contentions into the picture – that Ayer himself gives exactly the same answer, adding the significant proviso, to which we shall need to return, 'if the question . . . is taken as a question of fact'. But then Ayer, surprisingly, goes much further, and asks: 'does the argument [from illusion] prove even that there are *any* cases of perception in which such a belief would be mistaken?'⁵ This is surely a most surprising question to raise. For one thing, we have noted already that no sensible plain man does, in fact, believe that what he ('directly') perceives is *always* 'a material thing'; as he gazes up into a clear blue sky, for example, he would be most unlikely to say for his own part, and probably most reluctant to accept as a suggestion, that he is directly (or in any other way) 'perceiving a material thing' – for surely the sky is not 'a material thing'. Nor is a rainbow, for another example. Argument is scarcely necessary to disprove what no one believes. But apart from that, surely at least some of the standard instances of (so-called) illusion can properly be taken to establish at least something; most of them, indeed – such as cases of perspective, refraction, and 'optical illusion' – have indeed no tendency to show that what is perceived, and taken to be perceived, is 'not a material thing', but surely there are *some* cases at least – some cases of hallucination, for example – in which the subject really does, or at any rate very well may, believe that he perceives some material thing, and be mistaken in thinking so. But Ayer goes further still: it has not been shown by the traditional argument, he suggests, that – quite apart from such rather extreme cases as hallucination – *any* of our perceptions is 'delusive' in any way, even that of the familiar stick which looks bent in water. But that seems to amount to saying not only that such 'illusions' do not prove all that they have been supposed to but that they simply do not occur. Can Ayer really mean that?

Well, no, he does not; and what he does mean, as Austin goes on to point out, is of considerable interest. We must recall the proviso noted earlier: 'if the question . . . is taken as a question of fact'. The claim that Ayer is really making here is not that a stick which is really straight never looks as if it were bent, for example, but in some way that the question whether it is 'really' straight or bent is *not a question of fact*. And similarly with other cases; even when I hallucinate pink rats, it is not a question of fact whether there are or are not rats to be seen and which I see.

It is Ayer's way of explaining this further point that Austin finds particularly remarkable. At first sight, of course, one would think that what he is saying is just untrue, for in any ordinary sense, clearly, it *is* a question of fact whether a stick, looking bent and partly immersed in water, is a straight stick or a stick with a kink in it. It may even be quite an important fact, since an oarsman, for example, will wish to be firmly assured that he is not being expected to row with a crooked oar. Furthermore, though the fact that a crooked-looking oar is really straight can be established by, and as a fact of, common observation, it is a fact also capable of fairly elaborate scientific explanation, as fitting in with, indeed following from, other things that we know about light and (some) transparent substances. Why then does Ayer suggest that these questions are *not* questions of fact?

The answer, as Austin sees it, is both simple and startling: what Ayer turns out to be saying is that there just *are* no facts about 'material things', neither scientific facts nor facts of common observation. If I say that the oar looks bent but is straight, and you say that it is bent, it is Ayer's thesis that 'as far as the facts are concerned, there is really no dispute between us';[6] if I say that you and I see the same thing, and you 'prefer to say' that I see one thing and you another, 'the facts to which these expressions are intended to refer are in either case the same'. The construction to be put on these surprising remarks is this: the only fact – the only *fact* that there ever is – is that certain sense-experiences occur; all other questions, questions not about the actual occurrences of sense-experiences, are properly to be seen as not questions of fact but, broadly, questions of what we are to *say*, of how we are to describe things, even of what we 'prefer' or 'choose' to say. The only genuine statements of fact, or statements of genuine fact, are those starkly recording that such-and-such sense-experiences occur; in all other forms of discourse we are speaking, at best, *as if* there were facts other than these.

It is Austin's justified complaint, at this quite early point, not (yet) that this contention of Ayer's is untrue or incoherent, but that it appears, a couple of hundred pages later in his book, to be more or less the *conclusion* at which he eventually arrives.[7] If so, it is decidedly disconcerting to find it asserted, and in effect assumed, at so early a stage, in exposition of part of the argument supposed to lead to that very conclusion. And more immediately, it is surely distressing to find the contention that the issues are never factual, but concern only choices of terminology, supported not by argument but simply on the assertion that that is so. Nor, in fact, does that bold contention really mean quite what it says; for the liberal licence to choose our preferred terminology is issued, so to speak, only *after* hard facts have been restricted to being facts about 'phenomena', or sense-experiences; if the plain man 'preferred to say', as he most probably would, that by the exercise of his senses he sometimes became apprised of facts about tables and chairs, Ayer would surely be obliged to say he was *mistaken* – for there *are* no such facts.

We may deal very briefly with the next turn of the argument. Having contended that the 'argument from illusion' does not, when rightly understood in the way he sets out, establish any matter of fact, Ayer goes on to ask whether perhaps it does establish something about our language: 'does it not prove that we need to make at any rate some alteration in our ordinary way of speaking if we are to be able to describe all the empirical facts?'[8] Ayer believes that 'even this limited claim' is not well founded; but he supports this view in ways which Austin – while not dissenting from the view itself – again finds highly objectionable.

The point to grasp is, Ayer contends, that 'our ordinary way of speaking' is more versatile, more flexible, than it is sometimes given credit for. There is, he uncontroversially and rightly observes, a 'correct and familiar' usage of the word 'perceive' – and of other verbs of perception, such as 'see' or 'hear' – in which 'to say of an object that it is perceived does carry the implication that it exists': if I saw a fox, then there was a fox to be seen; but, he claims, there is another sense, or usage, of these verbs, also 'perfectly correct and familiar', in which 'to say of an object that it is perceived does not entail saying that it exists in any sense at all'.[9] Similarly, he says, there is a sense of, for example, the word 'see' in which it is not possible that what is seen 'should seem to have qualities that it does not really have'; but there is also another 'sense' in which that is indeed possible. Thus, with these resources, the ordinary speaker need never be stuck for something to say. For example, the sufferer from double vision may, with a single piece of paper before him, deny that he really sees two pieces of paper (though perhaps he seems to); but it is also open to him to say, in another 'correct and familiar' sense, that he really does see two. If confronted with the straight stick refracted in water, he may, it is suggested, deny that he sees the stick (since 'it is not possible that [anything seen] should seem to have qualities that it does not really have'); but it is also open to him to insist that he does see it, in that other sense in which it is 'not necessary that it should have the qualities that it appears to have'. These are indeed, Ayer says, 'ambiguities' in ordinary language; but they are 'not ordinarily a source of confusion to us':[10] this 'variety of senses' is, after all, 'familiar'.

Austin does not disagree with the thesis put forward on these grounds – that the 'argument from illusion' does not confront 'ordinary language' with phenomena which it is incapable of describing, of dealing with coherently. He holds, however, correctly, that the grounds thus offered are, in effect, mere linguistic fantasy. The quite difficult question, how it is to be established that a given word has 'different senses' and if so *what* different senses and how many, is not explicitly raised; it is clear, nevertheless, that at least some of the 'senses' proposed, and said to be 'correct and familiar', are purely fictitious. There is, for example, *no* 'sense' of the word 'see' such that to say that something is seen 'does not entail saying that it exists in any sense at all'. If there is no fox to be seen, on that ground alone it cannot be the case that I see a fox. I may indeed say of the hallucinating drunkard that he 'sees pink rats', when I know that there are actually no rats to be seen in his vicinity; but this shows nothing more than that the phrase 'seeing pink rats' is an accepted, rather short-hand way of characterizing a species of hallucinatory experience, which will not mislead only so long as all concerned are aware that it is hallucinatory experience that is in question; it does not show that there is, in general, any such special 'sense' of the verb 'see'. In general, that somebody saw rats certainly does entail that there were actual rats to be seen. There is, again, *no* sense of the word 'see' which is such that what is seen cannot 'seem to have qualities that it does not really have'; there may possibly be some particular items – after-images perhaps (*if* those are *seen*) – as to which there is really no distinction between how they 'seem' and how they really are; but that does not tend to show that there is, in general, any special sense of 'see'. In general, that somebody sees something is always compatible with the supposition, the possibility, of its really being in some respect other than the way it looked or appeared to him. And how in any case, Austin asks, could there possibly be a *single* sense of 'see' in which what is seen (1) must have the qualities it seems to have, but (2) may not exist? '*What* must have the qualities it seems to have?'[11] A language incorporating such a 'sense' would indeed be in some trouble.

I said at the beginning of this chapter that *Sense and Sensibilia* is liable to perplex in part because of the wispiness, or instability, of its dialectical target. It is at this point in Austin's progress that he calls attention explicitly to this phenomenon. We considered first the allegation, familiar in the tradition, that the plain, unphilosophical person espouses and expresses in his judgments of perception beliefs that are in fact mistaken – that the argument from illusion shows that to be true, and thereby makes the case for the philosopher's remedial intervention. Ayer himself comes to the conclusion that that idea is ill-founded, and Austin - though not indeed for the same reasons – concurs. We then moved on to the alternative idea that the argument from illusion perhaps exposes some serious deficiency in the plain man's language, that is in our ordinary language. Ayer again concludes that the suggestion is ill-founded: armed with 'different senses', all 'correct and familiar', of verbs of perception, the plain man need never be at a linguistic loss in describing the sensory phenomena which he may encounter. However, Ayer now says, although that is in his opinion so, the case is made out that the plain man's terminology does at any rate incorporate 'ambiguities'; and although these may not be misleading for most ordinary purposes, the philosopher finds their elimination 'desirable'. He thus may reasonably decide to espouse or latch on to *one* (alleged) 'sense' of verbs of perception – that in which the perceived item must exist and must have the qualities it appears to have. He decides to use verbs of perception unambiguously in *that* sense. But he of course finds that, in that sense, perceived items cannot be 'material things'; for material things of course may sometimes appear to have qualities or characteristics which really they have not, and may even seem to exist when and where they do not. So finally the philosopher introduces a special new term, 'sense-datum', to stand for that which *is* perceived in the philosopher's chosen sense: a sense-datum is to be such that it can neither seem to exist when it does not, nor appear to have qualities which really it does not have, and can therefore be – as nothing else can – the object of perception in the philosopher's sense. That – avoidance of ambiguity – is put forward as the real motive for the philosopher's terminological intervention.

Austin's response to all this is a rather complex matter. He first says, correctly, that this suggested motivation must actually be bogus, for the sufficient reason that there are in fact, in our ordinary language, no such ambiguities as it is the philosopher's supposed intention to eliminate. But he goes on to make what might seem to be the startling claim that the bogusness of that suggested motivation does not really matter – that in fact the avoidance of ambiguity is not Ayer's concern at all, and that the driving-force, so to speak, behind his philosophical manoeuvrings is actually something quite different, to which the convolutions of the argument from illusion and its 'interpretation', no less than the fantasy about different senses of verbs, are in fact wholly irrelevant.

The suggestion that Ayer has thus misstated the motivation of his own argument might seem surprising. Austin is, however, quite right; and it is noteworthy that, in his own critical comments on *Sense and Sensibilia*, Ayer seems to have himself conceded, by tacit implication, that that is so. He says there that the whole argument from illusion, however deployed or 'interpreted', is really quite irrelevant to his real point:

> we do not need to rely on the empirical fact that illusions . . . actually occur. That is, it is not necessary for this purpose [i.e. his purpose] that we should ever actually be deceived by appearances or even that anything should ever actually appear in any way different from what it is. It is enough that these things be possible.[12]

And a little earlier he says that 'as I have construed expressions like "directly see", it would be *contradictory* [my italics] to speak of directly seeing material things, or any parts of them'; and it needs no empirical argument, of course, to show that a proposition which is actually self-contradictory is false. We thus have the very strange dialectical position that in his later comments Ayer appears willing to concede that every-thing – or almost everything – that Austin has so far said is true or at least may very well be true, and therefore that a good many things which he himself had said were not, but puts up as a riposte that that is really of little importance, since in any case all the issues about illusion and delusion, refraction and reflection and hallucination, about our ordinary language and its real or imagined ambiguities, are beside the point, irrelevant to any position he really wishes to propound. Austin would have felt inclined to comment, I believe, that even if certain propositions are really irrelevant to some major thesis not yet disclosed, it must surely be as well to observe – it is not merely obtuse and obstructive to observe – that they are actually not true; and in any case that, if the argument from illusion and its interpretation is really the irrelevance which Ayer has later declared it to be, much time and trouble would have been saved by his saying so at an earlier stage.

At this point in Austin's discussion – the beginning of Chapter X of *Sense and Sensibilia* – the argument substantially changes gear. It becomes clear that (if I may put things for a moment in my own way) Ayer, in a sense, is not really interested in perception at all: this is no doubt largely why he later maintained such equanimity in face of the complaint that some of the things he says about it are untrue; he differs in this, incidentally, both from Price,[13] who really was extremely interested in perception itself, and of course from Austin. His real interest (attested by the fact that it actually gives his book its title) is in 'the foundations of empirical knowledge'; and while it is taken for granted, reasonably enough, that empirical knowledge presupposes the occurrence of sense-experience of some sort, it really does matter very little, I think, to Ayer's thesis *what* sort of senses, or even how many senses, we actually have, what their enjoyment or employment is actually like, or even, as we have seen, whether they ever actually betray us into error, and if so how and why. The interest and the terms of the debate from here onwards concern not perception but the theory of knowledge. Accordingly I shall first try to state, no doubt too briefly, what Ayer's position was on this, and will then turn to the quite tricky question of assessing the impact upon it of Austin's criticism. It is quite clear that he regards the position, as Ayer expounds it, as at least misstated in important respects; how much further his objections go, and why, is not so readily apparent.

Ayer's package of propositions can be stated with reasonable fairness, I think, in such terms as the following. We have sense-experiences – for example, that of sitting in a deck-chair while hearing a cuckoo in the adjacent copse. But it is in principle possible that one should be in exactly that sensory state – that it should be exactly *as if* one were sitting in a deck-chair, etc. – when in fact one is not. (Ayer need not, as he insists, assert that this ever actually happens, only that it is in principle possible.) In such a case, though there would be perhaps no deck-chair, no cuckoo, no copse, the sense-experience itself could in principle be exactly the same. To have a sense-experience is by definition to be 'directly', or 'immediately', aware of a sense-datum. Now a judgment, were one to be made, simply about the sense-datum itself would be verifiable conclusively – would be, in fact, 'directly' verified by the occurrence of the sense-experience of being directly aware of it. And such a judgment would be 'incorrigible', in that, since its scope is restricted, so to speak, to just that sense-datum, no other experiences, whether one's own or other people's, no judgments about anything else, could be of any relevance to it, and *a fortiori* they could not show it to be false or compel its retractation. Such a judgment, being thus conclusively verifiable and indeed incorrigible, can of course be certain; and its terms, Ayer adds, can be said to be 'precise', in that it is just this specific sense-datum and nothing else to which they refer.

Any judgment about a 'material object' (which effectively means, in this context, about *anything* other than a specific sense-datum) stands in contrast with this at every point. My judgment that I hear a cuckoo – that it is not merely *as if* I do but that I do in fact – necessarily 'goes beyond' the sense-experience that I here and now have, since it commits me to the availability, to the at least possible occurrence not just of this present sense-experience but of a large (Ayer says, of an infinitely large) array of appropriate sense-experiences of my own or of other people. A material thing such as a cuckoo is both enduring and public, open to observation by anybody; accordingly, if I judge, on the basis of my present sense-experience, that I hear a cuckoo, I therein 'infer', or 'assume', or take for granted that the appropriate other items of sense-experience, my own or other people's, will, or would, or anyway in principle could, all be available. If so, such a judgment cannot be verified 'directly', for the sense-experience on the basis of which it is made is not by itself a sufficient condition of its truth; it cannot indeed be verified *conclusively* at all, for the implied, or assumed, array of further available sense-experiences is not finite: however many I may find to be consistent with the judgment that I hear a cuckoo, it remains possible that further experience will, or would, negate that judgment, by being in some way of the 'wrong' sort. Such judgments can therefore, in principle, never be 'certain'; and they are inevitably, Ayer adds, 'vague in their application to phenomena', since it is not possible to stipulate any definite congeries of sense-experiences whose availability would provide necessary and sufficient conditions of their truth.

We must recognize, then, Ayer contends, that empirical knowledge has a certain *structure*. The *foundations* of empirical knowledge are sense-experiences (whatever their precise nature may contingently be), or, perhaps more exactly, are propositions about the individual sense-data of which in sense-experience we are or might be immediately, 'directly' aware. These propositions rest on no evidence, but are directly, and indeed conclusively, verifiable; they are certain, incorrigible, precise. *Everything* else is, no doubt in varying degrees, theory, inference, hypothesis, extrapolation. For propositions about material things (that is, about anything else) go beyond the data; they are not directly verifiable, therefore must rest upon evidence or inference or assumption, are in principle always corrigible and never certain, and are (in some sense) vague.

Let us first consider what Austin's objections to all this are, and then take up the more difficult question of what they amount to, what is their real 'effect'.

First, he argues that propositions about sense-data could not in fact be, as such, *incorrigible*. It is not perfectly clear, of course – it is a major unsatisfactoriness of the whole discussion that it is not clear – what a 'sense-datum proposition' would actually look like, what its terms would be (I had a go at making this clear in my book about Berkeley, but we see in the last chapter of *Sense and Sensibilia* that Austin did not think much of that particular effort);[14] but we are told in general terms that the sense, or content, of a sense-datum proposition is such that its truth or falsehood is to rest solely upon that very sense-datum itself, is to run no inferential or extrapolatory risk, is to be logically insulated from, and thereby invulnerable to, anything else. Let that be granted. But still, if its propounder is saying anything at all, he is saying that his present sense-datum is of a certain character; and how could it be that, in principle, he *could* not in any way be mistaken in saying so? Extrapolatory risks are not the only risks there are. There is the possibility of misdescription, misclassification, misidentification, not merely through perhaps insignificant slips of the tongue or harmlessly idiosyncratic usage of some descriptive term, but through such deplorably familiar causes of real error as hastiness, casualness, lack of due attention and care, perhaps also lack of experience or skill. How, we might ask - whatever exactly a sense-datum is supposed to be – could *any* kind of item be such as to guarantee that a fallible being could, in principle, never be mistaken in any way in his judgment about it? He may be, by definition of this case, exempt from the possibility of a certain kind of error – the kind that often ensues upon risky assumption or unwarranted inference. But he may in other significant ways fall into error, and so be liable to correction, if only, perhaps, in some cases by himself.

So sense-datum propositions, whatever they are, are not as such incorrigible. Nor are they, Austin adds, as such 'precise'. Ayer's suggestion appears to be that such propositions are 'precise' in that their 'reference' is to be, by definition, absolutely specific: when I propound such a proposition, it is 'about' just *this* sense-datum and nothing else whatever. But precision (to put Austin's point with impoverishing brevity) is actually a matter not of what I am talking about, but of what I am saying about it. You ask me what is in that glass on the table, and let us suppose it to be absolutely clear that my answer refers to that and to nothing else at all; I might answer, vaguely – it being absolutely clear, however, what I am talking about – that it is a reddish liquid of some sort, or, more precisely, that it is a Médoc, Château Terre Rouge, of 1981. Similarly a remark about a sense-datum could, surely, be as vague as you like – 'sort of pinkish', perhaps, or even 'some dark colour or other'.

> A difficulty here is that it is never made really clear whether Ayer regards the 'sense-datum language' as something which already exists and which we use, or whether he thinks of it as a merely possible language which could in principle be invented; for this reason one never knows quite what one is supposed to be considering, or where to look for examples.[15]

But until we are told, in fact, what the vocabulary of sense-datum propositions is actually to be, the question whether such propositions are precise or vague cannot really be raised at all. But, Austin notes, if the characterization of sense-data *is* to be always 'precise', then its chances of being incorrigible are thereby diminished. We 'take refuge' in vagueness when we wish to minimize the chances of error; to be extremely precise is to run the risk of getting it wrong.

What, then, of the catch-all antithesis to sense-datum propositions, propositions about 'material things'? These are said to be never incorrigible, not conclusively verifiable; they can be, and always need to be, supported by 'evidence', but such evidence can never be sufficient to make their truth certain. Austin has objections to make to all of this. First, the thesis that such propositions can never be conclusively verified appears to rest upon the supposition that any proposition about a material object must remain, ineluctably and for ever, vulnerable to falsification by the occurrence of some unexpected, recalcitrant, untoward sense-experience – its 'commitment' in that respect to the future, and indeed to the present, is in principle infinite. But is this true? Suppose that I have lived on terms of close and equable companionship with a certain animal for several years, and that I and others take, and always have taken, this animal to be a cat. Is it really the case that our future experience might at any time oblige us all to conclude that we have been all along mistaken? It is in principle conceivable, no doubt, that quite extraordinary things might occur – the animal gradually becomes wiry-haired and begins to bark, or to talk French, shrinks to the size of a mouse, or vanishes inexplicably before our very eyes. But would we then be obliged to conclude that it *never was* a cat? Surely not. We may say, with amazement, that it seems to be turning into a dog, or we may be left, with even more amazement, completely at a loss for words; but we need not question that for years it undoubtedly *was*, as we all took it to be, a cat. That was established conclusively, not indeed by an infinite number of tests, but in the experience of all of us over a number of years. To be sure – conclusively sure – that some object is of a certain familiar sort, we need to have *enough* experience of it, in some cases to carry out *enough* tests or checks; and when we are thus sufficiently assured that this thing is, say, a telephone, then, though the future course of events may conceivably disconcert and astonish us, it need not – will not – oblige us to drop that proposition as false, as one that – as it turns out – we were from the start mistaken in accepting. We knew and we know that, at any rate, it *was* a telephone.

The 'evidence', then, needed to establish such a proposition conclusively is not infinite in amount (and for that reason never completely obtainable). Enough is enough. But are all such propositions, in any case, put forward upon the basis of 'evidence'? It seems wholly unnatural to say so. The police may indeed conclude, on the basis of certain evidence, that the malefactor whom they wish to assist them with their enquiries is now somewhere in London. But suppose they then go to London and actually find the malefactor; is his presence before them more *evidence* that he is there? Surely not – they have now got for the proposition that he is in London something much better than evidence: namely, the physical presence of the person himself. (They may subsequently state, *in* evidence, that he was there; but their evidence then is *that he was there*, not that they had evidence that he was there.) I am holding at this moment a pen in my right hand; I do not have evidence, even very good evidence, that a pen is there, I can see and feel it.

Austin has a general point here, and a point of importance. It is that it is a mistake in principle to suppose that we can usefully talk in any of these terms about *kinds of propositions*. Take, for instance, the proposition that Simpkin is a cat. We can ask, if we like, what 'kind' of proposition that is; we can say, if we like, that the kind of proposition it is, is an empirical, contingent proposition about a material object. Now, given only that it is a proposition of *that kind*, we clearly cannot sensibly purport to answer the question: is it true or false? For of course, so far as that goes, it might be either: true if the item referred to as 'Simpkin' is indeed a cat, otherwise not. But it is Austin's contention that exactly the same goes for the questions: is it certain or only probable? Does it need to be verified? Could it be verified or not? Does it rest on evidence? How strong is the evidence? Does it *provide* evidence? Might it turn out at some later date to be untrue? For all of these questions turn, not on what kind of proposition we are talking about, but on – broadly and briefly speaking – the particular *circumstances* in which the proposition is propounded. Said by me of my own pet of ten years' standing, it is certainly true that Simpkin is a cat; for that proposition I need neither evidence nor verification. If an acquaintance speaks to me of his own pet Simpkin, I may think it probably true that Simpkin is a cat, on the evidence, perhaps, that the name 'Simpkin' is known to be

one often given to cats; and I might go on, if it concerned me, to verify
that supposition. Again, that Simpkin is a cat might in some cases be
'evidence', for example, for someone's supposition that I am fond of
animals. And so on. If so, it must surely be an undertaking misconceived
in principle, having identified (let us suppose) two kinds or classes of
propositions, one about 'sense-data', another about 'material objects', to
ask which *kind* is, *as such*, certain or uncertain, corrigible or not, verifiable or not, based on evidence or evidence-providing – or true or false.
There can be no answer to such questions. And Austin here makes the
bold remark, which we shall need to consider, that 'if the Theory of
Knowledge consists in finding grounds for such an answer, there is no
such thing.'[16]

It is typical of the dialectical oddity of this whole business that Ayer, in
the piece defending his position which I mentioned earlier, actually
concedes (rather impatiently) almost all of this, but argues once again
that it does not really matter.[17] That ordinary judgments about ordinary
objects of perception, such as that I now have a pen in my right hand,
can be and often are certain 'is true, so far as it goes'. Austin argues
that, as I see and feel the pen as I do, I would not be said to have
evidence that I am holding a pen, nor does the proposition that I do, in
the circumstances, stand in need of verification; 'all this may be accepted,
as a comment on ordinary usage'. When I look at the pen and put out
my hand to pick it up, I do not conclude by *inference* that I shall feel
it in my hand; 'this is true, but not to the purpose'. It is probably true
that 'experiential statements' are not incorrigible, at any rate 'I do not
wish to commit myself to the view' that they are; and as to the view
that other sorts of statements are never conclusively verifiable, 'Austin
objects to this way of speaking, I think justifiably'. Whether it is proper
to speak of different 'senses' of 'see', and other verbs of perception, 'is
immaterial'; and while it is true that many of the cases cited under the
title 'argument from illusion' are not cases of *illusion*, 'these points are
unimportant'. Let us admit that the claims and theses to which Austin
objects are sometimes untrue, often misleadingly stated, often outrage
ordinary usage, or use ordinary terms in under-explained 'technical'
senses. All that does not really matter; for there remains, Ayer says,
made in these perhaps rather less than felicitous ways, a logical point, a
logical thesis, which Austin's (pedantic?) critical objections leave quite
untouched. This is, we are now told, that 'the occurrence of the experience which gives rise to the perceptual judgment is logically consistent
with the judgment's being false'; the judgment 'claims more than is
contained in the experience which gives rise to it'; 'our judgments of
perception go beyond the data on which they are based'. 'Statements
about physical objects are at a theoretical level with respect to experiential

statements.' And if one were to object that it does not look much like a *theory* to say that there are tables and chairs, no doubt it would be replied that that statement too just makes the same 'logical point' – perhaps misleadingly, but what of that?

How effective is this defence? Well, first, it is certain that Austin would not have taken kindly to Ayer's remarkable supposition that untruth, misdescription, misclassification, misleading language, unannounced deviations from 'ordinary usage', and the rest, are unimportant or immaterial. At the very least, here as elsewhere in philosophy, while such deficiencies in felicity and accuracy of statement and expression may be 'irrelevant' to some point that is really at issue, they are quite sure to make it unnecessarily difficult to see clearly what that 'real' point actually is, and to generate a fog or smog of bogus perplexities which, one might say, simply waste time and make trouble. In Austin's words, 'there is nothing so plain boring as the constant repetition of assertions that are not true, and sometimes not even faintly sensible; if we can reduce this a bit, it will be all to the good.'[18]

But what about the 'logical point' that Ayer does think important? 'The occurrence of the experience which gives rise to the perceptual judgment is logically consistent with the judgment's being false.' For example, I might be in a state such that it is exactly *as if* I heard a cuckoo, and I might for that reason take it that I heard a cuckoo, but actually I did not; perhaps I heard something else, or even nothing at all. Does Austin wish to deny that that is so? Surely not; for that that is (logically) possible seems to be not only true, but even a truism. But Ayer, of course, for his part does not wish merely to assert that this is true; he wants to maintain that it is also *important* – important not, presumably, in that by itself it solves any philosophical problem, but rather in that it at least raises an important problem, and allows it to be succinctly formulated and discussed. Historically, 'the' problem has been stated in various terms. What is the relation between 'ideas of sensation' and external 'bodies'? between 'impressions' and external objects? between sense-data and material things? between sense-experience and 'empirical knowledge'? In his book Ayer formulates the problem in more formal terms: what is the relation between 'the sense-datum language' and 'material-object language'? If material-object language 'goes beyond' sense-datum language, how do we effect the transition, as it were, from one to the other? The ground, it seems clear, of his considerable impatience with Austin's criticism is that he sees it as amounting to a mere refusal to address the 'real' problem at all, a refusal even to allow it to be formulated, perhaps indeed to an attempted denial of the problem's existence. If we are flatly forbidden to introduce the term 'sense-datum', how are we ever to address the question how sense-data are related to material things? It is not enough just to refuse to confront the problem altogether.

This is, in my submission, to misunderstand Austin's position. This is certainly not that there is just no 'problem' at all – that so long as we speak carefully and exactly in ordinary language, we shall find absolutely nothing in the general area of perception which gives occasion for any sort of philosophical perplexity. No doubt he did think (and rightly so) that the tradition of philosophical debate in this area was indeed burdened with a train of more or less bogus perplexities generated by carelessness as to facts, by infelicity of expression, by mechanical repetition of unexamined 'examples', by simple muddle; but he certainly would not have wished to assert so dogmatic a thesis as that if such bogus perplexities were avoided or cleared away, there would be nothing left for a rational philosopher to worry his head about. The real burden of his book is that, as posed in the terms employed by Ayer in 1940 (and of course in at least similar terms by a host of earlier writers), 'the problem' seemed to him to have the air of mere fantasy. We are purportedly to consider the relation between 'the sense-datum language' and 'material-object language', between propositions about sense-data and propositions about material things. But in fact *we do not know what these are.* The term 'material object' is not well-defined. It looks fairly certain that if it were to be well-defined, there would be a sizeable residuum of items which, while not 'sense-data', would not be material things either; what about them? Then 'propositions about' material things are not well-defined either; or at least, if they are – if they are simply to be *any* propositions at all 'about' material things, or even more liberally, any empirical propositions *not* about 'sense-data' – they will constitute a class of vast and almost limitless diversity. *What are we talking about?* Again, a sense-datum is purportedly to be the object, or perhaps the content, of a sense-experience. But what is that? How *many* sense-data crop up in, say, thirty seconds? Which sense are we talking about? All of them indifferently? (What is 'a sense'? What is an 'experience'?) When we are not attempting to say simply how things are in the world, but in one way or another bring ourselves and our 'experience', or our 'impressions', into the picture, there is not just *one* sort of thing available to us to say. Our language is very rich in different words, different idioms, different turns of phrase; how much of it is supposed to constitute *the* 'sense-datum language'? Or if none of it really does, what exactly is the new language to be? Once again, *what are we talking about?* It is not the supposition that there are problems that Austin takes issue with; no doubt there are, as there always are; it is the suggestion that we are actually in possession of, have identifiably and clearly before us, *two languages,* such that we can profitably settle down to consider 'the problem' of how the one is related to the other. If one actually looks at the things we say, and that are available to us to say, about the things (not *one* kind of things!) that we perceive and our 'experience' (not *one* kind of experience!) in perceiving them, the notion of 'two languages' looks like mere fantasy, presumably unrecognized as such because of its venerable pedigree; and if that notion is fantasy, then 'the problem' *stated in those terms* will be, not so much obviously non-existent, as not intelligibly posed. This is what Austin meant by 'dismantling the whole doctrine before it gets off the ground' (the very last phrase of *Sense and Sensibilia*). He did not mean: refuse to discuss, or deny that there are, any problems. He meant: do not succumb to the fantasy of formulating your problems *as if* there were 'two languages' whose relations we are to scrutinize. If we pose it in that way, we almost literally do not know what we are talking about. To succumb to that fantasy – if I may bring in here a phrase he used in another connection – is 'simply barking our way up the wrong gum-tree'.[19]

Very similarly – in conclusion – with his *obiter dictum* about the Theory of Knowledge: if you ask what kind of sentence it is in which are expressed propositions which, uniquely, are incorrigibly certain; which, uniquely, can be known; which, uniquely, constitute evidence for other propositions; which, uniquely, can be conclusively or 'directly' verified – and so on: then, since there is *no* such *kind of sentence, if* the Theory of Knowledge were supposed to be the answer to *that* question, there would be no such thing. Austin would not, of course, have wished flatly to deny that there were questions or problems which might usefully be labelled as constituting the Theory of Knowledge; but he would have wished for a clear, coherent, unfantasizing statement of what those questions and problems actually were.

I should mention one final matter. It has sometimes been said in criticism of Austin that he was not entitled to his wholesale rejection of 'the sense-datum theory', or to his rejection of the term 'sense-datum' itself, since by his own admission he does not consider at all *one* of the standard ways in which that term, or some equivalent, has been sought to be introduced. He concentrates his fire on the deployment for this purpose of the argument from illusion; but he does not consider, and indeed explicitly omits from consideration,[20] a quite different tradition of argument which takes as its premise that perception is some sort of causal transaction. In a nutshell: if to see a tomato is to be causally affected by a tomato, *what is the effect?* What is it that is caused? According to H. H. Price,[21] for example, that I am perceptually aware of (e.g. that I see) some object is to say that that object 'causes a sense-datum with which I am acquainted'; and is it not at least arguable that some such term as 'sense-datum' is absolutely required, if the causal transaction of, say, seeing is to be illuminatingly analysed, or even described? But if so, we are not entitled to wholesale rejection of the term 'sense-datum' simply on the ground that the battered weaponry of the argument from illusion does not require any such coinage.

I am inclined to think, as a matter of fact, that these 'causal' consider-ations, which Austin avowedly does leave out of account, probably can be made the basis for a much stronger 'case for sense-data' than can the arguments which Austin has in his sights.[22] However, while it may be regrettable that Austin did not examine the case that might be made in that way, I do not see that his not doing so undermines what he *does* say in *Sense and Sensibilia*. For he surely does not seek to show in that book that such a term as 'sense-datum' was supposed to be could not be shown, by any species of argumentation whatever, to be desirable or even admissible as a piece of philosophical neologism; his view was simply that, by the sorts of arguments he did consider, the thing had not actually been done. If one had put it to him that the thing might be done satisfactorily in some quite different way, he would of course have encouraged one to go ahead – to try to do it. He might have been sceptical perhaps, but not dogmatically prohibitive.

III

Knowledge and Other Minds

Austin's earliest published paper was 'Are there a priori concepts?', a contribution to a three-paper symposium held at the Joint Session of the Mind Association and Aristotelian Society in 1939. That paper – except for its unusually determined insistence on distinguishing one question from another, and its marked scepticism as to the merits of most philosophical answers – is not particularly characteristic of Austin's work; in it he showed more readiness than he usually did to join in the debate more or less within the terms, and terminology, conventionally adopted, and he referred rather freely, as later he seldom did, to the subject's history. He began, however, with a remark that really is revealingly characteristic: 'frankly, I still do not understand what the question before us *means*: and since I hold, *nevertheless*, no strong views as to how it should be answered, . . .'.[1] His paper 'Other minds', a contribution in 1946 to another symposium, begins rather similarly; his policy will be, he says, that 'of splitting hairs to save starting them'.[2] The 'problem' of 'other minds' consists, no doubt, in perplexity as to how one knows – how one possibly could know – what is in someone else's mind, what he is thinking, what his feelings are, for example whether he is angry. Austin begins, not with this perhaps obviously somewhat problematic sort of case, but with more general consideration of the question 'How do you know?'

First, for me to be asked quite properly and naturally how I know, it need not be the case that I have said explicitly that I do. For if I make any assertion, any unqualified assertion, as for instance that there's a goldfinch in the garden, there is a sense in which by so doing I 'imply' that I know that to be true, so that the question how I know it can naturally arise. But I might, of course, concede, or say, in spite of that usual implication, that I don't know it, but that anyway I *think* there is; and if so, I might be asked to say why I think so.

The two cases are very different. If my answers are judged to be unsatisfactory, it will be objected in the one case that I do not know it, but in the other that while I no doubt do believe there's a goldfinch in the garden, I ought not to believe it, have no good reason to. 'Why do you think so?' does not question the 'existence' of my belief though it may question its validity or grounds. 'How do you know?' may put the 'existence' of my alleged knowledge in question. If it is not, or there is not, a goldfinch, I may well of course think that it is or that there is; but I certainly do not – could not – know it, if it isn't so.

To the question 'How do you know?', answers of very different kinds are possible. I may claim general competence in matters of this sort: 'I'm an ornithologist'; or particularly favourable present conditions of exercise of such competence as I have: 'I saw it very clearly'. I may mention what, in general, identifies certain birds as goldfinches; or I may say on what basis I so identified this particular bird. Or, of course, I may refer to authority: 'The gardener told me.' Naturally in so answering I take for granted that the gardener himself knew, but there is nothing in the least exceptional about such a case; no doubt by far the greatest part of what each of us knows is known 'because', or by way of the fact that, someone else said so, in print or otherwise.

On this question of 'authority', Austin's next paragraph seems to me rather confusingly to run together two points which, though both important, are importantly distinct.

> The occurrence of a piece of human testimony radically alters the situation. We say 'We shall never know what Caesar's feelings were on the field of the battle of Philippi', because he did not pen an account of them: *if* he *had*, then to say 'We shall never know' won't do in the same way . . . [3]

But that seems to make two points at once, both of which we shall come back to. The first, which Austin mentions, is that 'it is fundamental in talking (as in other matters) that we are entitled to trust others, except in so far as there is some concrete reason to distrust them': when a person speaks or otherwise pronounces on some matter, it is not to be treated as, always and in principle, a merely and completely open question whether he is to be believed. But his particular example surely takes much of its force from a different point: that an individual is in a position to speak with quite special and peculiar authority on the question how he himself feels, what his feelings are or were. If Caesar had told us *that*, the situation would be indeed radically altered in that we would have had not only 'a piece of human testimony', but testimony provided by the only person in a position really authoritatively to provide it.

If I say that I could tell the bird was a goldfinch, identify it as a goldfinch, 'by its red head', my questioner might reply that that's 'not enough: plenty of other birds have red heads'. I need not in fact always be abashed by this, even if I admit it to be true, for the (usefully) vague expression 'by its red head' does not mean simply 'by the fact that its head was red'. If I had said the latter, I would indeed have implied, no doubt mistakenly, that no other (small British) kind of bird has a red head; but 'by its red head' is more naturally and properly taken as saying only that there was *something* about its red head, not necessarily just its being red – and I may be quite unable further to specify what – which enabled me to tell that this was a goldfinch. However, 'That's not enough' may often be a perfectly justified comment – *provided*, Austin insists, that the objector has in mind 'some more or less definite lack';[4] if he has no idea *why* it's not enough, is quite unable to specify in what way the answer falls short of adequacy for the purpose, then for him to go on saying 'That's not enough' is just pointless and silly. Further, enough, Austin insists, *is* enough: if I am to be justified in saying I know, I need some basis for saying so that, *within reason*, excludes the possibility of its not being so. We are, Austin later says, fallible beings: it is seldom, perhaps never, *inconceivable* that we should be mistaken, even in the most favourable-seeming case.[5] But to suggest that I don't know – that my answer to 'How do you know?' is not good enough – is not, at least if the suggestion is to be of any interest, merely to point out that I am a fallible being who could conceivably err; it is to imply some concrete reason for supposing that I might be mistaken (or have omitted some precaution, etc.) in this case. If so, then, though fallible, I shall in fact often be justified in saying that I know; and, Austin importantly adds, may be perfectly justified in saying so, even if I actually turn out to have been wrong. In such a case, indeed, I didn't know (as it turns out); but it does not follow that I was not justified in saying that I did. To be mistaken in saying something is not necessarily to be unjustified in saying it.

We may note here that Austin takes up a couple of points which we have come across before (see p. 24). It is sometimes suggested – in this case by one of the other symposiasts, John Wisdom – that there is a particular sort of case in which, since it does not involve 'prediction', I *cannot* be wrong – at least in any of the ways in which I usually can be.[6] This is the case of 'a man's knowledge of his own sensations'. Of course a man may say falsely that he has a certain sensation; but that is lying, not being mistaken. Or he may misname his sensation, whether inadvertently or through some idiosyncrasy of linguistic usage; but that is 'verbal' error only. In 'the most favoured sense', if he is, say, in pain and says that he is, then surely it is not possible for him to be wrong. Austin demurs.[7] Of course, in vastly many such cases, there will indeed be no serious question of a man's being wrong; but there is no sound basis for the idea that he never could be. The phrase 'knowing my own sensations', Austin points out, is – if it is really an acceptable construction at all – not grammatically analogous with, say, 'eating my own lettuces'; 'my own sensations' are not analogously the direct object of the verb 'know', so that my sensations are literally and completely known by me as my lettuces may be literally and completely eaten by me. To 'know my sensations', if the phrase is allowable at all, must mean 'to know what my sensations are'; and once we have seen that, it must look highly unpersuasive to say that I necessarily *must* know and could never be wrong. Perhaps I cannot identify, recognize my 'sensation' at all – 'I simply don't know what it is: I've never tasted anything remotely like it before.'[8] Or I may be uncertain whether I have got it right – it isn't *quite* right for the taste of pineapple. Or I may just get it wrong, perhaps through sheer carelessness – I say 'magenta' when the look (to me now) just is not magenta (as perhaps I may subsequently realize). Austin adds for good measure that more ordinary statements are not – at any rate not on the ground that they involve 'prediction' – in some special and different way prone to incurable *un*certainty.[9] If I say, gazing over the desert, 'There's an oasis', I am perhaps in saying so predicting - betting, assuming, taking for granted – that it will not turn out to be a mirage, that we shall actually find water when we get there; and of course in such a case I may turn out to be mistaken. But if we then do get there and do find water, surely I am not 'predicting' any longer, I could not be – it *is* an oasis, as we have now established. Of course *conceivably* the future may still throw me into speechless confusion – the 'water' may burst into flames, or turn pink, or the whole scene may vanish. But then that is what would happen – I would be thrown into speechless confusion, at a loss for words. It would not mean that, in saying it was an oasis, I was wrong before.

The next section of Austin's paper has attracted more attention than any other; and it is indeed interesting, though also, I believe, in this context really unprofitable and misguided.

Austin had been interested, he later said,[10] since 1939 in the phenomenon of what he came to call 'performative' utterance: utterance the role or function of which is not (merely) to *say* something but (primarily) to *do* something, as 'I bet you sixpence it will rain tomorrow' is to make a bet, not (merely, if at all) to say that I do. This became the topic, of course, of *How to Do Things with Words*, and will fall to be examined in detail in due course (pp. 105ff.). But Austin records that he 'made use' of some of his thoughts on this topic in 'Other minds', a good many years before the lectures as now printed were delivered.

His object in bringing in these thoughts is to try to throw more light on the popular but not perspicuous dictum 'If I know, I can't be wrong'. Austin notes, of course correctly, that this cannot sensibly be taken to mean that only an infallible being could know anything – a being that in general, in espousing any view, could never be wrong. The way in which the dictum makes, he says, 'perfectly good sense' is rather like this:

> you are prohibited from saying 'I know it is so, but I may be wrong', just as you are prohibited from saying 'I promise I will, but I may fail'. If you are aware you may be mistaken, you ought not to say you know, just as, if you are aware you may break your word, you have no business to promise.

Now 'I promise' is, of course, typically a performative utterance; in saying it I do not (merely, if at all) make an assertion, I make a promise. 'The parallel', Austin says, 'between saying "I know" and saying "I promise" may be elaborated.'[11]

First, there is a certain parallel between any assertion 'S is P' and an utterance of the form 'I shall do A'. If I assert that S is P, I 'imply' at least that I believe it, even that I am quite sure of it; if I say 'I shall do A', I imply at least that I hope (or expect) to do it, perhaps even that I fully intend to and am sure that I can. If I say that S is P when I do not believe it, or that I shall do A when I have no expectation or intention of doing any such thing, then I am deliberately deceiving; if I say that S is P when I believe it is but am not quite sure, or that I shall do A when I do not quite fully intend to or am not sure that I can, I may indeed mislead, but am not deceiving my hearer in the same black-and-white way.

Now suppose that I say not just 'I shall do A', but 'I promise to do A'. To say this, Austin rightly says, is to take 'a new plunge'[12] – 'by using this formula (performing this ritual)', I do not merely avow my intention, even my full and firm intention, to do A – I *bind* myself to the promisee, I stake my credit, I take on a commitment, in a new and special way. I do not merely lead him to, but *entitle* him to, count on my performance. 'Similarly, saying "I know" is taking a new plunge.' It is not merely avowing my belief, or even my full conviction – still less professing something *more* than full conviction, for there *is* nothing more 'in that scale'. 'When I say "I know", I *give others my word: I give others my authority for saying* that S is P.' If I take this special plunge, if I promise, I *can't fail* – meaning, of course, not that non-performance is impossible, but that I am *committed* to performance; you are *entitled* to expect, rely on, and indeed demand that: if I say 'I know', I *can't be wrong* – meaning, not that my pronouncements are infallibly correct, but that I am specifically committed to the proposition that S is P, and that you are entitled to rely on that and indeed to say, on my authority, that you know it too. 'Hence, if I say it lightly, I may be *responsible* for getting *you* into trouble.'[13]

36

There is, however, Austin noted, a natural enough 'objection to saying that "I know" performs the same sort of function as "I promise".' They seem to work rather differently. If in due course I do not do A as I promised to, you may complain: 'You didn't do it, although you *did* promise.' But if it turns out that S is not P though I said that I knew it was, your complaint is: 'It turns out that you were wrong, so you *didn't* know.' Austin says, in my submission unfortunately, that this contrast is 'more apparent than real. The sense in which you "did promise" is that you did *say* you promised . . . and you did *say* you knew.'[14] We shall come back to this.

Austin goes on to make a few general remarks about 'performatives'. We are talking, he says, about 'ritual phrases'; and 'utterance of obvious ritual phrases, in the appropriate circumstances, is not *describing* the action we are doing, but *doing* it'.[15] Of course the attendant circumstances must be right for the purpose. 'In these "ritual" cases, the approved case is one where *in the appropriate circumstances*, I say a certain formula': 'I will' at the prescribed point in a ceremony of marriage, 'I give' when whatever it is is mine to give, 'I order' when I have the authority to issue an order to the addressee; and so on. But now, he goes on, if it turns out that the circumstances are not at all, or at least not fully, appropriate, 'we tend to be rather hesitant about how to put it'. If for instance he was married already, then the second ceremony was not really a marriage, was 'null and void'; he did tell me to do it, but if he had no authority was that really an order? And so on. 'But the essential factors are (a) You said you knew: you said you promised; (b) You were mistaken: you didn't perform. The hesitancy concerns only the precise way in which we are to round on the original "I know" or "I promise".' And finally: 'To suppose that "I know" is a descriptive phrase is only one example of the *descriptive fallacy*, so common in philosophy.'[16]

I believe that this extended comparison, while of great interest at the time as introducing Austin's fertile topic of performative utterance, is both unilluminating and indeed misleading about knowledge.

'You are prohibited from saying "I know it is so, but I may be wrong", just as you are prohibited from saying "I promise I will, but I may fail".'[17] We can see that at least the phrase 'just as' is wrong here, if we change the grammatical person. I myself indeed cannot properly say 'I promise, but I may fail'; you, on the other hand, can perfectly well say *of* me 'He promises; – or 'has promised' – 'but he may fail': I have undertaken a commitment which *you* are not sure that I shall (be able to) actually carry out, and there is nothing off-colour about that. That, however, does not work for 'know'. As before, I cannot properly say 'I know, but I may be wrong'; but neither can you or anyone else say *of* me 'He knows, but he may be wrong': if you think I may be wrong, then your saying that I know is 'ruled out' no less firmly than is my saying so, if *I* think that.

Why is that? Well, to say 'I promise to do A' is to make a promise, to undertake, 'ritually' to commit myself, to do A in due time. If so, to say 'I promise to do A, but I may fail' can only be a pretty self-defeating performance; the first clause issues a commitment, a guarantee of performance, which the second clause proceeds to retract. But that presents no problem to somebody speaking *of* me. For in saying of me 'He promises' – as Austin rightly insists – another speaker himself issues no commitment; he merely says that I do; and it is of course perfectly consistent for *him* to say that I make a commitment and that I may fail to carry it out. The case of 'know' is quite different from that. 'I know that S is P' *entails* (of course among other things) that S is P, that I am correct in holding that S is P. If so, to say 'I know that S is P, but I may be wrong' is not just an ineffectual, self-defeating performance; it is actually the utterance of a self-contradictory proposition; and that being so, it can no more properly be said of me by somebody else than of me by myself. If it may not be true that S is P, then, simply, it cannot be the case that I know that S is P – whoever may say that I do, myself or anybody else, or even if nobody says it.

This is of course the (valid) ground of the objection which Austin regrettably underplays as 'more apparent than real'. It can be true that I promised but failed to perform, since it can of course, unproblematically if regrettably, be the case that I undertook a commitment which I subsequently failed to fulfil. But since 'I know that S is P' entails that S is P, then necessarily, if it turns out that S is not P, it has to be untrue that I knew that S is P – however positively, or indeed with however much justification, I or anybody else may beforehand have said that I did. In this case, there is at least this respect in which there is no hesitancy at all as to 'the precise way in which we are to round on the original "I know" '. We may argue about whether, or how far, I was justified in saying I knew; but actually I did *not* know, there is no room for argument, or any occasion for hesitancy, about that.

The performative comparison at least temporarily misleads Austin, I believe, in another respect. With a genuine performative, a 'ritual' formula, we can properly raise the question what one who issues it (in appropriate circumstances) *does*; it is, so to speak, specifically 'for' doing some particular thing, and we may ask (it will often be obvious) what that thing is. Austin unfortunately – if only temporarily – suggests that we can do this also for 'I know'. 'When I say "I know", I *give others my word*: *I give others my authority for saying* that S is P.'[18] But that – as some of his own earlier examples show – fits only some of the cases. If you ask me as a doctor whether I am sure that the prescribed medicine is safe for children, I may reply that I know that it is; and in so replying

I give you my word as a medical man, my professional authority, for that: that is what I *do*. But what if you tell me that George is coming to lunch, and I say unexcitedly 'Yes, I know'? In so saying I surely do not 'give you my authority': in such a case, after all, you do not *need* my authority, since you for your part already know (perfectly well) that George is coming to lunch, as you have told me: all *I* have done is to *tell* you that I know that too. Besides authoritatively, for example as a doctor, pronouncing or declaring that I know, I may for instance shamefacedly admit, or reluctantly confess, or unguardedly disclose that I know, and no doubt do scores of other things too – including, as in the case cited, just colourlessly 'saying' that I know some fact that may already be known to all my hearers and not remotely the subject of any doubt or dispute. Compare Austin's own example: 'I know, I *know*, I've seen it a hundred times, don't keep on telling me.'[19] There is clearly no question of 'giving others my authority' there.

The fact surely is that 'I know' is not, in Austin's sense, an 'obvious ritual phrase' at all, a phrase by the (appropriate) utterance of which some particular thing is 'ceremonially' done. It is of course glaringly obvious that whereas to say 'I promise' is to promise, to say 'I bet' is to bet, and so on, to say 'I know' is *not* to *know*; but neither is it, in itself, to do anything else in particular, except of course to *say*, truly or maybe falsely, *that* I know. It seems to me that Austin actually gives no reason for his striking conclusion that it is a mistake, an example of the 'descriptive fallacy', to suppose that 'I know' is 'a descriptive phrase';[20] but I think I see how he came to be misled into that conclusion. His ritual, performative phrases, 'I promise' and so on, are indeed phrases in whose utterance something is *done*. He had observed, of course quite correctly, that in saying 'I know' something is *done*. And that made it seem to him at the time that 'I know' must itself be a sort of, or akin to a, ritual phrase. I believe that, in 1946, Austin had not yet clearly seen that, besides his special class of performatives, in *all* (normal) utterance, including the utterance of undoubted descriptive phrases, *something* is done; in that sense *any* (normal) utterance is in a way performative, has its performative aspect if you like, but may nevertheless be quite ordinarily, standardly descriptive. But, that being so, that I do something (or other) in saying 'I know' has no tendency to show that it is not a descriptive phrase.

In this whole passage Austin seems to have rather forgotten a point he had actually made, and correctly made, right at the outset: namely, that I may know something, and perhaps be quite naturally asked whether I know it or how I know it, without necessarily saying or ever having said *that* I know it. Promising, betting, and the rest consist (nearly enough) essentially in saying something – if I am to do the thing, I have actually to utter the prescribed 'ritual phrase'; but to know something is not necessarily, and certainly not essentially, to say anything at all. It has been true of me all day today, for example, that I know that today is Wednesday; yet I have had no occasion, as it happens, to *say* that today is Wednesday, still less any occasion to say that I know that it is. (It could be true of me, incidentally, that I know that today is Wednesday, not only in spite of the fact that I have had no occasion to say so, but even if I have actually never given the matter a thought. If you were to ask 'Do you suppose he knows what day of the week it is?' the answer 'Yes, I'm sure he does' does not necessarily presuppose that the question has ever actually entered my head: something can be 'within my knowledge' without ever being actually in my thoughts, let alone on my lips.) The comparison with promising leads Austin, temporarily and unhappily, to concentrate on the case of someone's actually *saying* 'I know', in spite of his being, really, perfectly well aware both that someone who knows does not necessarily say that, and also that someone who (even justifiably) says it perhaps does not know.

So what is to be said about 'If I know, I can't be wrong'? The reason, surely, why that makes 'perfectly good sense' is a good deal simpler than Austin makes it out to be. It is not a matter – or not *just* a matter – of what I am committed to by *saying* that I know; it is simply that a proposition's being known *entails* that it is true, so that, if a proposition is or turns out to be false, any assertion that anybody knew it must be retracted. And that, of course, is why 'He knows it, but it isn't so' is every bit as wrong, and for just the same reason, as 'I know it, but it isn't so'.

In the last four pages of his paper Austin confronts directly the official topic of the symposium 'Other minds'. 'How can I know what is in another person's mind?' Very cautiously, he says that it 'seems likely' that the question covers a number of significantly different cases: how can I tell what someone thinks (or perhaps 'really' thinks) about the next election, about my chances of promotion, or the immortality of the soul? How can I tell what he is thinking about here and now? How can I tell what his sensations are? Or what his feelings are, or his intentions, or his likes and dislikes, or his mood? He will consider, he says, the case of 'feelings and emotions, with special reference to anger'.[21]

Of course, as he sensibly observes, quite often the answer will be that I can't tell and don't know; but there is no reason to be distressed by, or to boggle at, that; for no one supposes that we always *do* know 'what is in another person's mind', or even that we could find out. There are kinds of people – 'royalty, for example, or fakirs or bushmen or Wykehamists or simple eccentrics'[22] – whose feelings may be very hard or impossible for us to divine. Even more than in the case of the gold-finch, we may need, and may actually lack, some prior experience of both this kind of individual and probably this particular individual. Sitting opposite a total stranger on a Turkish railway, why should I *expect* to be able to tell what he is thinking?

It seems to be a special point about feelings that, if I am really to know what you are feeling, I must be able to imagine, or 'appreciate', what you are feeling – and this may perhaps even amount to the requirement that I must have felt the same way myself. Otherwise, while I might know quite well what your feeling is *called*, we might well wish to say that I don't really know 'what it is like', what it is to have that feeling – real physical fear, for example, or acute hunger. I may even hesitate to say that I know that his motive is, say, ambition, if I am conscious that I myself have never felt such a thing, and do not really know 'what it is like' to feel it.

It is tempting to say – and to pose the 'problem' in this way – that an angry man *feels* anger 'in his mind', but that the rest of us can be aware, at best, only of 'signs' of his anger; how then are we to make a reliable transition from the signs to the feeling? Austin finds this way of stating the case misleading.[23]

First, the ordinary notion of a sign, in general, he says, stands in contrast with that of the manifest presence of the thing itself. Much as, when I find the malefactor in London, that is not (even very good) *evidence* that he is there,[24] so finding a fox in the chicken-run is not a (particularly good) *sign* that a fox has got in. Thus 'signs of anger' tend, Austin says, to mean signs of rising, or impending, or suppressed anger; and they tend to stand in contrast, not with the 'feeling' of anger, but with the actual explosion, the display or manifestation or exhibition of anger. Certainly, if we had only the signs to go on, we might hesitate to say that we know (yet) that he is angry; but the case is different when the anger is actually displayed, much as it is when we actually find the fox in the chicken-run.

It is an over-simplification to say that (an emotion like) anger is essentially just an inner feeling, with which certain detectable 'signs' are more or less reliably associated. That leaves out of the picture the 'displays' of anger, and other things too. There is in fact, Austin suggests, a fairly complex 'pattern', or package, in such a case, made up of various elements.[25] There are occasions, or circumstances, which naturally tend, and would be expected, understandably to arouse anger: there are ways of behaving, even of looking, to which an angry person is naturally inclined, which are not just signs of, but express or give vent to, his anger. Being angry is not *just*, purely and simply, having a certain feeling, quite apart from any thoughts about the situation you are in, or 'any impulse, however vague, to vent the anger in the natural way'. That is why, Austin notes, a person who says he is angry may 'sometimes accept corrections from outsiders'; whatever 'the feeling' he has, taking more careful note of the circumstances and the rest of the 'pattern' may bring him to agree that he was really not so much angry as, say, indignant, or jealous, or resentful.[26] It is important to remember that we learn to say we are angry by noting what goes on when others say *they* are angry, and what goes on when others say of us that *we* are angry. 'Mere' feelings, if there are such, without natural occasions or natural ways of expression, would certainly be 'very hard to be sure about': but emotions, in general, are certainly not 'mere' feelings in that sense.

There are of course, Austin goes on, special difficulties about emotions, that do not arise in the case of knowing that it's a goldfinch. An emotion *may* be suppressed: a person may really be angry while deliberately not displaying anger in any natural (or any other) way. Also, an emotion may be feigned: a person may convincingly put up a display of, say, anger though not really angry at all. Again, if I do not know a person well, or even if I do, I may misunderstand him – misread, so to speak, the parts of the pattern that I observe in his demeanour or behaviour. I may even be unsure, in my own case, what my own feelings really are – whether I may not be, as it were to myself, feigning or suppressing, or misunderstanding myself. But, Austin insists, there are ways of trying to deal with such difficult cases, not *wholly* unlike ways of trying to deal with uncertainties about birds: ways of establishing that he really was, or was not really, angry; sometimes at least we can do that, though of course not always. 'There is no suggestion that I *never* know what other people's emotions are, nor yet that in particular cases I might be wrong for no special reason or in no special way.'[27]

But finally, there is one further special feature. 'The goldfinch, the material object, is . . . uninscribed and *mute*; but the man *speaks*.' Two distinguishable issues arise here. The first is that, as Austin says, 'a peculiar place is occupied by the man's own statement as to what his feelings are. In the usual case, we accept this statement without question.'[28] Why is that? Austin seems to feel, and I think he is right, that for him at least no particular mystery is here involved. Of course he does not hold that, in saying how he feels, a man could not be wrong, so that his statement holds 'a peculiar place' for that reason, is 'incorrigible'. Certainly, in fairly complex cases like that of the emotions, a person may misidentify his own feeling, and may even be brought, as we have said, by other people to realize that he has. (That is so, Austin of course insists, even if it is only his *sensations* that are in question.) Again, he may be a habitual fantasizer or self-deceiver, or in a particular case be obviously liable to fantasy or self-deception: in such a case we should be happy enough to reject his statement, or at any rate not feel particularly inclined to accept it. We may say perhaps two pertinent things. One is that although a person is by no means an infallible appraiser and reporter of his own feelings, in the ordinary way he is at least as well placed as possible to get it right; he is, so to speak, his own perpetual eyewitness, and is not handicapped, as others may be, by any mere lack of opportunity for discerning how things are with him. It may be worth mentioning too that, very often perhaps, there is simply no point or interest in questioning what he says; if he says he felt a spark of irritation, it would normally be pointless and unprofitable not simply to accept that he did. Why argue about it?

But second, and finally, Austin raises, and recognizes that 'as philosophers' we shall certainly wish to raise, the different question: when a person speaks, what reason have we to believe him *ever*? What justifies us in supposing, *ever*, that when a person speaks what he says is even more likely to be true than not? 'What "justification" is there for supposing that there is another mind communicating with you at all?'[29] How do you *know*, how *could* you know, that you are not the only human inhabitant in a world of robots? Some philosophers would say that the 'real' problem about other minds is precisely that.

What Austin has to say on this no doubt important matter is extremely brief and rather cryptic. There are, he says, tempting replies that will not really do. We may be tempted to say that, quite often, we do actually find out in all sorts of unproblematic cases that what people say is true, so that, though our experience in that respect is not quite invariably reassuring, it is possible to construct a kind of inductive argument which makes it rational, in general, to believe them rather than not. That, however, does not, presumably, rule out the theoretical possibility that 'they' are all robots; but here we may be tempted to say that the supposition that what seem to be people really are people is a *theory*, or hypothesis, that explains rather well the course of our experience, and is to be preferred to the robot hypothesis as a good deal simpler and less fantastic. What Austin means, I think, by holding that such replies will not really do is that though tempting and even in a way obvious, they are too thin, too feeble, too academic, to fit the case. It seems to be 'a distortion' to suggest that we are disposed in general to accept what people say because we have – or that we are 'justified' in so doing only in so far as there is – an inductive argument which shows that to be the rational thing to do. The question, *in general*, simply does not arise in that way. And it seems fantastic to suggest that our 'belief' that there are people besides ourselves with whom communication is possible is just a *theory* that fits in well with the experience we have. 'It seems, rather,' Austin says, 'that believing in other persons, in authority and testimony, is an essential part of the act of communicating, an act which we all constantly perform.' It cannot be treated as a completely, genuinely open question whether the business of communicating – which provides us, incidentally, with all the terms in which we ourselves think as well as talk – is aimed, so to speak, at the communication of truth.

Believing other persons – unless we have particular reason not to – is, Austin says, 'an irreducible part of our experience'.[30] It cannot sensibly be treated coolly, as something that we may or may not be 'justified' in doing, or that stands in any need of argumentative justification. Not to do it, one might almost say, if it were really possible would be a kind of madness, a gross and fundamental deviation from human normality. If I were *really*, suddenly, afflicted with the suspicion that my wife, say, and all my colleagues might actually be robots, to try to argue me out of it would be to misread the situation. I would stand in need not of an argument but of a spell of sabbatical leave or a course of therapy. It is pretty clear, I think, that something of that sort is what Austin had in mind.

IV

Truth

Austin's paper 'Truth', which was the first contribution to a three-paper symposium at the Joint Session of 1950, has been the occasion of as much sharp controversy as any of his writings. I shall not sift through this controversial fall-out in detail, since much of it was, I believe, beside the point – sometimes insisting upon things that Austin did not deny, sometimes firmly denying things that he did not assert, and sometimes debating issues that, to the main issue, do not much matter. It will be as well, however, to glance at some of these points by way of one or two preliminary observations.

First, then, it is noteworthy that in this connection Austin very clearly and definitely does *not* make the sort of mistake, as I have taken it to be, into which he temporarily deviated in writing about knowledge. There, as we have seen, he gave a temporarily conspicuous place to the question what one who says 'I know . . .' *does* in saying so – not, of course, an improper question in itself, for no doubt one who speaks so always does something; also, however, not a very useful question since, depending on the circumstances, one who speaks so may be doing any of a number of different things. Nor does the question bear at all on the central matter of what it is for it to be true of him that he knows – whether he himself says that he does, or other people say that, or even if that he knows is never *said* by anyone at all. Austin, it will be remembered, in this case misleads himself so far as to say that 'I know' is not 'a descriptive phrase' at all – by which he seems clearly to imply (what else *could* he mean?) the surely manifest falsehood that 'I know that . . .', anyway when said by me of myself, makes no assertion at all and can be neither true nor false. Now it would not have been very surprising if, with his keen and characteristic interest in the 'performative' aspect of speech, he had sought illumination about truth by asking what a speaker who says '. . . is true' therein does. In fact, however, in this case he firmly and explicitly declines that gambit. It is no doubt the case,

45

he says, that to say that some proposition p is true will be, depending on the circumstances, to do one or other of quite a number of things – to confirm that p, for example, or to insist, or concede, or grant, or emphasize, or acknowledge that p. But it does not follow from that, he rightly says, that to say that p is true is not *also* to make some assertion about p; and it leaves on our hands the central question what it is that is therein asserted. In fact, p's being true, he says – and of course one might wish that he had said the same (which he perfectly well knew to be true) about p's being known – does not necessarily involve anyone's *saying* anything at all. And his last word in the paper is the explicit suggestion, which he clearly holds to be correct, that '. . . is true', notwithstanding its multifarious possible performative roles, *is* a 'descriptive phrase'.[1] That part of the controversy, then, which consists in suggesting that Austin had somehow failed to see, had culpably overlooked, that '. . . is true' has (many) performative roles, is beside the point. Austin saw that quite clearly, but saw also, and said, that it is substantially irrelevant to the question, as one might put it, what '. . . is true' *means*. It is ironic that in this case other people seem to have been led astray exactly as one might have feared that Austin would be, but he was not.

Second, there arose from Austin's paper much sharp argument about 'facts'. It was argued immediately and strongly by Strawson that it could not be profitable to seek to illuminate the notion of truth by considering a supposed relation between truths and facts, since that relation is too close, too formal, and therefore too trivial, to be illuminating.[2] If it is true that p, then, trivially, it is a fact that p; but the fact that p is not something 'in the world' which 'makes' it true that p; it is simply what the statement that p states (if it is true), and it is an inevitably unilluminating truism to say so. The dialectical picture is somewhat obscured here by the circumstance that Austin was at great pains to dissent from this, at least in part. In his later paper 'Unfair to facts'[3] (written in 1954 but not published at that time) he raises a quite elaborate battery of objections to the fairly obscure thesis that facts are not 'in the world', or are 'pseudo-entities'. I think it clear, however, that to the assessment of the central thesis of his paper 'Truth', this particular line of controversy is really irrelevant. His 'definition' – if that is what it is – of truth in that paper actually makes no mention of 'facts'; and indeed he goes on, immediately after producing it, to say explicitly that 'trouble arises' from the use of the word 'facts', so that it had better be avoided.[4] Here then we have another case, I think, of ill-targeted shooting.

It may be said, though – and this is my last preliminary observation – that he rather invited misunderstanding here by indicating general approval of the 'correspondence theory' of truth, and by saying that 'when it corresponds to the facts' is a perfectly good answer to the

46

question 'When is a statement true?' 'As a piece of standard English this can hardly be wrong. Indeed, I must confess I do not really think it is wrong at all: the theory of truth is a series of truisms.'[5] But he adds: 'Still, it can be misleading', and so it can be; for, as he immediately goes on to say, a statement's being true, as he sees it, is not a matter of its standing in some single relation – to be called 'correspondence' – to some single other term – 'the facts' – but more than one relationship between, as he puts it, 'the words' and 'the world', relationships in the account of which 'the facts' do not substantively figure.

I believe it will be helpful to introduce further examination of his views about truth by looking first at another paper, the very strange piece called 'How to talk: some simple ways'. It is true that this piece was written, or at any rate published, some three years later than 'Truth'; it is true also that its avowed object was not to throw light on the notion of truth, but to advance our understanding of a certain (quite small) class of 'speech-acts'. But 'How to talk' does incorporate, more or less inexplicitly, a distinctive, highly simplified 'picture' of what truth is. It is, I think, much more than likely that Austin already had this picture in mind when he was writing 'Truth'; in any case, if we look first at the simplified picture, certain features of the earlier account seem to me to become easier to understand.[6]

'How to talk' is, as I have said, a very strange piece. Its declared purpose, indeed, is not surprising: 'we are engaged', Austin says, 'to elucidate some of our ordinary language about speech-acts'.[7] But usually, when he wished to 'elucidate some of our ordinary language', he did so, as one might say, directly, by examining in detail the uses of certain ordinary phrases or expressions in the sort of circumstances and contexts in which they ordinarily and naturally occur. His procedure here is absolutely different. He asks us to imagine an almost extravagantly artificial 'world', and a 'language' to go with it stripped, or simplified, to the near-minimum of resources that could count as a language at all, and then to consider, in that clear but bleakly schematic setting, what speech-acts are distinguishable. Presumably this most uncharacteristic way of proceeding was adopted, in this unique instance, as a methodological experiment; and perhaps we may infer, from the fact that he never tried it again, that he did not judge the experiment to have been particularly successful. I think, however, it may prove instructive for our present purposes.

We are to imagine, then, what Austin calls 'Speech-situation S_0'. The 'world', in this situation, is to consist of an indefinite number of individual 'items', each of one and only one definite 'type': an array, as a rough instance perhaps, of colour-patches each of some distinct and specific shade of colour, or each of some distinct and specific geometrical shape.

(We are to ignore the point that the colour-patches have shapes, or that the shapes have colours; we may suppose that the colour-patches all have the same – therefore uninteresting, unremarkable – shape, or that the shapes are all of the same – therefore insignificant – colour.) Each item is to be 'totally and equally distinct' from every other item, each type 'totally and equally different' from every other type.[8] Numerous items may be of the same type but, as we have said, none of more than one. Both items and types are to be apprehended by simple inspection.

The 'language' we are to imagine, in this situation, consists of expressions of three and only three mutually exclusive sorts. First, there are 'I-words', for example numerals, each of which is assigned uniquely as a 'reference' to – in *some* ways rather like a proper name of – its own individual item. Second, there are 'T-words', vocables each uniquely associated with its own item-type (say, a colour or a shape). Third, there is 'is a', which we may call the 'assertive link'. The language permits the formation of sentences of one and only one form, namely 'I is a T', for example '1227 is a rhombus'. Nothing else will be a sentence in S_o. '1227' is attached by 'conventions of reference' to its individual item; it is purely conventional that *this* item is to be so referred to. 'Rhombus' is attached by 'conventions of sense' to its particular type; it is purely conventional that *that* type should be assigned that particular name. It is thus purely conventional that the sentence '1227 is a rhombus' has in S_o the meaning that it has; and it is purely by convention that, when that sentence is uttered by way of assertion, the assertion made is that 1227 is a rhombus. But it is of course *not* a question of convention, but of simple fact, whether or not 1227 *is* a rhombus.

It is, I think, Austin's main purpose to show that, even in this starkly simple world and employing this highly minimal language, the possibilities for speech-acts are more numerous than one might expect. In using any I-word, for example '1227', I am of course *referring* to an individual item; and in using any T-word, for example, 'rhombus', I am (what Austin rather oddly calls) *naming* a type. But one might think that, in producing the whole utterance '1227 is a rhombus', there is one and only one thing that I can be doing – simply saying, asserting, stating, that 1227 is a rhombus. It is, Austin says, not so simple as that: perhaps I am always 'asserting' that 1227 is a rhombus, but there are, he says, four distinct ways of doing so – 'four species, if you like, of the generic speech-act of asserting'.[9]

I shall not go into this in great detail because it lies rather off the track of our present concern, but in summary what Austin has in mind is this. First, I may start off, so to speak, with a given item before me, say 1227, and have to find a pattern to match it, that is to settle its type; if I succeed, I say '1227 is a *rhombus*'. Austin calls this 'placing' or sometimes 'cap-fitting': I fit the cap *rhombus* to the given item. Second, I may start off with a given type, say rhombus, and have to find a sample or specimen to fit it; if I succeed, I say '1227 is a rhombus'. Austin calls this 'casting' or 'bill-filling': as a rhombus, the item 1227 fills the bill. Third, there is what he calls 'stating': I have this given item, and I have to find a pattern, not to match to it as in 'placing', but to match it to. And finally 'instancing': I have a given pattern, and have to find an item, not to fit to it as in 'casting', but to fit it to. We have four species, it seems, because, in saying 'I is a T', we fit the name to the item or the item to the name on the ground that the *type* of the item and the *sense* of the name *match*';[10] but in matching there is a distinction in *onus of match*: matching type to sense is distinguishable from matching sense to type (just as, or much as, fitting item to name is distinguishable from fitting name to item).

However that may be (I have damaged it a little, I suspect, in the cause of brevity), let us raise the question of current interest: what is it for an assertion in S_o to be *true*? Note first that in S_o, simple though it is, we must yet distinguish a *sentence* – say '1227 is a rhombus' – from the assertion that 1227 is rhombus; I might, for instance, utter or write the sentence '1227 is a rhombus' not by way of asserting that 1227 is a rhombus, but, say, in practising the formation and utterance of sentences, or giving instances of word-strings that are well-formed sentences in S_o. In such cases I am not (really) referring to or naming anything, but merely, for some reason or other, producing a sentence. If, however, in producing the sentence '1227 is a rhombus', I *do* (really) refer and name, then, in S_o, there is no further question of what I have therein asserted, what 'statement' I have made; for it is a stipulated feature of S_o that '1227', if used to refer, refers always and uniquely (or, more strictly, the speaker so refers) to *the* item 1227; and it is stipulated that 'rhombus' names one and only one type; so that in every assertive utterance of '1227 is a rhombus' any speaker says the same thing about the same thing, namely of 1227 that 1227 is a rhombus. In these circumstances to utter assertively the same sentence is always to make the same assertion. So what is it for the assertion to be true (not, we may remark, for it to be *said* to be true, since S_o provides no means of saying any such thing)? Well: the assertion that 1227 is a rhombus is true (Austin also says 'satisfactory') when the item referred to by the I-word – '1227' – is of a type which matches the sense of the T-word – 'rhombus'. Or let us put the question in this way: in order for me to be in a position to see – and perhaps, in a language more richly equipped than that of S_o, to say – that it is true that 1227 is a rhombus, what do I need to know? Two things, it seems. First, I need to know, in virtue of the language's conventions of reference, what item, or which item, it is pertinent to the question on hand to inspect; and second, I need to know, in virtue of the language's conventions of sense, what it is that that item is said to be. In S_o no great problem can arise in either case: the I-word '1227' makes a reference uniquely to the item 1227, so that that is the item pertinently to be inspected; and the assertive linking of the T-word 'rhombus' says quite unambiguously of the item referred to that it is a rhombus. If on inspection I see that it is indeed a rhombus, then I see that the assertion that 1227 is a rhombus is *true*. The crucial questions are: (1) what to inspect, and (2) what it is said to be, and also of course finally (3) whether it *is* what it is said to be.

Let us turn back now to the paper 'Truth', in which we are to consider 'the use, or certain uses' of 'true', not now with reference only to the starkly simplified language and 'world' of S_o, but in 'ordinary' languages and the 'real' world. We shall find that Austin's account resembles quite closely the account of truth that we have extracted from S_o – it has much the same 'shape', as it were – but with certain differences which, if we bear S_o in mind, will become, I think, rather easier to understand.

First, what is it of which truth can be predicated? Well, Austin says, not sentences. We have seen that, even in S_o, it was necessary to distinguish the sentence '1227 is a rhombus' from the assertion that 1227 is a rhombus – on the ground (and there perhaps only on the ground) that the sentence might be produced non-assertively, perhaps simply as an instance of a well-formed sentence, in which case no question of truth arises; but of course, in S_o, if a given sentence *is* assertively produced, there is no room for uncertainty as to what assertion is therein made – any assertive utterance of the sentence '1227 is a rhombus' can be *only* the assertion that 1227 is a rhombus. In a natural language the distinction between sentence and assertion is more patently necessary; for of course the same sentence may be uttered in making different assertions – 'My cat is a tabby' said by two or more different owners of cats; and the same assertion may be made in different sentences, as I may assert that my cat is a tabby in both French and English. Moreover, in natural languages, but not in S_o, words and sentences may be ambiguous. If so, what is true (or not) cannot be the sentence 'My cat is a tabby'; what is true (or not) is what some particular use of that sentence (or of other sentences) asserts to be the case: namely, that the particular cat referred to is a tabby. Austin elects, not at all fervently, to say that what are true (or not) are *statements*; and there seems no particular reason to object to that usage, provided that we distinguish statements, in this sense, not only from the sentences in which they are or might be made, but also from the datable occasions ('statings' perhaps) of their being made – and provided we remember also that a statement, in this sense, need not in fact be *made* at all: that pigs can fly – the 'statement' that pigs can fly – may of course be true (or not), whether or not it has ever been stated by anyone that pigs can fly.[11] The question 'Is it true that pigs can fly?'

perhaps *suggests*, or implies, that somebody has stated that they can; for
if no such statement has been made or even envisaged, it would be more
natural, perhaps, simply to raise the question 'Can pigs fly?' Nevertheless, it would obviously be wrong to suggest that it can *be true* (or not)
that pigs can fly, only if someone or other has stated that they can (or
not).

Austin then turns to the question, what are the conditions necessary
for there 'to be communication of the sort that we achieve by language
at all'. First, he says, there must be 'a stock of symbols of some kind'
which a 'speaker' can produce and an 'audience' observe. We may call
these 'words', though of course it is a contingent matter that *our* 'stock'
consists of the sort of complex sounds and inscriptions that are ordinarily
so called. Then there must be something besides (though including) the
words, which the words are to be used to communicate about: call this
a 'world'.

And finally (for present purposes – of course there are other
conditions to be satisfied too) there must be two sets of conventions:
  Descriptive conventions correlating the words (= sentences) with
the *types* of situation, thing, event, etc., to be found in the world.
  Demonstrative conventions correlating the words (= statements)
with the *historic* situations, etc., to be found in the world.
  A statement is said to be true when the historic state of affairs to
which it is correlated by the demonstrative conventions (the one to
which it 'refers') is of a type with which the sentence used in making
it is correlated by the descriptive conventions.[12]

Now this is clearly reminiscent of, and rather like, what Austin had to
say (or, historically speaking, later said) about 'Speech situation S_0'.
There too we had 'a stock of symbols' on the one hand, and 'a world'
on the other; and there too we had 'two sets of conventions', there called,
not 'descriptive' and 'demonstrative' conventions, but 'conventions of
sense' and 'conventions of reference'. But there is a notable difference.
In S_0, the so-called conventions of sense correlated with 'types', not
'words (= sentences)', but *some* of the words, namely T-Words, *parts*
of sentences; and the conventions of reference correlated with individuals, not 'words (= statements)', but, again, some of the words, in
this case I-words, parts of sentences. Why, in 'Truth', does Austin put
it differently?

The answer, I believe, is clear enough, and may even be obvious. It
is that the 'words' of natural languages cannot be neatly and exclusively
divided into, and indeed do not really include, I-words and T-words.
In S_0, I-words, the numerals, had no 'sense'; their use, and their *only*
use, was to refer, each unequivocally and always to its own individual
item; and such words, and only such, invariably appeared in the subject-

place in the only kind of sentence which S₀ permitted. Similarly, T-words had senses, but could never be used to refer, and invariably appeared – naming 'types' – in the predicate-place in the only permitted sentences. Natural languages contain no such classes of mutually exclusive words – certainly not proper names (there have been scores of different people, and some animals, called 'Napoleon'). Again, in natural languages most (all?) of the words that can occur in the predicate-place in subject-predicate sentences can permissibly also occur in the subject-place; we have not only 'This is a cat', but also 'This cat is black'; we have 'Black is' – or, as some pedantically insist, is not – 'a colour', and 'The black cat is a tom'.

But that does not take us all the way. It may be agreed that natural languages do not contain I-words and T-words – words wholly without 'sense' that can be used only in making absolutely unique references, and other words with 'senses' that can be used only in unambiguous predication. However, one might say, although it follows from that that 'demonstrative conventions' do not in natural language govern the use of a specifiable class of *words*, do they not, nevertheless, govern the use of identifiable *parts* of sentences? In such a sentence as 'The black cat is a tom', though the phrase 'the black cat' has sense and is admittedly not an I-word in the sense of S₀, surely it *is* that part of the sentence which, when the sentence is uttered in asserting, refers (or, is used in referring); and though 'tom', or 'a tom', is admittedly not a T-word, is it not in this case that part of the sentence which 'describes', which assigns the thing referred to to a certain 'type'? If so, then should not Austin's two sets of conventions, in 'Truth', be seen as applying, not indeed to mutually exclusive classes of words as in S₀, but to, as one might say, distinguishable functions – demonstrative conventions to those part of sentences which (while normally having descriptive meanings too) are used in referring, descriptive conventions to those parts of sentences in which predication is done? It has in fact been said to be a serious mistake on Austin's part to suggest, as he does, that there is anything at all to which *whole sentences* 'refer', in anything like the way in which, in 'The black cat is a tom', *part* of that sentence refers, unproblematically, to a particular black cat.

Well, mistake or not, I think it is perfectly clear why Austin puts the case as he does, and *not* as it is thus suggested that he should have put it. We must notice here another respect in which natural languages differ from the simplified model language of S₀. In that model, every sentence was of exactly the same form, 'I is a T'; every sentence had an I-word as its grammatical subject, and a T-word as predicate; accordingly, the distinct functions of referring and describing ('naming') could always be assigned to distinct parts of sentences, the subject and the predicate. In natural languages, however, not only are there no I-words or T-words

– there is also no single form of permissible sentence; not every sentence is of the subject-predicate form, in which part of the sentence could be said to refer to something, and another part to predicate something of the item so referred to. Thus, if we are to have an even tolerably general account of what it is for a statement to be true, that account must not be put in terms which restrict it *only* to subject-predicate sentences, sentences in which the roles of referring and describing can be assigned to distinct parts of those sentences. If so, it seems that demonstrative conventions do indeed need to 'operate', so to speak, not on parts of sentences – since many sentences contain no appropriately distinguishable parts – but on sentences as wholes.

Yes, it may be said, no doubt something of this sort is what Austin's account *needs*, if it is not to come out, unacceptably, as 'fitting' only one particular sentence-form. But is it clear that what is needed can intelligibly be supplied? It has been suggested that the sort of account which Austin offers actually does fit, intelligibly, only subject-predicate sentences, however much he may have wished, and attempted, to make it cover other cases besides.

I believe that this suggestion can be shown to be wrong. Let us go back again for a moment to the simple model of S_o. In S_o, a statement is made, for example that 1227 is a rhombus; and I ask – perhaps I ask myself, silently – whether that is true. As we said earlier, if I am to be in a position to answer that question, there are two things that I essentially need to know: I need to know, first, what, or which, item it is relevant to the question at issue to inspect, and second, what it is that that item is stated to be. I need to know that it is irrelevant what 1225 may be, or 193, or 2215 – that 1227 only is pertinent to the issue; and I need to be able to recognize the type 'rhombus'. Now in S_o these matters are settled easily enough. If I know the language, I know straight off that 1227, and only that, is in question – nothing else, after all, could be so referred to; and I know unambiguously what that item is said to be. I know, as one might put it, where to look, namely at 1227; and I know also what I am looking *for*, namely the type that it is said to be, and its being (or, as it may turn out, its not being) of that type, that is, a rhombus.

In natural languages things, even when pretty simple, are never *so* simple. Suppose the statement to be made that Felix is asleep. If I know the language, I know pretty well what sort of situation is thereby alleged to obtain: 'Felix' is a proper name, presumably of some animal or person, and that animal or person is said to be asleep. But no doubt many people and animals are called 'Felix', and in order to know whose current state is actually relevant to the truth or falsity of the statement made, I need to know who, or what, is being referred to by the name 'Felix' on this particular occasion. But that can be done; and, assuming that it is done, we have a simple situation much resembling that of S_o. I know where to look, namely at (let us say) this particular person, and what to look *for*, namely his being (or, as it may turn out, his not being) asleep.

But now consider a statement of a very different kind – for example, the statement that the dodo is extinct. No statement of anything like this sort occurred in S_o; for whereas in S_o every statement referred to, was 'about', a specific individual, this statement (notwithstanding the singular form of its grammatical subject) is not 'about' any individual dodo, nor yet any particular group of dodos; and whereas in S_o every statement 'described' the item referred to in a specific way, assigned it to a type, this statement says nothing at all as to what dodos are (or the dodo is) *like*. What the statement says is that there once existed some dodos and now there are none. There is in this statement nothing corresponding to the reference and predication of '1227 is a rhombus', or 'Felix is asleep'. One might think, then, that in this case, since there is no question of what or which individual, or even what or which individuals, are being talked about, there is nothing at all for 'demonstrative conventions' to do; that, in order to be in a position to investigate whether the statement is true, all that we need to know is what – in virtue of 'descriptive' conventions – the sentence used in making it *means*. It is easy to see, however, that that cannot be right. Let us suppose that the dodo became extinct in 1713. Then the statement that the dodo is extinct, made in 1712, would have been false; whereas the statement made today, in a sentence having exactly the same meaning, is true. And that is to say that in this case, just as much as in the case of the statement that Felix is asleep, I need to know, in setting out to investigate whether the statement is true, what it is pertinent to that issue to investigate, to 'inspect'. Demonstrative conventions 'correlate' the statement made in 1712, not indeed to any specific individuals, but to the state of the world – its fauna-content, so to speak – at and prior to that date. Did it at that date contain any dodos? If it did, the statement is false. If the statement is made today, then it is pertinent to investigate the state of the world at and prior to *this* date; if there were dodos around at some earlier date and now there are none, then the statement that the dodo is extinct is true, and it is nothing to the purpose that a statement made in the same words at an earlier date might have been false – except, of course, that such a statement at *some* earlier date *must* have been false, if it is to be true today that the dodo is extinct. (Unicorns are not 'extinct'.)

It is particularly to be noted here that we are confronting matters that did not arise in S_o, not only because 'The dodo is extinct' is a sentence-form that S_o did not provide for, but also because the 'world' in which we and natural languages dwell is unlike that of S_o in one enormously important respect: namely, it *changes*. It was in fact taken for granted, or stipulated, in S_o that, if, say, 1227 is a rhombus, it also always was and always will be a rhombus – for which reason the language had no tenses or other indications of time, and for the question whether it is true that 1227 is a rhombus, it did not matter in the least when that statement was made. But our world and things in our world change; and therefore, in considering whether some statement is true, we need crucially to know to the state of affairs at what time or times it relates; this we may know sometimes from the terms in which the statement is made, or, more commonly, from the time at which it is made. And of course, a statement made at a certain time may be true, and a statement made in identical words at another time may be false – if things have changed.

Let me try to put Austin's point in the most general way. In considering whether or not some statement is true, he is saying, there are always two distinct kinds of things that we need to know: we might put it like this, rather as we did a moment ago – one is what to look *for*, the other is what to look *at*. In S_0 this is a simple matter. Every statement says that some item is of a certain type: an instance of being of that type (or not) is always what we are looking *for*, and the T-word always 'names' the type in question; and we always know from the I-word what to look *at*, namely the specific individual to which the given I-word uniquely and invariably refers. In natural languages things are not so simple. Statements may be of many forms, not just of one form; and not only do *words* not divide tidily into mutually exclusive classes of referring-words and characterizing-words but it is not even true that every sentence has distinguishable referring and characterizing 'parts'. But we can put it like this: when a statement is made in a use of a given sentence, we can hope to tell from the *sentence*, by exploiting descriptive conventions, what the sentence *means*, that is what *type* of situation in the world it 'describes' – that is what we are to look *for*; and we can hope to tell, by exploiting (various sorts of) demonstrative conventions, *where and when* a situation of that type is, on this occasion of the use of the sentence, stated to obtain – and that is what we are to look *at*, to see whether it does or does not instantiate the 'type'.[13] Of course there is no question in this context (unlike that of S_0) of saying, in general, what sort of thing a 'situation', or 'state of affairs', is, what sort of thing an instance of a type will be; for of course it will depend what the statement is. Sometimes what we are to look *at* will be simply the present state of some individual ('Felix is asleep'); but sometimes it will be the habitual behaviour of a class of individuals ('Tigers growl'); or a wide variety of happenings in a large region over a period ('The rate of inflation in Brazil is rising'); or even the state of the whole world both at and before a certain date ('The dodo is extinct'). But what can be said to be common to all the cases is that, in considering whether a given statement is true, we need to know what we are looking for, what sort of state of affairs the sentence 'describes', and what (it is relevant to the question at issue) to look *at*, to see whether or not the actual state of affairs is of that sort, is as it is described or said to be. If the statement is of completely unrestricted generality, we may even be called upon to 'look at' *everything* – at the state of affairs at every time and place – in order to see whether things are as they are said to be – which has always been well recognized to be, at least, a difficult task to carry out.

I ought to append some remarks on some further matters, two simple enough and two much more perplexing. Let us dispatch the comparatively simple ones first.

Besides saying from time to time that this or that is the case, we also have occasion from time to time to say that such-and-such is *not* the case. Rather surprisingly, Austin says something about this in 'How to talk', but almost nothing about it in 'Truth'; and it is a fair comment that what he says in the latter paper about 'when a statement is said to be true' actually fits the case only of affirmative statements. One might try to argue that this is not so, perhaps. Take the statement that Felix is not asleep. Could we perhaps hold that the 'type' of state of affairs thus said to obtain is that of 'Felix's not being asleep', and that the statement is true when the relevant historic state of affairs – that is, the relevant Felix's present state – *is* of that type? This would be to say that, for every 'type' of state of affairs as so far envisaged, for example some object's being pink, there is another contrasted and indeed opposed 'type' of state of affairs, for example the object's not being pink; and that what any so-called negative statement really does is to *affirm* that some historic situation *is* of the latter sort of type. (In other words, every statement is really affirmative.) I shall not try to decide, and am indeed not in the least sure how to, whether in general this would be a conceivably workable line to take; but I am quite sure, in any case, that Austin would not have wished to take it. In 'How to talk', where he does explicitly though briefly consider negative statements, he does not suggest that these can be accommodated *in* S$_o$ – that a so-called negative statement could be held still to be of the form 'I is a T', provided that the class of T-words was expanded to include, for instance, 'not a rhombus' or 'non-rhombus' as well as 'rhombus'. His reason for not favouring that suggestion must have been, I think, simply that it would seem too grossly artificial and awkward to regard such a phrase as 'not a rhombus' as a way of saying of what type some item *is*: if we were so to regard it, we should have to say, surely unhappily, that a hexagon, a circle, a triangle, and an ellipse, for example, are in this respect all of *the same* type: 'not a rhombus' is truly affirmable of them all. But surely I do not say of what type some item *is*, in saying that it is not a so-and-so.[14] What Austin does in 'How to talk' is to envisage a new speech situation called S$_{ON}$' in which, as well as the I-words and T-words and the assertive link 'is a', we have available what might be called the negative-assertive link, 'is not a'. It is true, then, that I is not a T when the type of the item referred to by 'I' and the sense named by 'T' do *not* match. And this is taken to be, surely rightly, a kind of case for which the original speech-situation S_o did not make provision. If so, then 'Truth' does not make provision for it either; and we ought to add that a negative statement is said to be true when the historic state of affairs to which it 'refers' is *not* of a type with which the un-negated version of the sentence used in making it is correlated by the descriptive conventions. Exactly how, in natural languages, negative statements are to be *identified* is a separate question, which I think we need not go into here.[15]

The next (I think) uncontroversial point is this.[16] It was built into the model of S_o that every statement made, or capable of being made, in that situation was, quite definitely, *either* true *or* false. T-words were to have completely firm, specific 'senses'; and every item was either quite definitely to be, or quite definitely not to be, of any given 'type'; it was also taken for granted that for every I-word there *is* the item to which that word purports to refer; if so, then every statement that I is a T is either (exactly) true or (definitely) not. Our actual situation is of course not at all like that. Possible (and actual) states of affairs mostly do not, in the real world, fall neatly into quite specific and sharply distinct 'types';[17] it is often, even usually, a matter of penumbral gradations over a range of not identical but also not wholly different cases. Further, it is possible to purport to speak about some individual or state of affairs (etc.) which actually does not exist at all. And hugely many of the words in natural languages do not have absolutely precise, closely and sharply demarcated senses. (Think of all the possible states of human heads between absolute hairlessness and a rich crop of hair; think of the vagueness of what is meant by 'bald'.) If so, we may have a 'problem' that could not arise in S_o: when some state of affairs is said to be so-and-so, it may be not merely hard to decide, but genuinely indeterminate, whether it *is* (to be called) so-and-so or not. We have a decently clear idea of what a typical bald head is; we are often in no doubt that a given head is or is not bald; but what about *this* head? Is it near *enough* to a 'typical' bald head to be (fairly) said to be bald? Or has it enough hair for it to be said (unmisleadingly, or perhaps without flattery) *not* to be bald? Thus in reality, though not in S_o, we have the possibility of statements being made, or that could be made, as to which it is just not possible to pronounce straightforwardly and confidently either that they *are* true, or that they are *not*: the words neither fit the situation clearly, nor clearly do not fit; often there will be not much point, or even no point at all, in labouring to make a choice between those stark alternatives; and sometimes, if we think that some state of affairs is close *enough* to some 'typical' state of affairs for it to be said to be true that so-and-so, the question will arise for what purpose we may judge it to be close 'enough'.[18] To take an example of Austin's: what about the statement that the galaxy is the shape of a fried egg? or, elsewhere, that France is hexagonal? These may be good 'enough' for many purposes, but probably not if we are doing astronomy or cartography. Then there is the different case of statements which may be judged undoubtedly true or false if certain *other* conditions are satisfied; but what if they are not? It will often be clearly true, and often clearly false, that Smith is at home; but what if he has just died in his bed? Is it *then* true or false that he is at home?

Austin adds that it is 'jejune to suppose that all a statement aims to be is "true" '. I am in fact not quite sure what he had in mind in saying this, but he at least may have had in mind the point that truth – even, so to speak, at its best and clearest – is not the all-sufficient virtue of statement-making. He once said, in a much-quoted dictum that was cited in an earlier chapter, that 'importance is not important: truth is'; and one can see what he meant by that. He may here have had in mind to add that truth is not *necessarily* important; and of course one can see what is meant by that too. A 'good' statement should be not just true ('a bare minimum', he says[19]) but also, for one or another of a wide range of possible reasons, *worth making*, or proper to make – apt, relevant, interesting, informative, pertinent, or something of the sort. If I do not mind how trivial, boring, or irrelevant my statements are, nothing would be easier than to ensure that absolutely every statement I make is true.

I turn now to a more perplexing matter. If has often been objected that Austin's account of 'when a statement is said to be true' is inadequate *at least* in that it is too narrowly restricted – it fits, at best, only some of the cases. I have already partly conceded that this is so – it certainly does not, as it stands, fit negative statements, in which some state of affairs is said, perhaps truly, *not* to be such-and-such; but that, I believe, could be accommodated without much difficulty. The most frequent objection – that it fits only statements of subject-predicate form, in which some thing or things is or are referred to and 'described' in some way – is, I have argued, ill-founded; that restriction is indeed present (and perfectly acceptable) in the 'account' of truth that we might elicit from S_o, but I have tried to argue that the account in 'Truth' brings in differences from the S_o model whose effect is precisely to free it from that particular restriction. So far as I can see, the account works perfectly well for such statements as that there are camels in Australia, that there are such things as camels, or that all camels are, say, malodorous. But Austin admits to 'uneasiness' about another case, that of hypotheticals.[20] Understandably so; for when I make a hypothetical statement, I do not appear to be saying that any 'historic state of affairs' *is* (or is not) of a certain sort, but that *if* a state of affairs is, or was, or were to be, of a certain sort, then some other state of affairs is, or was, or would be, of a certain sort. It may be that neither state of affairs actually, 'historically', obtains, or ever did or will. Yet we are often happy enough to say that such statements are true. I shall not pursue that particular difficult topic – except to say that one conceivable escape-route, namely a fully truth-functional analysis of hypotheticals, would not, I believe, have looked attractive to Austin's eye. I want to discuss another sort of restrictedness which is, I think, quite incontestably there in Austin's account, but about which, as it seems to me rather surprisingly, he says not quite nothing, but very little indeed.

What I have in mind is that Austin's account of 'when a statement is said to be true' does surely fit the case – and seems quite deliberately to have been designed to fit the case – only of statements whose truth or falsehood is a *contingent* matter. When truth is in question, as here represented, we have a sentence depicting ('correlated with') a 'type' of 'situation, thing, event, etc., to be found in the world'; we have to identify what, or which, '*historic*' state of affairs . . . to be found in the world' is relevantly involved in this case; and finally, to see whether that historic state of affairs in fact is, or is not, of the type depicted. We are represented as always finishing up, so to speak, by inspecting 'the world', or some spatial or temporal part or region or aspect of the world; and such inspection is always crucial in determining whether the statement is in fact true or not. But now - what about *necessary* truth? What about the 'statements' that the angles at the base of an isosceles triangle are equal, that brothers are male, that bachelors are unmarried? What about necessary falsehood? A schoolmaster once wrote to me of a certain boy that he was 'unique in having two brothers in the school': surely I did not need to inspect 'the world' – any school or its pupils – to see that this was untrue (for if *he* had two brothers in the school, so also did each of his brothers). In such cases, 'historic states of affairs' are surely not involved at all – in determining either truth or falsehood, they have no role to play. Yet surely we are dealing here with truths and falsehoods, are we not?

I think there are actually clues enough to establish what Austin wanted to say about this, very little though he *does* say. He asks: 'When is a statement not a statement?' And answers: 'When it is a formula in a calculus . . .'[21] And a few lines later: 'It was only so long as the real nature of arithmetical formulae, say, or of geometrical axioms remained unrecognized, and they were thought to record information about the world, that it was reasonable to call them "true" . . .'. These remarks do not quite cover the cases of 'A bachelor is unmarried', or 'No boy can be unique in having two brothers': these are neither exactly 'formulae' nor of course axioms; but I suppose that these and other such necessary 'truths' could be said to be of essentially the same nature as 'formulae in a calculus' – if we have some well-defined system of connected terms such as 'bachelor', 'married', 'brother', 'uncle', 'aunt', and so on, then we can play around with them to produce various 'formulae' of the sort that are sometimes said to be 'true by definition'. Austin really wishes to hold, I believe – and I believe this is the heart of the matter – to three points. The first is the idea that there is a central, fundamental, 'classic' case of language-use in which something is affirmed about 'the world' or some part or region or constituent of 'the world'; this gives us the central, fundamental, 'classic' case of *statement*; and what it is for statements of that sort to be *true* gives us the central, fundamental, 'classic' concept of truth. The second is that it is possible in any natural language (not in S_o) to formulate sentences which formally resemble, look linguistically perhaps just like, the sentences in which 'classic' statements are made; but the more clearly we realize that they are not and cannot be used in making 'classic' statements, the less we shall be, and should be, inclined to described them as making statements at all. And the third point is that while 'it is a matter for decision . . . how widely we should be prepared to extend the uses of "true" and "false" in "different senses" ',[22] the more clearly, once again, we realize that certain sentences are not used in 'classic' statement-making, the less we shall be, and should be, inclined to comment on uses of them as 'true' or 'false'. If we think that it *is* 'reasonable' to label, say, 'No boy can be unique in having two brothers' as true, that may be because, besides superficially resembling such a 'classic' statement as that no boy in the school ever breaks any rules, it is, as that statement is if true, perfectly 'satisfactory' – it conflicts after all with nothing, accords with everything. I do not know that Austin would have strongly denied that that was reasonable.

In any case, I am sure that this is what Austin believed, though he does not produce much argument in support of it. His basic idea – some would say, his 'intuition' – was that, in seeking to understand better the notion of truth, we should not, so to speak, put into the same pot *every* use of 'true' that actually occurs: we should leave aside, at any rate to begin with, not only 'true friend', 'true love', 'true Pekinese', 'true democracy', and so on, but also at least some of the uses of 'true' in application to things sayable or said. There is, he supposes, a pretty clearly identifiable *central case* – that in which in certain words something informative, factual, empirical, contingent is said, or sayable, of 'the world'; and the question arises whether *that* is *true*. The central aim, at any rate to begin with, should be to try to reach a better understanding of that central case; and if we can do that, then we may go on to allow, or resist, or at any rate also to understand better, uses of 'true' by analogy or extension, in the various non-central cases. I think he would have held that, if we seek to find something that will fit, or cover, *every* use of 'true' that actually occurs, we shall be liable to come up with something no better, at best, than some sort of synonym or paraphrase, whose use we shall actually *understand* no better than that of 'true' itself. For my own part I find this persuasive, and I think there are points to be urged in support of it. One might observe, for example that some moral philosophers have thought it important to maintain – and Austin, rather parenthetically, seems inclined to agree with them – that 'value-judgments' ought not to be labelled 'true' or 'false'. But what, one may ask, is this argument about? It is incontestable that, in the ordinary use of ordinary language, evaluative judgments very commonly *are* said to be true or false; no one would suggest that to speak so is an obvious solecism; so what could motivate the contention that this very commonly accepted usage ought to be objected to? The answer seems reasonably clear. These philosophers evidently have some such idea as this: the central, paradigmatic, most approvable case of 'true' is its use in application to statements of *fact*;[23] and they wish to urge that 'evaluative judgments' are not sufficiently *like* statements of that sort (whatever that sort is) to make desirable, or even tolerable, the use of 'true' or 'false' with reference to them. It may not be clear what the merits of such an argument would be, but it is relevant to our present point that the issue can even be intelligibly raised. If there were not *some* such central, paradigmatic notion of truth, and a question of how closely certain other sorts of cases do or should resemble that central case, it would be hard to see what the argument could possibly be about.

One question remains which is not, I think, easily answered, though I am also not sure that it is particularly important. One might put it like this: what exactly, in 'Truth', did Austin undertake to do, and suppose that he had done? Alternatively: what are we to make of the closing words of Austin's paper?

> If it is admitted (*if*) that the rather boring yet satisfactory relation
> between words and world which has here been discussed does
> genuinely occur, why should the phrase 'is true' not be our way of
> describing it? And if it is not, what else is?

This looks a little strange. the 'relation between words and world' which has been discussed may perhaps be 'boring yet satisfactory', but it is also of some considerable complexity, and it seems rather odd to suggest that 'is true' *describes* that relation. But I suppose that, rather strange though the wording may be, what Austin means is this. He has said that a statement is true 'when' it (or the words in which it is made) is 'related' in a fairly complex way to 'the world'. But if 'is true' is 'a descriptive phrase', then to say that a statement is true is itself to say something (true or false) *about* that statement. His question is: does the statement that a given statement is true *mean*, and therefore *state*, that the words in which the given statement is made are so related to 'the world'? And it is pretty clear that his preferred answer is: yes.

To go into this at all thoroughly would be a lengthy business. To give good grounds for a specific answer to such a question as 'What does the phrase "is true" *mean?*' might involve – presumably should involve – some general consideration of what 'mean' itself means, what meaning is, how for any word or phrase we are to seek answers to the question what its *meaning* is (as distinct from other questions about it or its uses).[24] Perhaps it may be enough for present purposes to point out that Strawson, Austin's first and most persistent critic on this whole topic, first held (in 1950) that Austin's preferred answer was obviously and indeed disastrously wrong, and seems later (in 1964) to have come, with much less fervour, to the conclusion that probably it was not so bad after all.

Strawson's first view, expressed in direct and immediate comment on Austin's paper, is clear enough. He urges then that while it is obviously correct, for what it is worth, to say that such a statement as 'What Felix said is true' is 'about' a statement, namely the statement that Felix made, that is really nothing more than a trivial point of grammar; it really says no more than that the sentence 'What Felix said is true' has a subject and predicate, and that its grammatical subject is 'what Felix said'. If, not content with this unilluminating though no doubt incontestable point of grammar, we press the question what the statement that what Felix said is true is really, substantially about, the only possible sensible answer, Strawson says, is that it is about whatever Felix's statement was about: if Felix says that the French Revolution was a terrible affair, and I say 'That's true', we both say something, and indeed the same thing, about the French Revolution. More specifically: if what Felix said is true, then 'it is, *of course*, necessary that the words used by [Felix] in making the statement should stand in a certain conventional (semantical) relationship with the world'; but Felix himself did not in *his* statement *say that* these semantic conditions were fulfilled – it would be absurd to suggest that he did; but no *less* absurd to suppose that I say some such thing, in saying 'That's true'. In saying 'That's true', I am of course *doing* something other than what Felix did; for he made a statement, whereas I expressed agreement with the statement he made. But to suggest that our remarks are 'about' fundamentally different matters – that his was about the French Revolution, and mine about words and their semantic relations to the world – is, Strawson says roundly, *'patently* false'.[25] Austin has propounded, he say, a 'fundamental confusion . . . between: (a) the semantic conditions which must be satisfied for the statement that

62

a certain statement is true to be itself true; and (b) what is asserted when a certain statement is stated to be true.'[26]

To put Strawson's point in Austin's terms: the phrase 'is true' does not 'describe' *any* relation, whether boring or otherwise, between words and world; it does not 'describe' anything; the occurrence of the phrase 'signalizes, without commenting on, the occurrence of a certain way of using language';[27] it 'signalizes' the occurrence of some bit of fact-stating, but says nothing *about* that, nor indeed about anything unless, as we have seen, what the original statement was about. And finally: Austin

> describes the conditions which must obtain if we are correctly to declare a statement true. . . . The central mistake is to suppose that in using the word 'true' we are asserting such conditions to obtain. . . . What supremely confuses the issue is the failure to distinguish between the task of elucidating the nature of a certain type of communication (the empirically informative) from the problem of the actual functioning of the word 'true'within the framework of that type of communication.[28]

I have not been able to find much in Strawson's 1950 paper as to *why* he held that the line taken by Austin 'supremely confuses the issue', or why it was thought to be so damaging. I think the fact of the matter is simply that, at that time, what Austin said seemed to Strawson to be 'patently false'; even conceding that, when some statement is true, certain words (used in making it) are related in the ways described to 'the world', it just seemed patently obvious that we do not *say that* they are so related, in saying just ordinarily that the statement is true. Now the sort of mistake that Strawson here seeks to pin on Austin is indeed sometimes made; indeed, he had himself, in his then very recent article 'On referring',[29] famously accused – and, some would say, convicted – Russell of making a mistake of exactly that sort. For the statement that the present King of France is bald to be true, it is one of the conditions that must be satisfied – a 'presupposition' – that there should be a present King of France; but it may well seem 'patently false' to suggest that the statement that the present King of France is bald, among other things, *says that* there is a King of France. That suggestion, further, might be held seriously to 'confuse the issue' by muddling up subject-predicate propositions with existential propositions. But the difficulty is simply that, to my eye, Austin's suggestion about 'true' does *not* look 'patently false' in at all the same way. It is no doubt the case that a person who says just ordinarily 'That's true' does not usually *have in mind* any elaborate thoughts, or any thoughts at all, about semantic relations; he may well 'have in mind' only what he is *doing*, say, expressing his agreement, as he might well have been happy to do in some quite different form of words. But that of course is not conclusive as to what 'what he said' could be properly held to *mean*. And in this case the supposition that what *it is* for a statement to be true may also be what *is meant by saying* that it is true can hardly be pronounced to be *obviously* false.

In any case, as I mentioned, we may end with the pacificatory observation that Strawson himself, in 1964, seems to have resiled from his earlier uncompromising position. He writes:

> In the above I have not been at pains to distinguish (1) what a statement's . . . *being true* is a matter of, (2) what is meant (or what is stated) by a statement (or by someone who states) that a certain statement *is true* and (3) what the meaning (the sense) of the phrase '*is true*' is; but have taken it that the answer to any one of these questions carries directly with it the answer to the others. . . . If someone wishes to contend that we do not *really*, or do not *fully*, know the *meaning* of 'is true' unless we know what types of conventional relation obtain between words and things when something true is stated or otherwise expressed in words, then the contention seems to me by no means extravagant.[30]

Of course, to say that a suggestion like Austin's is by no means extravagant is not at all to say that it is absolutely correct. But we may leave it at that, on a comparatively peaceful note.

V

Excuses and Accusations

The paper 'A plea for excuses' has long been regarded, I think rightly, as one of Austin's best, most fertile, and most characteristic contributions to philosophy. Perhaps nothing that he wrote is more closely packed with food for thought. (It goes along with, and should be read in conjunction with, the posthumous paper 'Three ways of spilling ink',[1] which deals with the opposite side of the same coin: if I have done some more or less objectionable thing, an 'excuse' may be offered by way of getting me out of trouble – yes, I did it, but, say, inadvertently; the other paper deals with expressions that may keep me firmly *in* trouble, may even make matters worse – I not only did it, but I did it, say, on purpose.) However, closely packed though these papers are with food for thought, they present a considerable difficulty for critical assessment – for a reason of which Austin himself was clearly well aware. As he says in the very first sentence, 'the subject of this paper, Excuses, is one not to be treated, but only to be introduced, within such limits'.[2] The fact is that in the early 1950s Austin gave several times a whole series of classes on this subject, in the course of which he went over the whole field, point by point in successive weeks, in what he himself calls 'congenial' detail; 'much of the amusement', he goes on to say, 'and of the instruction, comes in drawing the coverts of the microglot, in hounding down the minutiae', but 'to this I can do no more here' – that is, in 'A plea for excuses' – 'than incite you'. He is reducing a long series of seminars into a single paper. The result of this is that the thirteen numbered paragraphs which succeed the 'programmatic' introductory pages (fairly briefly discussed in the first chapter of this book) successively compress into single-paragraph dimensions topics each of which, in his classes, had been allotted at least a couple of hours of discussion; and quite often there is scarcely space enough for him to do more than to indicate what the topic is and to commend it for consideration. We get the questions, so to speak, but not the answers – or sometimes the answers too, but not many of the reasons for the answers. This seems to me to make the paper as a whole, while remarkably stimulating to thought, somewhat recalcitrant to commentary. I am not in the least sure that, in the pages that follow, I have picked out for discussion what Austin would have thought most worthy of attention; and I have certainly left out much that *might* have been discussed. The truth no doubt is, as Austin said of his own paper, that the subject 'is one not to be *treated* . . . within such limits'. But we must do our best.

In everyday life we make pretty free use of the nouns 'action' or 'act', and of the verbs 'act' or 'do', usually of course without perplexity or confusion. Sometimes there is an expressed or implied contrast with something else: 'actions speak louder than words'; 'this is no time to argue – we must act!' We say that the law concerns itself (or should) with actions, not thoughts; and so on. And of course we constantly report or otherwise discuss, and often make the subject of favourable or unfavourable comment, what people (including ourselves) do or are doing, did or have done, or are likely or intend to do. But what is it to *do* something? What is 'an action'? Can actions be individuated and counted, and if so, what constitutes, how are we to pick out, *one* action? Austin's several discussions of such questions as these were intended to contribute, often rather obliquely, to 'the development of a cautious, latter-day version of conduct'.[3] But I think that he was much less concerned to come up with answers to questions of such daunting, or possibly tempting, abstractness and generality, than to discourage the idea that adequate answers are already to hand.

Two thoughts that may be briefly tempting may also be briefly dismissed. There is, Austin says,

> a vague and comforting idea in the background that, after all, in the last analysis, doing an action must come down to the making of physical movements with parts of the body; but this is about as true as that saying something must, in the last analysis, come down to making movements of the tongue.[4]

There are some physical movements, for example of the heart, which are clearly not 'actions' that a person 'does': and if it is objected that movements of the heart are not movements that we 'make', that merely raises, without answering, the question how making a movement, for example bending one's leg, is to be distinguished from a movement's occurring – one's leg bending. It is of course quite obvious that hardly any 'actions' are *just* the making of physical movements; in saying what a person 'did' we very often bring in, in one way or another, his intentions – even striking a match is to make certain movements with the *intention* of generating a flame; or we bring in (as for example in buying a box of matches) a more or less elaborate background of conventions and practices without which the very notion of 'buying' would have no sense. It is not even clear, really, that to do something must always involve making any physical movement at all. Is thinking an action? Or (by *in*action) permitting something to happen? Or waiting for the traffic lights to change? But these are things that people do.

The manifest unhelpfulness of that 'vague and comforting idea' may lend a certain attraction – which in fact Austin thinks not wholly spurious – to another, namely that 'doing' something, 'doing an action', can be regarded as merely a sort of dummy, 'a stand-in used in the place of any . . . verb with a personal subject'. The suggestion would be that, to the question 'What did he do?', *any* sentence of the form 'He . . .', with a past-tense verb, could be an acceptable answer. But although this notion, Austin thinks, 'has no doubt some uses' – there is a certain 'dummy' aspect to 'do', as there is to 'thing' – it has manifest deficiencies also. For one thing, it is not really true that just *any* verb with a personal subject would comfortably be taken as ascribing an 'action' to a person. 'He caught a cold', or 'He fell off his bicycle', seem rather to tell us what happened to him, than what he did. If told that someone has died, it would be eccentric to remark 'What an injudicious thing to do!' or even to enquire when he did that. But if so, we are left with the question *what* range or classes of verbs, and why, can specify actions, things that people do. Further, if we think of an action simply as an answer to the question what a person does, we may be tempted to suppose that all actions, as such, are somehow

> equal, composing a quarrel with striking a match, winning a war with sneezing: worse still, we assimilate them one and all to the supposedly most obvious and easy cases, such as posting letters or moving fingers, just as we assimilate all 'things' to horses or beds.[5]

As a way of at least beginning to seek some clarification of these matters, Austin recommends the study of what he calls 'excuses'. What are these? When are excuses offered?

> In general, the situation is one where someone is *accused* of having done something, or (if that will keep it any cleaner) where someone is *said* to have done something which is bad, wrong, inept, unwelcome, or in some other of the numerous possible ways untoward.[6]

In such a case the accused person may, of course, flatly deny that he did the thing in question. Alternatively, he may admit, even cheerfully accept, that he did indeed do it, but go on to argue that it was not in any way objectionable, perhaps even that it was a good, right, sensible, or desirable thing to do – that is, he may seek to *justify* the thing that he did, or himself for having done it. But differently from either of these, he may accept that he did it and that what he did was indeed in some way objectionable, but claim it as, say, unfair to say baldly, without qualification, that he did it – it was an accident, perhaps, or inadvertent, or unintentional. This is to put forward what Austin calls an 'excuse'. 'In the one defence, briefly, we accept responsibility but deny that it was bad: in the other, we admit that it was bad but don't accept full, or even any, responsibility.'[7] Sometimes, Austin notes, our offer of an excuse may really amount to no more than, as it were, pleading guilty to a lesser charge: if I have wrecked your transistor by leaving it out in the rain, I may be glad to accept an accusation of thoughtlessness, as at any rate less painful than that of having (simply) wrecked your transistor. (Incidentally, 'what I did' in this case – wrecked your transistor – did not consist in physical movements but in their *omission* – I *failed* to bring it indoors.) 'The average excuse, in a poor situation, gets us only out of the fire into the frying pan – but still, of course, any frying pan in a fire.'[8]

Why does Austin adjure us to think about, to distinguish and disentangle, the ways in which we make excuses for things we have done, rather than to think directly about the notion of action itself? Part of the answer is, I am sure, simply that he found the topic of excuses enjoyable and congenial, exactly to his taste. How exactly are we to distinguish 'inadvertently' from 'unwittingly', 'accident' from 'mistake', 'negligently' from 'recklessly', 'carelessly', or 'unintentionally'? Or, on the other side, 'intentionally' from 'on purpose', and both from 'deliberately'? In the words I quoted earlier 'much, of course, of the amusement . . . comes in drawing the coverts of the microglot, in hounding down the minutiae'. This sort of thing, to Austin, was philosophical fun. But he thought also that 'ordinary' action – as also, for instance, ordinary, everyday saying, or seeing – is apt to confront us with a 'blinding veil of ease and obviousness that hides the mechanisms of the natural successful act'[9]; in what is overwhelmingly familiar and ordinarily unproblematic, it is easy to miss the complexity of what is actually going on. When an excuse is offered or called for, something has 'gone wrong', and in noting the wide variety of things that *can* go wrong, we may better appreciate how their ordinarily going right is not such a simple matter. Austin makes the same claim for the study of *pretending*; pretending to do something, like doing something accidentally, is one of the 'possible ways and varieties of *not exactly doing things*', and that, he says, is a topic that needs to be thoroughly investigated 'if we are ever to understand properly what doing things is'.[10] If the car is running smoothly we are apt not to give much thought, if any, to what is going on under the bonnet; it is when things go wrong that we need to examine the machinery.

Another suggestion which Austin throws out, very briefly, is that thinking about excuses may help us with 'the problem of Freedom' (though he does not here say much about what exactly that problem is). I believe that what he has chiefly in mind here is a point concerning, as one might put it, the onus of proof or, perhaps, the proper direction of argument. If a philosopher asks 'Do we (ever) act *freely*?' – and Austin makes clear that he has in mind 'the philosopher's use', a question asked by a philosopher rather than one that crops up in ordinary life – it may seem as though, in response, we should try to find some component in, or some feature or property of, acting, the presence of which would invariably, and would alone, justify the assertion that a person so acting acts 'freely'. We might then conclude (or not) that such cases do some-times occur; 'freely', that is, is treated as a 'positive' term, as ascribing some positive feature or characteristic to an action, and the question is whether that feature is (ever) rightly ascribed. Austin's slightly guarded suggestion ('there is little doubt . . .', he says) is that this puts the dialectical boot on the wrong foot. If it is agreed that X did A, then we should not see ourselves as required to look for some specific, extra ground for the conclusion that he acted 'freely'; we are entitled to say to the philosopher that, yes, he acted 'freely' *unless* some particular reason is shown for saying otherwise – that he did A under duress, or by mistake, or inadvertently, or something of that sort.[11] To establish, that, say, a cigarette is a 'real' cigarette I do not have to establish, 'positively', something more than that it is a cigarette; I have to exclude (if I take the question seriously) one or more of the ways in which the item in question might *not* be a real cigarette (but an exploding joke-cigarette, a chocolate cigarette, and so on). The philosopher's 'free', Austin suggests, perhaps works in the same way; if it is agreed that people do things, then they sometimes act 'freely' if there is sometimes no reason to qualify in any special way, or modify, the statement that they do those things.

I think it is clear that this suggestion has some illuminating force – even outside philosophy. It seems helpful, for example, to the understanding of the 'logic' of legal proceedings to say that an accused person's 'responsibility' for some act that he has done does not need, and is not treated as needing – beyond establishing that he did it – to be 'positively' established, but stands as a general and fundamental presumption about human action *unless* some counter-plea (of duress, say, or accident, or insanity) is entered and itself positively contended for; and it may be thought that, in looking at the matter that way round, so to speak, the law simply embodies a fundamental ordinary-life presumption about 'agents' and the things they do. But it is of course very much less clear – as Austin would no doubt have agreed – that the philosopher's 'real problem' of Freedom is thereby comprehensively solved, or eliminated.

There too, however, the point may well be thought to have the considerable merit of locating the burden of argument in the right place. If it is agreed that people very often do things not under duress, not in trances or under hypnosis, not by reason of insanity, not accidentally, not unwittingly, not in any way deviantly or abnormally, then, if a philosopher insists that his 'real problem' of Freedom remains untouched, and that nevertheless perhaps no one ever acts 'freely', at least it is very clearly incumbent upon him to set out exactly what he takes the 'real' issue to be.

Is it, then, right to say – or, at least, to say until reason is offered for saying otherwise – that, in the absolutely ordinary, everyday case of a person's doing something, he acts 'freely'? It is Austin's view that this would certainly *not* be the right thing to say. In the particular case of 'freely', since he has suggested that 'in the philosopher's use' the function of that adverb may be 'only . . . to rule out the suggestion of some or all of its recognized antitheses', its use would presumably be uncalled for if no such suggestion were made or contemplated. But Austin puts forward, very briefly, a more general proposition than this, in the words 'No modification without aberration': that is, he holds that, in the absolutely ordinary, everyday case, *no* 'modifying' expression – whether of the 'excuses' group, such as 'inadvertently', or the 'aggravating' group, such as 'on purpose' – is properly usable at all: 'no modifying expression is required or even permissible . . . It is bedtime, I am alone, I yawn: but I do not yawn involuntarily (or voluntarily!), nor yet deliberately. To yawn in any such peculiar way is just not to just yawn.'[12]

This is not a straightforward business, though I think it is clear enough, up to a point at any rate, what Austin is saying here. He is making a point about what he calls 'the natural economy of language': a rather rough-and-ready point indeed, but I think a clearly correct one so far as it goes. We have a class of what he calls, pretty vaguely, 'normal' verbs, which *mean* things – things of all sorts – that people in everyday life frequently, normally, just 'naturally' do, such as sitting down, starting cars, opening letters, yawning, answering questions, opening doors. We may say that, for any such verb – without trying to be precise about *which* verbs are thus 'normal' – there is something like a 'standard case' of doing whatever it may be, of sitting down in a chair or starting a car, a case which is, so to speak, centrally representative or illustrative of what the word means. If so, then, if we have a case of a person just naturally, ordinarily doing something of this sort, then there is (of course) no more to be said than simply that he does it: if he just naturally, ordinarily sits down in his chair, then that's that: that is exactly what the words 'He sat down in his chair' are, so to speak, tailor-made for, there is no more to be said.

I sit in my chair, in the usual way – I am not in a daze or influenced by threats or the like: here, it will not do to say either that I sat in it intentionally or that I did not sit in it intentionally, nor yet that I sat in it automatically or from habit or what you will.[13]

If no 'aberration', no 'modification'.

Beyond this stage, however, I think it is not too clear at all exactly what point Austin is making. This is partly inevitable, on his own view of the nature of the case; for his point is about verbs, or about 'the great majority' of verbs, which 'name actions', and of course it was one of his points right at the beginning that we are not antecedently in possession of any clear conception of what exactly those verbs would be. But then, further, as we have seen, he limits the application of his thesis to 'normal' verbs, and one may well wonder, while respecting his caution, what he really means by that. It is not, I hope, too pedantic to ask whether, in fact, he really means to be talking about *verbs* at all. He suggests that 'murder' is perhaps not one of his 'great majority'; but, while we may no doubt readily concede that murdering is not (in our society) a normal, ordinary, everyday sort of thing to *do* – are there circumstances 'in which such an act is naturally done'? – it is not at all obvious that 'murder' is not a perfectly normal *verb*. But then, if we say that he presumably has in mind, not some philological concept of what would or would not be a 'normal verb', but some plain though of course rather vague notion of what would be an ordinary sort of thing to *do*, some uncertainties still lurk; for ordinary sorts of things to do are 'named' often – usually? – not by verbs alone, but by verbal phrases; eating sandwiches is an ordinary thing to do, eating the day's newspaper is not – eating, by itself, seems unclassifiable as either one or the other. (And what about eating *someone else's* sandwiches?) The picture wobbles a little.

A more serious perplexity is this. It seems not unfair to say that Austin appears to be putting forward some *one* thesis, a general thesis about verbs that name actions ('normal' verbs!) and about expressions 'modifying' the verb: the thesis, namely, that, in virtue of 'the natural economy of language', in 'the *standard* case' of a person's doing the action named, 'no modifying expression is required or even permissible'; normally, no modifying expression is 'called for, or even in order'. But this really, straight off, looks like two *different* theses: for it is surely a very different matter to say that the use of some expression is not 'required' or not 'called for', from saying that it is not 'permissible' or not 'in order'. The former suggestion would seem to be that, in the standard case, any modifying expression would be unnecessary, superfluous, and as such an offence against 'the natural economy of language'; but the latter suggestion seems stronger, the suggestion that in the standard case a modifying expression is, not just not needed, but not allowed, is not superfluous, but 'wrong' in some way. But there again the further question arises: if, in 'the standard case', use of some modifying expression is actually wrong, *why* is it wrong? If it is somehow ruled out, ruled out by what?

I am inclined to think that, if one pursues this tack a bit further, the at-first-sight 'unity' of Austin's thesis begins to disintegrate: that one may well come to doubt whether there is anything much to be said about action-verbs and modifying expressions *in general*. It seems to depend too much on exactly which modifying expressions, and indeed which verbs or range of verbs, one chooses to consider. One might be tempted, for a start, to try to clear the decks a little in this way. Surely, one might think, we can readily agree that, in the standard case of a person's doing some ordinary thing, at any rate all the 'excusing' modifiers are naturally ruled out; for to do something accidentally, inadvertently, by mistake presumably *is* an 'aberration', so that to characterize the standard case in that way will always yield a simple *falsehood*. Why, when in the ordinary way I put my breakfast egg into the boiling water, would it be 'wrong' to say that I do so accidentally, or by mistake? It would be wrong, surely, just because it would be untrue. I do *not* do it either accidentally or by mistake; and the same surely would go for any other 'adverb of aberration', in such a case.

I think that there is some merit in that contention. If, as it seems reasonable to say, the various excuse-offering modifiers *mean* that there was something odd, not absolutely straightforward, about the performance in question, then it must be right to say that they will (obviously) be out of place when, *ex hypothesi*, the performance is 'standard', a completely ordinary case. But in fact even this simple-seeming point does not work in quite the same way for *all* the excuse-offering modifiers. For there is the complication that, given some ordinary action done in the ordinary way, the importation of a modifying expression into its description will actually yield a quite straightforward falsehood only if attachment of the *particular* modifier to the *particular* verb at least makes sense; and, as Austin himself remarks in his next paragraph on the same page, that condition is by no means always satisfied;

> given any adverb of excuse . . . it will not be found that it makes good sense to attach it to any and every verb of 'action' in any and every context: indeed, it will often apply only to a comparatively narrow range of such verbs.[14]

The sentence 'He dropped the egg into the saucepan accidentally' at least makes good sense (he *might* have done it accidentally); and what it says may therefore be said to be simply untrue in the standard case of one's boiling an egg. But suppose that 'what I did' was, for example, to sentence the accused malefactor to a fine of £50: that seems to be something that one might be said to do by mistake – perhaps the sentence was 'meant' to be, I had previously resolved that it should be, fifty days, or £500 – so that, if I get it right, it is untrue to say that I so sentence him by mistake. But what about 'accidentally'? Sentencing someone to a fine or a term of imprisonment surely seems (for some reason) to be not the kind of thing that *could* be done accidentally, or by accident; and if so, to add 'accidentally' to the statement of what I did in this case is something even worse than untrue – it is not really understandable. Thus, although it seems that it must indeed be right to say that 'adverbs of excuse' must always be out of place in any absolutely ordinary, standard case of doing something – where *ex hypothesi* there is no aberration – there is not, even here, where the sailing seems to be comparatively plain, any simple, quite general diagnosis of what goes wrong. In such a case, to attach *some* modifiers to *some* verbs will result in ordinary falsehood – it is not true that I dropped my egg into the pan accidentally; but other modifiers and verbs may give us something not just (or at all) untrue, but something not really (or not at all) intelligible.

But, in any case, this is surely not the more interesting side of the argument. For since 'adverbs of excuse' are employed – by definition, one might say – to suggest that the action is not just *done* in the ordinary, unqualified sort of way, there is obviously not the slightest temptation to think that any of *them* could always, and properly, be employed in 'the standard case'; obviously they must all be 'out of order' in some way or other, even if not for just the same reason in every case. Austin must, then, surely have been chiefly concerned at this point with adverbs from, so to speak, the other bag – what he calls 'the opposite numbers of excuses – the expressions that *aggravate*, such as "deliberately", "on purpose", and so on'.[15] Here, in fact, it is 'intentionally' that seems most likely to generate debate: for there does seem to be real temptation in the idea that the standard, ordinary case of doing this or that just *is* the case of doing it intentionally, and so that it must always be more or less 'in order' to say so.

Here again the cases differ. Take 'deliberately', for a start. I would be inclined to say here (and I think Austin would have agreed) that, when one just ordinarily does something, it is in fact neither true nor false that one does it deliberately: the question *does not arise*. Roughly speaking, to do something deliberately – as, for instance, deliberately exposing oneself to the enemy's fire – is to do something after taking into account, in awareness of but in spite of, certain considerations against doing it, as for instance the danger of being shot. To do the thing not deliberately would be to do it in ignorance of, or not taking into account, such considerations. But if there are no such considerations in the case, surely the question does not arise at all. If asked 'Did you do that deliberately?', I shall be wholly at a loss to answer either way, until I have some idea of what you take to have been the objection to my doing it. If I have eaten your sandwich, I might answer (brazenly) 'Yes', or (apologetically) 'No – I'm afraid I thought it was mine'. But if it *was* my own sandwich, neither answer seems to fill the bill.

It is not at all clear, though, that 'intentionally' works in this way. It is certainly true that, when I give the cat his dinner, say, it would usually be extraordinary and puzzling for me (or anyone) to *say* that I gave him his dinner intentionally. But is this perhaps like the case of my being asked what day of the week it is, and answering 'It's Monday'? Here, it would be extraordinary and puzzling for me to say 'I know that it's Monday'; but that is not because I do *not* know – unquestionably I do – but because it is wholly superfluous, uncalled for, pointless, to *say* that I know, in answering such a simple question in the ordinary way. I believe that Austin was inclined to take this view of 'intentionally', at any rate in some cases. Take this passage from 'Three ways of spilling ink':

> The notice says, 'Do not feed the penguins'. I, however, feed them peanuts. Now peanuts happen to be, and these prove, fatal to these birds. Did I feed them peanuts intentionally? Beyond a doubt: I am no casual peanut shedder. But deliberately? Well, that seems perhaps to raise the question, 'Had I read the notice?' Why does it? Or 'on purpose'? That seems to insinuate that I knew what fatal results would ensue.[16]

Here we have three different cases (or issues anyway) which might be roughly distinguished as follows. I deliberately fed peanuts to the penguins *if* I was aware of, and chose for some good or bad reason (or for none) to disregard, the notice specifically forbidding feeding the penguins: if I had not seen the notice, and knew of no objection to my feeding them, I should resist the charge that I deliberately fed them peanuts. I fed them on purpose, if my aim was to bring about their death. But did I feed them peanuts intentionally? 'Beyond a doubt', Austin says without hesitation: whether I had read the notice or not, and whether or not I knew of, or aimed at, fatal effects, in feeding them peanuts I was certainly acting intentionally. 'I am no casual peanut shedder.' This seems to be exactly the view that, in the standard case of doing some such ordinary thing, it is certainly *true* that we do the thing intentionally, though usually there would be no particular occasion to *say* so. It is far from clear, however, that Austin was quite happy with this in other cases; in the case, for instance, where 'I sit in my chair, in the usual way', he says not only that 'it will not do to *say*' that I sat in it intentionally, but that the suggestion that I *did* sit in it intentionally should be 'repudiated' – meaning presumably that that is not *true*, not merely not worth saying. Perhaps, again, the sad truth really is, as so often, just that cases differ. Perhaps there are some things – sitting down might be an example – which are ordinarily done, not unintentionally of course, but genuinely not intentionally either: the sitter-down, while not unaware of what he is doing, gives absolutely no thought or attention to it, still less to the question whether to do it or not; and perhaps there are other things, equally ordinary things – like feeding peanuts to birds perhaps – which demand at least some attention (though not deliberation) and so ordinarily *are*, if done, intentionally done. I believe that Austin would have accepted this. We may bring in here a case from 'Three ways of spilling ink'.

> Suppose I tie a string across a stairhead. A fragile relative . . . trips over it, falls, and perishes. Should we ask whether I tied the string there intentionally? Well, but it's hard to see how I could have done such a thing unintentionally, or even . . . not done it intentionally.

This seems to imply that there are some *sorts of things* which, if ordinarily done, *are* done intentionally. Sitting down perhaps – or yawning – is not that 'sort of thing'.[17]

The upshot of all this may seem rather disappointing (and perhaps we have spent more time on it than it deserves). Austin's slogan is 'No modification without aberration'. The one thing that seems incontestable is that, as we converse ordinarily about the things that people ordinarily do, we *do not* attach any 'modifying' adverb or adverbial phrase to the assertion that they do those things. It is only in more or less special cases, when the plain assertion of the doing of the thing will not quite do as it stands, that some 'modification' comes in. But it seems to emerge that, if we go on to ask *why* this is so, there is no strong, simple, single answer to be found. The penalty, as it were, for intrusion of a modifying phrase in the 'standard case' seems in some cases to be falsehood, in others lack of clear sense, in yet others perhaps just superfluity: there is no 'general theory', we have to take the cases one by one. Whether or not, in his reference to 'the natural economy of language', Austin meant to put forward, or took himself to be putting forward, some general theory is to me unclear. His phrase there is in any case, one might think, somewhat ambiguous: has he in mind some point about language itself, or about the circumstances in which, and reasons for which, language is used? Is he making a point about language, or about the use of language in discourse, or both? The point about language might be that the 'name' of an action just *means* the 'standard case' of so acting, and therefore properly stands unadorned, so to speak, or unqualified, when the standard case is what we have before us. The point about discourse might be that one does not mention what is not worth mentioning, so that – though people ordinarily do act, say, intentionally – there is only in special cases any reason to say so. The notion of 'economy' seems appropriate enough for both.

A particularly instructive case to which Austin draws attention is that of *Regina* v. *Finney* (1874), a 'somewhat distressing favourite', he says, in classes conducted in Oxford with H. L. A. Hart. The case was as follows:

> Prisoner was indicted for the manslaughter of Thomas Watkins.
> The prisoner was an attendant at a lunatic asylum. Being in charge of a lunatic, who was bathing, he turned on hot water into the bath, and thereby scalded him to death. The facts appeared to be truly set forth in the statement of the prisoner made before the committing magistrate, as follows: 'I had bathed Watkins, and had loosed the bath out. I intended putting in a clean bath, and asked Watkins if he would get out. At this time my attention was drawn to the next bath by the new attendant, who was asking me a question; and my attention was taken from the bath where Watkins was. I put my hand down to turn water on in the bath where Thomas Watkins was. I did not intend to turn the hot water, and I made a mistake in the tap. I did not know what I had done until I heard Thomas Watkins shout out; and I did not find my mistake out till I saw the steam from the water. You cannot get water in this bath when they are drawing water at the other bath; but at other times it shoots out like a water gun when the other baths are not in use.[18]

The first point to notice here is the comparative complexity of the specification even of a fairly straightforward 'action'. What, to begin with, was Finney's *intention*? He 'intended putting in a clean bath'. But it is clear from the story that, further, as a part of that intention or as a subsidiary intention, he intended to refill an *unoccupied* bath, and for that reason asked Watkins to get out. It appears to be true, also, that he intended to refill the bath by first turning on the cold tap – at any rate, he states explicitly that he did *not* intend to turn the hot water on. But now, in the execution of that intention, or those intentions, two things went wrong: he evidently did not notice, or realize, that Watkins had not got out; and secondly, he 'made a mistake in the tap'. Finney offers in explanation (or as part of his 'excuse') that his *attention* was distracted from what he was doing by the new attendant's question, so that he did not, as one might put it, oversee as he ordinarily would have done the incidentals and circumstances of his doing, or setting out to do, what he intended. Thus, until he heard Watkins's shout, he 'did not know what [he] had done' – did not know, presumably, that he had caused grave injury to Watkins; and he did not 'find his mistake out', namely that he

76

had turned the hot tap as he did not intend to do, until he saw the steam. Finally, his troubles were compounded by the other baths not being in use, so that hot water shot out 'like a water gun'. It is not clear whether or not Finney knew at the time that the other baths were not in use; but in any case, since it was his intention to run cold water into an empty bath, he would not have thought that point particularly significant.

Finney's counsel contended on his behalf that Watkins's death 'resulted from accident', and that, though Finney might have made a 'culpable mistake', there was no 'negligence' so gross as to be reckless. The judge, after summarizing what happened, went on to say to the jury 'if you think it inadvertence not amounting to culpability – i.e., what is properly termed an accident – then the prisoner is not liable'. (The jury decided that he was not.) It is noticeable that both use expressions not used by Finney himself; he, perhaps naturally, had not confessed to negligence or recklessness, but he had also made no mention of accident or indavertence – his turning on the hot tap was *not intended*, he *made a mistake*. It is also, in the judge's remarks, particularly unclear exactly what the jury is being invited to consider: 'if you think that indicates gross carelessness', 'if you think it inadvertence . . . what is properly termed an accident'; but to what, we must ask, do 'that' and 'it' refer? It is no use seeking to answer that question by saying that the judge is talking about 'what Finney did', for obviously what he did could be specified in many radically different ways: for example, step by step – he bathed Watkins; he loosed out the bath; he told Watkins to get out – or compendiously – he caused Watkins's death. Was the judge suggesting that it might be considered gross carelessness on Finney's part not to have noticed that Watkins was still in the bath? or to have turned the wrong tap? Does he suggest that perhaps Finney turned on the hot tap inadvertently? *and* accidentally? Both of those suggestions in any case, if made, would seem to be wrong: 'inadvertently' would suggest that, in the course of doing something quite different, Finney had turned on the tap without realizing, or registering, that he was doing so; 'accidentally', that he had, say, knocked the tap with his hammer while trying to mend a pipe. Finney, correctly, said neither: he turned the *wrong* tap, not the tap he intended to turn; at that point he *made a mistake*. Possibly the whole transaction, the (of course unintended by anybody) death of Watkins, might be properly termed 'an accident'; but the death did not, contrary to counsel's phrase, 'result from' accident, at any rate if that means that it resulted from something that Finney did by accident, or accidentally – for what *did* he do that could be qualified in that particular way? The morals to be drawn from all this are principally three. First, the question what a person did can almost always be answered, for different purposes or for different reasons, in many different ways – and, further, there are different ways in which that may be so. We may say

77

that, for instance, he painted a picture of Westminster Bridge; or, we may, so to speak, break down that pretty complex and protracted 'action' into component phases: he laid on this stroke of paint, then that. . . . We may mention things that he did 'incidentally' to the action, perhaps without noticing (particularly, or even at all) that he was doing them, such as putting down a tube of paint in a particular place. Differently, we may bring into the statement of what he did a smaller or larger stretch of 'what happened', often bringing in happenings which were unforeseen and unintended by the agent, of which he may even never have become aware: I could, for example, without intending to, ruin your business by innocently informing a ruthless competitor of your trade secrets, perhaps without ever realizing that that – ruining your business – was what I had done. Second, and consequentially, if we are usefully to discuss whether the agent did 'it', say, intentionally or not, it is clearly absolutely essential to be clear what 'it', for the purposes of that discussion, is to be taken to be. It may be that I intentionally informed an enquirer of your trade secrets, perhaps innocently answering a question from what I took to be a disinterested party; but I did not intentionally (or deliberately) ruin your business. Finney turned on the hot tap by mistake; but he did not scald Watkins by mistake – which would suggest that he had meant to scald somebody else, or possibly to injure Watkins in some other way. And third, it must be stressed that terms of excuse – and their 'opposites', where those exist – are *different*, not freely and inconsequently interchangeable. Shooting your donkey by mistake is not the same as shooting your donkey accidentally.[19] Thoughtlessly betraying your secrets is not the same as doing so inadvertently, or unwittingly. It may be true that, in church, I intentionally (if also thoughtlessly) lit a cigarette, but not true that I deliberately lit a cigarette in church.

By way of penetrating 'the blinding veil of ease and obviousness' that is apt to obscure our view of what 'acting' is, Austin mentions several times what he calls the 'internal machinery' of doing actions, 'the departments into which the business of doing actions is organized':

> As I go through life, doing, as we suppose, one thing after another, I in general always have an idea – some idea, my idea, or picture, or notion, or conception – of what I'm up to, what I'm engaged in, what I'm about. . . . I must be supposed to have *as it were* a plan, an operation-order or something of the kind on which I'm acting, which I am seeking to put into effect, carry out in action: only of course nothing necessarily, or, usually, even faintly, so full-blooded as a plan proper. When we draw attention to this aspect of action, we use the words connected with intention.[20]

But in doing something, carrying out such a plan or 'plan', there are involved also (and here a rather military-looking model comes in) 'the receipt of intelligence, the appreciation of the situation, the invocation of principles, the planning, the control of execution' – and 'the rest'.[21] There are 'departments of intelligence and planning, of decision and resolve' – and again he gives particular emphasis to 'appreciation' of our situation, as something not reducible to mere information – 'a course of E. M. Forster and we see things differently: yet perhaps we know no more and are no cleverer'.[22] I think the suggestion here is not of course that in 'doing things' we often actually go through all these stages separately and self-consciously, but rather that, when things go wrong as they sometimes do – when charges may be levelled and excuses made – the particular charge, and perhaps excuse, will be seen as relating, not undiscriminatingly to 'what he did', but to some particular aspect of, or element in, 'what he did' rather than to others. In Finney's case, for example, his 'plan', what he was up to, what he was doing (in that sense) was perfectly all right – he was bathing lunatics as part of his job, no objection to that. His choice of 'ways and means' was all right too: he had bathed Watkins, loosed out the bath, and asked him to get out, so that the bath could be refilled for the next customer. It was at 'the executive stage' that things went wrong in two ways: in actually refilling the bath, Finney failed to notice that, contrary to his 'plan', Watkins had not got out of the bath; and, to make matters much worse, he also 'made a mistake in the tap', turning on the hot water instead of the cold. Finney sought to explain these mistakes in execution by saying that his attention was distracted by the new attendant; and it was evidently accepted that his mistakes were not culpable, or at any rate not culpable enough to sustain the manslaughter charge. The judge took the view, probably rightly, that it would have been a different matter if Finney had known that Watkins was still in the bath – presumably because, in that case, to have made 'a mistake in the tap' would have been much more culpable. It is, as Austin notes, characteristic of excuses to be, even when in a way believable, still 'unacceptable', not good enough; if I knock over the pepper-pot inadvertence will get me off the hook, but not if I knock over your Sèvres vase.

And there I leave it – being particularly conscious, as I noted earlier, of having only dipped into the rich store of food for thought which Austin's paper contains. In his paper he said that he did not so much 'treat' the subject, as seek to incite his readers to explore it in detail. In this chapter I, perhaps, have not so much critically surveyed 'A plea for excuses' as (I hope) incited readers to read it for themselves.

VI

Ifs and Cans

When the question arises whether someone has acted rightly or wrongly, and perhaps whether he is to be commended or blamed for acting as he did, the further question may always arise: could he have acted otherwise? Could he have done anything other than the thing that he did in fact do? (This question of course could be raised in any case at all, but seems particularly interesting and pertinent where an agent's credit is in some way involved.[1]) No doubt we all ordinarily assume an affirmative answer to that question, at any rate in a very large number of cases. The burglar, instead of culpably breaking into my house and stealing the silver, could have stayed innocently at home watching television; I could have worked in the garden yesterday afternoon instead of playing golf – and perhaps it does not greatly matter which I actually did; and so on. What is commonly taken to constitute a problem here is that, notwithstanding this completely natural propensity to suppose that people could, of course, very often have done something other than what they actually did, it is urged by some philosophers (and others) that there are grounds for holding, quite in general, that nothing ever could occur except what actually does occur, and therefore, among other things, that human agents can never act except as they actually do, and could not, in any case at all, have acted except as they actually did. Austin's 'Ifs and cans' take its start from some remarks of G. E. Moore's, in Chapter VI of his *Ethics*,[2] on this time-hallowed topic.

Moore starts with the following case. Suppose that I spent the morning working at my desk (and was not locked in, tethered, drugged, injured, or in any other way confined or disabled). Then it seems that these two things could truly be said of me: that, this morning, I could have walked a mile in twenty minutes (although in fact I did not), and that, by contrast, I could *not* have run 2 miles in five minutes. We note that these are evidently remarks about my physical capacities; walking a mile in twenty minutes is something that, in my state of this morning, I was physically well able to do, and so could have done, while neither I nor, come to that, anybody else could have covered (on foot) 2 miles in five minutes. If so, then there is at least some sense – *that* sense, whatever it is – in which it is at least sometimes true of a person that he could have done something which in fact he did not do.

But the objector – let us call him the 'determinist' – may not be satisfied with this. Let it be agreed (as surely it must on any showing be agreed) that something other than what I actually did this morning – for example, in this case, walking a mile in twenty minutes – was generally within my physical capacities at that time, and so was (in that sense at least) something that I could have done; it may still be held to be the case, all the same, that I could not actually have done it. For it may be held that, given all the circumstances as they actually were this morning, the actual course of events was thereby causally *determined* – given those exact circumstances and known (or even unknown) laws of nature, nothing could have occurred except what actually did occur; and so the alternative scenario, so to speak, of my going for a walk could not in fact have been realized, I could not have done it (it could not have been the case that I did it). I could not have done it, given all the circumstances as they actually were, even though it was something that was in general within my physical capacities to do.

Rather tentatively, Moore suggests that that is not the end of the matter. There is some reason, he thinks, to hold that, in such a case, 'could have' really means 'could have *if* I had chosen', or (as he suggests it might be 'preferable' to say, 'to avoid a possible complication') '*should* have if I had chosen'. But if that were right, the determinist might well – and even should – agree that I could have done it, even though I did not; for he might admit, and, surely, even must admit, that something could or would have occurred that did not actually occur, *if* the circumstances had been other than as they actually were, and therefore that, *if* I had chosen to (as I did not), maybe I could or should have walked a mile in twenty minutes this morning. That seems to amount to suggesting that 'could have', and presumably 'can', at least in such a case, are really *conditional;* and it is certainly at the very least consistent with the determinist's position to say that something other than what actually occurred could or would have occurred, *if* the actual circumstances or conditions prevailing had been different in a certain respect.

Well, Austin does not, at any rate for the time being, embroil himself directly in the debate with the determinist. He wishes in the first instance to argue with Moore.

First, what about 'could have' and 'should have'? Moore's position here is certainly enigmatic, to say the least. He suggests that perhaps 'could have' really means 'could have if I had chosen', but then goes on to say that it might be better – 'to avoid a possible complication' – to say 'should have if I had chosen'. But in fact that looks like saying something very different: 'what a man *could* do is not at all the same as what he *would* do: perhaps he could shoot you if you were within range, but that is not in the least to say that he would.' And if we take Moore's own case, 'I could have walked a mile in twenty minutes if I had chosen' is surely not synonymous with 'I should have walked a mile in twenty minutes if I had chosen'. Both might be true of me, but they do not say the same thing. The most natural way of reading the first would be as making a claim, or at least an assertion, about my physical abilities, whereas the second – which Austin regards as anyway a pretty strange and perplexing thing to say – is perhaps most naturally taken as saying something about my strength of character: if I had chosen to walk a mile in twenty minutes this morning, I should (jolly well) have done so.[3] Moore's suggestion that we may, and even that we had better, simply replace one form of words with the other is sadly unexplained, but in any case, in Austin's view, is certainly unjustified.

The next point is at least as serious a matter. It was evidently a key feature of Moore's suggestion that 'I could have', and presumably also 'I can', are really *conditional*. It seems that that must have been what he intended, since that is what his dialectical purpose, in debate with the determinist, evidently required; the determinist holds that, given all the circumstances, only what did occur could have (actually) occurred, but is quite ready to admit that something else could (or would) have occurred *if* the circumstances had been different – if some 'condition' had been satisfied that actually was not. Moore's tentative hypothesis is that 'I can if I choose' is a conditional sentence in that required sense, and that that is what 'I can' really means when fully set out. But *is* it 'conditional'? Well, we may say that it is, if that simply means that it contains a subordinate clause beginning with 'if'. But in other respects, as Austin proceeds to show, it differs strikingly from 'normal' conditionals.[4] By normal rules, if we have something of the form 'If p, then q', then, first, we may infer 'If not q, then not p'; and second, we of course cannot infer 'q' by itself. From 'If he's walking, he's going to be late', we may infer 'If he's not going to be late, he's not walking,' but not, of course, 'He's going to be late'; and to take an example with 'can': from 'He can do it if he's fully fit', we may infer 'If he can't do it, he's not fully fit', but not, of course, 'He can do it'; here, his ability is indeed said to be conditional upon something, namely upon his being fully fit. But 'I can if I choose' does not work in that 'normal' way. We certainly would *not* make the curious and perhaps senseless inference to 'If I can't, I don't choose to'; but it seems that we *can* infer 'I can, whether I choose to or not', and also, simply, 'I can', unconditionally. (My ability to do it, that I *can* do it, is certainly *not* said to be conditional upon my choosing to.) Such not-really-conditional 'ifs' are not, Austin points out, all that uncommon. 'There are biscuits on the sideboard if you want them' does imply – well, it *says* – that there are biscuits on the sideboard (whether in fact you want them or not), and certainly does *not* imply that if there are no biscuits, then you don't want them. 'I paid you yesterday, if you remember' does imply that I paid you yesterday whether you remember or not, and does *not* imply that, if I didn't pay you, you don't remember that I did – though of course, for a different reason, that would actually be true.

'I can if I choose,' then, and 'I could have if I had chosen' are not 'normal' conditionals – are not really conditionals at all – as Moore's argument appeared to require us to take them to be. What about 'I shall if I choose'? This is clearly rather different.[5] Certainly we cannot, from 'I shall if I choose', infer that I shall whether I choose to or not, or simply that I shall. So far, then, 'I shall if I choose' looks like a normal conditional. But what about 'if not q, not p'? Can we derive 'If I shall not, I don't choose to'? That certainly looks pretty strange, and Austin thinks it positively objectionable. His point, if I understand him, is that in 'I shall if I choose', 'I shall' is not (really, or merely) an assertion (prediction) that something – namely my doing it – will be the case, but rather is the announcement of a present intention, namely the intention to do it if I choose. It is thus pretty unclear what 'if I shan't' could be taken to mean: if it were meant to be the negation of 'I shall', it would not be merely the supposition of something's not occurring in the future; but if it is not that, what else could it be? I think that, significantly, if we try to make the inference work we find ourselves pushed into slightly changing the wording: 'Your grandfather will be greatly upset if you marry that man.' 'I shall marry him if I choose.' 'You surely won't do that, knowing how your grandfather feels?' 'If I don't, that will only be because I don't choose to.' In this rather disagreeable bit of dialogue (which, in effect, brusquely dismisses grandfather's feelings from the reckoning), it is noteworthy that 'I shall' is succeeded by 'If I *don't*', which is intelligible enough but perhaps not the straight negation of 'I shall' in the previous remark.

But to return to 'I could have, if I had chosen', which Moore tentatively proposed as the fully spelled-out version of 'I could have', and which, as we have seen, he evidently took to be an ordinary sort of conditional sentence. Austin suggests, surely rightly, that he may have been tempted into this position through failing to notice that 'could have' is actually ambiguous - or rather, as Austin more accurately puts it, that there are two distinct 'could haves', orthographically and phonetically identical but grammatically quite different.[6] One 'could have' really is conditional: 'I could have done it if I'd been fully fit' really does say that *I would have been able* to do it *if* a certain condition had been satisfied (as it was not), namely my being fully fit; it may be helpful to note here, as Austin does, that, if we were using Latin, we should have the subjunctive form *potuissem*. But it is also possible to say, quite unconditionally, 'I could have done it' – not that I would have been able to if . . . , but that I *was* able to (Latin *potui*). But once we see that 'could have' is sometimes simply the past *indicative* of 'can', the idea that it always requires an attendant 'if'-clause, or that there is always an 'if'-gap waiting to be filled in, does not look tempting at all. It is certainly grammatically allowable to append, as Moore does, to such an indicative 'could have' the phrase 'if I had chosen'; but that, as we have seen, does not turn the sentence into, or show it 'really' to be, a conditional: 'I could have if I had chosen' does not say that I would have been able to subject to some condition, but that I *was* able to, which is, of course, why we can derive from it that I could have, *simpliciter*. Similarly, 'I can do it if there's a following wind' really is conditional; 'I can do it if I choose' is not: it says flatly that I *am* able to do it.

If, then, there are, not all that uncommonly, these non-conditional 'ifs', what is to be said positively about their significance? They are surely not just *in*significant – though 'I can if I choose' does make the assertion that I can, it is hardly to be supposed that the addition of 'if I choose' makes absolutely no difference, is not really an addition at all but an absolute redundancy. This would be a large subject to investigate properly; it seems pretty clear that cases differ, and an all-embracing account might be hard to arrive at. Perhaps one might begin, at any rate, in this sort of way. In 'There are biscuits on the sideboard if you want them', it rather looks as if 'If you want them' has something to do, not with *there being* biscuits on the sideboard – for of course they are there whether you in fact want them or not – but rather with my *mentioning the fact* that there are biscuits on the sideboard: 'There are biscuits on the sideboard – which I think it pertinent to mention because you may possibly want them, and I don't know whether you do or not.' 'I paid you back yesterday, if you remember': what about 'I paid you back yesterday – as I hope you will remember now that I mention it, though (again) I don't know whether you will or not'? But it may well be that there are significantly different uses even of each of these. As to 'I can if I choose' Austin offers, merely as samples, eight slightly different possible interpretations, and observes that 'what is common to them all is simply that the *assertion*, positive and complete, that "I can", is linked to the *raising of the question* whether I choose to, which may be relevant in a variety of ways.'[7] All these 'ifs', of course, leave the question *open* – whether you want them, whether you remember, whether I choose to.

But now we must bring in an important distinction, which itself brings in a quite different topic. Austin says:

> There are *two* quite distinct and incompatible views that may be put forward concerning *ifs* and *cans*, which are fatally easy to confuse with each other. One view is that wherever we have *can* or *could have* as our main verb, an *if*-clause must always be understood or supplied, if it is not actually present, in order to complete the sense of the sentence. The other view is that the meaning of 'can' or 'could have' can be more clearly reproduced by *some other verb* (notably 'shall' or 'should have') with an *if*-clause appended to *it*. The first view is that an *if* is required to *complete* a *can*-sentence: the second view is that an *if* is required in the *analysis* of a *can*-sentence. The suggestion of Moore that 'could have' means 'could have if I had chosen' is a suggestion of the first kind: but the suggestion also made by Moore that it means 'should have if I had chosen' is a suggestion of the second kind.[8]

So far we have been considering, mainly at any rate, the first suggestion (though perhaps with one or two implicit side-swipes at the second, as for example in Austin's remark that in general 'could' is 'very different indeed' from 'should' or 'would'). That is, it has been mainly contended in Austin's argument that 'could have' is often a past *indicative*, 'was able to', and as such does not at all require to be 'completed' by a conditional *if*-clause; and further, that 'if I had chosen', while grammatically it may be appended in such a case, is, first, not always required, and is, second, in any case not a normal conditional *if*-clause when it *is* appended. However, as Austin now remarks, all of this leaves untouched suggestions of the *second* kind, namely that 'can' and 'could have', even when indicative, are to be *analysed* in the form 'shall', 'should', and 'should have', followed by some conditional 'if . . . .'. In fact he thinks this sort of suggestion to be not only as yet unrefuted but not implausible; 'there is some plausibility, for example, in the suggestion that "I can do X" means "I shall succeed in doing X, if I try".'[9]

Surprisingly, Austin immediately rejects this important suggestion ('plausibility, but no more'), but only in a footnote, and a footnote in which he also makes with surprising brevity some other notably substantial claims. We must look at this with some care, notwithstanding its apparently modest impingement, as presented, at the margins of his argument.

In the footnote he proposes for consideration the following case. On the golf course I miss a very short putt, and 'kick myself because I could have holed it'. Does that – that I could have holed it – *mean* that I should have holed it if I had tried? Not at all. Surely not; I *did* try after all, and missed. Is it then that I should have holed it if conditions had been different? Well, that might be so; but when I say, here and now, reproaching myself, that I could have holed it, I surely mean that I could have done so in *these* conditions, precisely as they were. Further, he goes on to ask, does 'I can hole it this time' *mean* 'I shall hole it this time if I try'? Again it seems not: for if I then do try, and miss, I shall not necessarily take that as showing that I *could* not have holed it. 'Indeed, further experiments may confirm my belief that I could have done it that time although I did not.'[10]

But now, if we accept Austin's description of the case and of my reactions therein, what exactly is thereby established? Clearly, his *main* point is correct. 'I can' (here anyway) certainly does not just *mean* 'I shall do it if I try'; for I may try and fail, and yet not be obliged or even willing to conclude that I was wrong to say 'I can'; indeed, it is only because I still think I was right to say that, that I may reproach myself for not bringing it off. But let us now ask: why in the first place did I say 'I can'? Or, retrospectively, when I say that I could have holed it, how do I know that? What justifies me in saying so? I think that (assuming that, in general, I, the green, the ball, the weather, etc. are not in any abnormal sort of state) there are two things that need to be mentioned in a case such as this. First, knocking the ball the short distance required to get it into the hole is obviously well within my, and almost anybody's, physical capacity; certainly I can hit a golf-ball, say, 2 feet. And second, I have skill enough with a putter to hit it adequately straight for the purpose: the hole is not all that small, after all, and 2 feet is a very short range; I have played putts of that sort of length many times, and nearly always succeeded. If asked then, in general, whether I can hole 2-foot putts, I should feel fully justified in replying 'Yes, I can' – not, of course, that if I try, I succeed *every time* (even Gary Player would scruple to make such a claim as that); but I succeed quite often enough for that to be an ability which I can unqualifiedly lay claim to. Thus, I can hole 2-foot putts; therefore – there being, we take it, no special or extraordinary difficulties in the present case – I can hole *that* putt; and, even if I fail this time (I don't succeed *every* time), I shall still say, remorsefully, that I could have holed it. I could quite properly have been *counted on* to succeed, and that is why I reproach myself.

But consider another case. My ball lies on the green some 30 feet, say, from the hole. Can I hole the putt? This is clearly not such plain sailing. Certainly I am physically capable of hitting the ball 30 feet, no doubt about that; but – into the hole? What about *that*? Can I hole 30-foot putts? Well, yes – that is to say, it's not physically beyond me, and indeed I have sometimes done it, perhaps once or twice in three or four rounds of golf. So can I hole *this* putt? Well, it's certainly not *impossible* that I should hole it – if I try, I may perhaps bring it off. Hope springs eternal in the golfer's breast. But that is about as far as I should be happy to go in this case; and I should certainly not want to say, unqualifiedly, that I can hole 30-foot putts, which would sound wildly boastful even on the lips of Gary Player. Incidentally, if I try but miss, I shall not in this case – not, at least, very reasonably – kick myself; for although it was indeed not impossible that I should have holed it, it would have been most unfair, not to say imprudent, to count on my doing so. However important it was, I can scarcely be blamed.

Briefly, another case: there is a cross-bunker 250 yards from the tee. Can I carry that bunker? In this case, flatly no: whatever my skill with a driver (we need not go into that), that particular shot is certainly beyond my physical capacity. I just cannot do it.

The point of all this is that I think Austin proceeds rather unfairly in dismissing quite so unceremoniously the suggested analysis of 'I can do X' as 'I shall succeed in doing X if I try'. Certainly this will not do if it is taken 'literally', that is, as claiming that 'I can', in general, means that, if I try, I succeed *every time;* or that 'I can (here and now)', simply means that if I try, I shall succeed *this* time. But one gets the impression that he would like to suggest more than this – that there is simply no particular connection at all between 'can' and 'could have' on the one hand, and questions about trying and success or failure on the other. And that looks highly questionable. When, in particular, we consider the 30-foot putt, it seems pretty clear that the issue is: when I try to do things more or less of that sort, do I succeed (not of course every time, but) *often enough* to justify the assertion that that is a thing I can do? Indeed, what else would be relevant to the question? And how, we may ask, do I *know* that I cannot carry a bunker 250 yards away? Well, trying, as I often have done, to hit the ball as far as I can, I have simply *never* succeeded in hitting it as far as that; so I can reasonably conclude that I am (physically) unable to do it; that is, in general, how one discovers what one's physical capacities are, what, so far as they are concerned, one can and cannot do. It is possible that it may also be unfair to read Austin in this way – that is, as repudiating any link between 'can' and 'if I try'; for as we saw, he says himself, of his own short-putt example, that 'further experiments may confirm my belief that I could have done it that time although I did not'; and what, one may ask, could such 'further experiments' consist in, other than trying a few times and succeeding? But if that is right, the short, unqualified, and certainly as such untenable proposed analysis might be thought to invite some amendment and sophistication, rather than to deserve a swift chop as nothing more than 'plausible'.

Other complex and important issues arise in the same brief footnote. If I tried (my hardest) and missed, Austin rhetorically asks, 'surely there *must* have been *something* that caused me to fail, that made me unable to succeed?' He suggests that 'a modern belief in science' may make us ready to assent to this; but that seems not quite right, or at any rate not entirely clear. The fact is that he has here raised two questions (and possibly three), not one. First, if I tried and failed, there is the question: must there have been something that caused me to fail? Well, a modern belief in science, if that is what it is, or at any rate a disbelief in uncaused happenings, may well lead us to assent to that: when I struck it the ball took a certain route (which was not what I hoped for and intended, that is I failed) and presumably something, or a combination of many things, caused it, as and when struck, to travel as it actually did and to confound my hopes. (Perhaps I twitched with the bottom hand, or lifted my head.) But second, there is the question: must there have been something that made me *unable to succeed?* It is far from clear that a belief in modern science, or indeed anything else, requires us to assent to that. A sudden heart attack, or being struck by lightning or paralysis or appalling jitters, might suddenly make me *unable* to hole a 2-foot putt; but what in the ordinary way causes me to miss does not make me *unable*, deprive me of the *ability*, to succeed – it simply brings it about that I *do* not succeed on this occasion. Austin goes on to make the important and interesting suggestion, to which we shall return in due course, that 'such a belief' – namely 'a modern belief in science, in there being a explanation of everything' – is

> not in line with the traditional beliefs enshrined in the word *can*:
> according to *them*, a human ability or power or capacity is
> inherently liable not to produce success, on occasion, and that for
> no reason (or are bad luck and bad form sometimes reasons?).

That is interesting, but it seems to me extremely doubtful whether it – or at least, whether all of it – is true. The idea of traditional beliefs being 'enshrined in [a] word' is itself a little puzzling; but presumably part of what Austin had in mind is that accepted, 'traditional' *use* of the word 'can' permits us to say that what a person *can* do he may, on occasion, not succeed in doing – even if, on occasion (not too often!), he fails, we may still say that he can. Well, that is certainly so; but surely 'modern belief in science' is perfectly consistent with that; for there is nothing in modern science, happily, which entails the quite preposterous belief that what, in general, a human being can do he must succeed in doing *every time* he tries. Presumably what 'modern science' might find uncongenial is the quite different idea that, sometimes at any rate, when he tries and fails, he fails *for no reason*, that there is simply no explanation for his failing on that occasion (allowing, of course, that we may very often not know what the explanation is, be unable actually to supply it). 'Modern science' supposes there must be an 'explanation'. But then, surely it is not at all clear that our unscientific 'traditional belief' really is that sometimes, when failure occurs, it occurs for no reason; one might think that most people, however unscientific, would tend to suppose that *something* must have 'gone wrong' to account for the failure, even if they had little or no notion of what it might be. (Perhaps nothing more specific than 'pressure of the big occasion'.) Perhaps, indeed, it depends which 'tradition' one looks at: ancient Greeks, for example, I think really did believe that some things, quite a lot of things, happen literally and in principle inexplicably, for no 'reason' at all, purely and simply 'by chance'; but it is surely not obvious that a tradition such as that is somehow encapsulated in the ordinary use of 'can'. Nor, I think, is it encapsulated, as Austin seems to suggest, in the notions of 'bad luck' and 'bad form'. It is certainly bad luck if, on a decent batting pitch, a batsman is out leg-before-wicket to a ball that suddenly comes through unexpectedly low; but only a highly superstitious batsman would suppose that the ball that got him kept low *for no reason;* nor of course did he miss it for no reason – it kept low. And if a batsman is going through a spell of bad form, as happens from time to time, he is not likely to suppose that he is coming unstuck for no reason; he is likely to be asking himself and perhaps his team-mates what he is doing wrong (though he, and they, of course, may not know the answer). Bad luck and bad form are not, one may agree, 'reasons' for failure – at any rate, not reasons of any explanatory potency; but readiness to use those convenient and useful notions does not commit one to the very strange belief that (some) failures occur for simply no reason at all. I suspect that we need, in fact, to bring in here yet a third question, which Austin in this footnote does not explicitly raise. There is the question: if he failed, must something have caused his failure, or caused him to fail? There is the different question: if he failed, must something have made him unable to succeed? But perhaps there is a third question: if he failed, must it have been impossible that he should have succeeded? Perhaps it is *that* question to which traditional belief and 'science' give different answers. We shall come back to that.

Finally, Austin takes up some remarks about 'He could have acted otherwise' offered by P. H. Nowell-Smith in his book *Ethics* (1954). These cover some old ground, but some new ground as well.

Nowell-Smith begins by saying that 'could have' is a 'modal phrase, and modal phrases are not normally used to make categorical statements'.[11] Austin, characteristically, declines discussion of what exactly a 'modal phrase' may be, but asks why 'He could have . . .' should be said to be not categorical, or at any rate, as Nowell-Smith also says, not 'a straightforward categorical statement'. *Part* of the ground for this claim seems to consist in a curiously tangled thesis about how 'He could have . . .' assertions are to be *verified*. For a start, Nowell-Smith makes the incorrect supposition that to say that a person could have done something is always to imply that he did not in fact do it; this is incorrect because, as Austin points out, it would be entirely proper to say that a person could have done something, for example committed a murder, when we do *not know* whether he actually did it or not, but are perfectly prepared, and perhaps even hope, to establish on further investigation that he did. This is pertinent because Nowell-Smith contends that the assertion 'He could have done it' is not straightforwardly categorical because it cannot be verified 'directly' – which seems to mean, at least in part, verified by establishing what he actually did; that may look fairly plausible (though, as we shall see, no more) when the question is whether he could have done something which in fact (we know that) he did not do; but if it is established that he did commit the murder, does not that show – and presumably 'directly', as a fact about what he actually did – that we were in this case *right* in saying that he could have done it? If so, that he could have done it sometimes at any rate *can* be verified 'directly', namely by establishing that in fact he did it.

But what about the case in which we say that he could have done something, it being known and agreed on all hands that actually he did not? Is it clear that *this* can never be verified 'directly'? Well, there are certainly some cases which seem to fit the sort of claim that Nowell-Smith is advancing. The case of the short putt, for example, which I miss and of which I say that I could have holed it; obviously, that I could have holed it is not 'verified' in any degree by the fact that I missed; but neither is it verified, really, by the mere fact that I did hole a similar putt on some other occasion – for in such a case we need to show, as Nowell-Smith puts it, that I have performed the feat 'sufficiently often to preclude the possibility of a fluke'.[12] The ability to hole (even very short) putts, we may say, is a matter of pretty consistent performance over a decently large number of cases; it cannot be established that I have it (or that I have not) by noting my performance in any single case; and perhaps that means that it cannot be established 'directly'. But caution is needed in generalizing from this sort of case. In particular, very curiously – a point not made by Austin – this picture of the case, though not too bad for the short putt, seems manifestly *not* to fit the very example that Nowell-Smith himself adduces in putting it forward. His example is: 'He could have read *Emma* in bed last night, though he actually read *Persuasion*.' We need to establish here that there was a copy of *Emma* to hand at the material time, but it seems to be agreed that that could be settled 'directly' – we see the book there. But if so, it seems overwhelmingly reasonable to say that at any rate *in this case* what he could have done though he did not, namely read *Emma, is* in fact shown conclusively by what he actually did, namely read *Persuasion*. How could that not be so? My ability to hole short putts is indeed not shown by what I did, by my actually missing one; but surely my ability to read one novel by Jane Austen *is* comprehensively established by my actually reading another. What could one possibly make of the remark 'Well, he certainly read *this* novel of hers, but that doesn't show that he could have read *that* one'? For what else – assuming both books to be available – is really involved except the ability to read English? (It is particularly curious that Nowell-Smith should not have noticed this, since in the same passage he actually gives 'He does not know German' as the reason why he could *not* have read *Werther*.) Nor, in this case at least, need we be bothered by the possibility of a 'fluke'; I may hole a putt – once, or occasionally – by a mere fluke, but what would it be to succeed, by a mere fluke, in *reading*?[13] The point that Austin himself makes is a slightly different one – surely, he says, that I could have, say, lifted my finger ten seconds ago is 'verified', not indeed by anything that I did ten seconds ago, but by my now proceeding to lift it; and that seems both conclusive enough, and 'direct' enough. Here too there seems to be no room for the suggestion that we need a run of consistent performances to rule out the possibility of a fluke. If so, we may perhaps conclude, in general, that Nowell-Smith's thesis fits only some of the cases. The thesis that what a person could have done cannot be established 'directly', that is by establishing what he in fact *did* do on some particular occasion, works rather well for such an ability as holing putts or making breaks of fifty at snooker, but not for others – including, oddly enough, the ability to read *Emma*, the very case that Nowell-Smith considers. If so, we are not thus apprised of a general truth about 'could have', but only a particular truth (perhaps) about certain sorts of abilities.

But in any case we need to ask: what if this thesis of Nowell-Smith's had been generally true? Suppose it were the case that, in general, 'He could have done it' could only be established by an 'inductive' argument, that is, by evidence as to what occurred, and did not occur, on adequately numerous (other) occasions: would that tend to show what it is apparently adduced as showing, namely, that 'He could have done it' is not 'categorical', or at any rate not straightforwardly categorical? Austin says, surely correctly, that it would not. The question whether a given proposition is categorical seems unrelated to the question, what sort of evidence or argument would be needed to establish its truth-value; to determine that the table I now write at is an antique I may need evidence, and presumably 'inductive' evidence, that it was made a fairly long time ago; the question perhaps cannot be settled 'directly'. But surely 'This table is an antique' is a categorical proposition. So is 'The sun will rise in the East tomorrow'.[14] It seems likely that Nowell-Smith's inclination to say that 'He could have done it' is not categorical was really attributable, not to his points about verification which certainly establish no such thing, but rather to two unclarities we have already encountered in the case of Moore – first, not seeing clearly that 'could have' can be, and often is, a past *indicative (potui)*, neither inviting nor requiring any conditional completion; and second, not seeing clearly that a proposition whose *analysis* comes out in conditional form is not thereby shown to *be*, itself, a conditional or non-categorical proposition. Nowell-Smith certainly wishes to hold that the *analysis* of 'could have' is of the form 'would have . . . if . . .'; and it looks very much as if he took that, incorrectly, as implying that 'could have' is itself not categorical.

So what about the *analysis* of 'can' and 'could have'? Nowell-Smith proceeds as follows. There is a certain conjunction of factors which is, he says, 'logically odd'[15] – namely that a person can do something, has the opportunity to do it, has a preponderant motive for doing it, but does not in fact do it. Well, first, *is* that (always) logically odd? Surprisingly, Austin does not raise that question here; he is content to argue that the contention does not justify the conclusion that Nowell-Smith draws from it, which we shall come on to in due course. But that is rather surprising because in fact – and it seems worth pointing this out – he had himself already produced a counter-example, at any rate given the interpretation that he is ready to put upon the obscure (then briefly fashionable) expression 'logically odd'. That a certain conjunction of propositions is logically odd Austin takes to mean simply that they cannot all be true together. But the following propositions, for example, *can* all be true together: (1) I can hole a 2-foot putt; (2) I shape up (have the opportunity) to hole a 2-foot putt; (3) I have a preponderant motive for holing it (it's an important match); and (4) I miss. There is nothing in the least logically odd about that. For of course, as Austin has himself pointed out, if I try (very hard) to hole a 2-foot putt and miss, we do not have to conclude that I could not have holed it; on the contrary, I may in such a case be overwhelmed with remorse precisely because I know that I *could* have holed it. The fact is that Nowell-Smith's conjunction of propositions, or rather his supposition that their conjunction is 'logically odd', implicitly incorporates a mistake that we noted at an earlier stage – the mistake, namely, of supposing that, if it is true that a person can do something, it must be true that he does it *every time* he tries. It may indeed be odd or unexpected that, say, Player, or even that I, trying hard, should miss a 2-foot putt; but it is not *logically* odd, let alone logically impossible.

But let us suppose, as Austin is willing to do, that Nowell-Smith is right thus far – that is, that it is 'logically odd', in one way or another will not do, to conjoin 'He can', 'He has the opportunity to', 'He (preponderantly) wants to', and 'He does not'. This is supposed to establish that 'He can' *means* that if he has the opportunity and preponderantly wants to, he does (or will). Austin is disposed to deny this, on two grounds. First, the form of argument relied on surely proves too much. The conjunction of four propositions is said to be impermissible: we are then invited to conclude that *one* of them, 'He can', *means* that if two others are true, the fourth – namely, that he does not – is false; that is, that he does (or will). But, as Austin puts it, the propositions 'all occupy parallel positions in the premiss'; and, if so, the same argument would lead to the conclusion that, for example, 'He wants to' *means* that if he can but does not, he has no opportunity to; or that 'He does not do it' *means* that if he can and has the opportunity, he does not want to. But these, as Austin says, as proposed analyses of *meaning* are 'fantastic suggestions'.[16] If I do not take my summer holiday in Iceland, it may well be true that I could but do not want to; but it would seem grotesque to offer 'He could have done but he did not want to' as what it *means* to say that I did not take my holiday there. But second, Austin points out that Nowell-Smith manages, in his proposed analysis of 'He can', to get to some proposition about what the agent does or will do only by introducing some reference to his *motives*, or to what he (preponderantly) wants – for how, indeed, could we say anything about what a person will do (or would have done) with no mention of what his motives for acting are (or were), or what he wants (or wanted)? But it is, he submits, clear that, if we are talking simply about what a person *can* do, any mention of his wants or motives is simply irrelevant. He goes on to concede, however, that, even if on these grounds Nowell-Smiths' particular thesis must be rejected, this does not show that *no* analysis of 'can' of the form 'will . . . if . . .' could be correct; in particular, it does not, he says, tell against the suggestion that 'He can' perhaps means 'He will if he tries', for that seems to leave it an entirely, and properly, open question whether or not he has, or ever will have, any inclination to try: 'here considerations of motive may be irrelevant', as he thinks they should be, in the analysis of 'can'. But we must remember, of course, though Austin does not remind us, that he has already offered *other* considerations against that analysis – as 'plausible, but no more' – at any rate in that bald unsophisticated form.

Let me now, in conclusion, venture a few remarks on my own account that may serve the purpose of tying up one or two loose ends. First, it seems to me important to bring firmly out into the open something which Austin mentions only briefly, in a footnote. 'I talk here and throughout', he says, 'of "ability" and "opportunity" only: but I realize that other abstract nouns like "capacity", "skill", and even "right" are equally involved. All these terms need listing and elucidating before we really get to grips with "can".'[17] I believe that this point, though thus unobtrusively introduced, is actually of central importance for the present topic. It is of central importance to recognize that cases differ – that when we speak of what a person can do or could have done, issues may be involved of many widely *different* sorts. Sometimes – can he walk? could he have walked a mile in twenty minutes? – of physical capacity. Sometimes – can he read? could he have read *Werther?* – of some 'mental' or intellectual ability. Sometimes – can he hole a 6-foot putt? could he have mended the engine? – of skill. Sometimes – can he stop me doing it? could he have compelled payment? – of legal power or right. And so on. It seems to be a constant cause of trouble that, so often, what a philosopher says about 'can' and 'could have' turns out to fit – and no doubt is derived from exclusive attention to – only some of the cases. If we have our eye on the case of a very simple physical capacity like lifting a finger, we think wrongly that 'He can' means 'He will (every time), if he tries'. If we think of an important and delicate skill like that of holing putts, we think wrongly that 'He can' can *never* be established by the simple fact that he did (because it might have been a fluke). If we think of the same sort of case, we may say, as Austin did, that 'ability' is 'inherently liable not to produce success, on occasion' – but would we be happy to say that about, for example, the ability to read? And if he can – has the legal power to – prevent my building a 10-foot-high wall in front of his house, does any question even arise of his *trying* to prevent me? If he chooses or decides to, in such a case, then he will. (If he has to *try*, it is, so far, uncertain whether he can.) Sometimes, then, the question of trying does not arise. Very often, the possibility of a 'fluke' does not arise. And of course – which is really the same point again – if we turn to the question what is required in order to *establish* or verify what a person can do, or could have done, we shall find again that cases crucially differ. To find out whether you can hole 6-foot putts, I take you out to the putting-green for a series of trials. To find out whether you can stop me building a wall, I consult my solicitor or some legal document. To find out whether you could have read *Emma*, I find out whether at the time you knew English, and could read. Some of these procedures, no doubt, are more 'direct' than others; some establish, but some do not, that you will, if you try.

If so, it is tempting, though perhaps not enormously illuminating, to suggest that what 'He can' *means* – means quite in general – can only be said to be something highly indeterminate, like: 'He has what it takes'.[18] That rather coarse formula, for which I certainly wish to make no extravagant claims, seems to me nevertheless to have at least these two important merits. First, it positively invites, and properly and usefully invites, attention to the question: what *does* it take? Of course there will be, and it is important that there is, no answer to that in general; but when it comes to cases the answer will usually be unmysterious. The context, or the circumstances, will usually make things clear. A general bodily capacity, perhaps; or a specific physical or intellectual skill (many skills are both); or a legally enforceable prerogative; or whatever it may be. Second, my coarse formula has the merit of bringing out, and of at least pointing the way to understanding, the insufficiently noticed fact that, very often, 'Can he?' or 'Could he have?' is actually not sensibly answerable at all with a straightforward 'Yes' or 'No' – for he may have, not all of or nothing of, but only *something* of, 'what it takes'. He certainly has the physical capacity needed to propel the ball into that hole: but has he the (sufficient) skill? He can do long division, but whether he can do one as complicated as that. . . . It is an interesting question what exactly is involved in possession and acquisition and exercise of a physical capacity; or of an ability; or of a skill; of 'know-how'; or of a power, privilege, prerogative, or right, and so on. It is an interesting question how ascription to a person of one or other of these may be justified or verified, refuted or attacked, and what expectations it entitles us to form as to his possible performances. But the central truth is that 'can' is at home in the *whole* of this extensive territory; and the temptation must be doggedly resisted of offering, as 'analysis' of 'can', observations that fit only this or that particular case. Austin himself, I fear, did not always resist that insidious temptation.

Finally, a word or two about 'opportunity', which Austin also mentions in the footnote just quoted. This too is a notion which, while it has been given a good and frequent run in proposed analyses of 'can', is really at home in only some of the cases. If I can speak Russian, I may from time to time, living in Oxford, have an opportunity to do so (my college entertains a visitor from the USSR). But when I take lunch with my colleagues in the ordinary way, it would be strange indeed to say that I then have an opportunity of speaking English – though I can, of course, and do. I believe that those who, like Nowell-Smith, have talked of 'opportunity' here have really had in mind a rather wider-ranging thought – the thought that, if it is to be fully true that he could, say, have read *Emma* last night, then not only must he have had at the time 'what it takes' to do so (namely knowledge of English and the ability to read); it must also be the case that nothing barred, ruled out, or excluded his actually exercising 'what it takes' on that occasion – such as, for example, there having been no copy of *Emma* available. If it is to be unqualifiedly true that, this morning, I could have walked a mile in twenty minutes, it must be true not only that I had 'what it takes' (the physical ability) to do so, but also – not quite that I had 'the opportunity' to do so, which would indeed be a strange thing to say – that nothing in the circumstances at the time ruled out the actual exercise by me of that ability.

But now, if that is on the right lines, it may be that we can bring more clearly into focus the divergence which Austin claimed (very tentatively) to discern between 'modern science', or 'determinism', and 'traditional belief'. He writes,

> It has been alleged by very serious philosophers (not only the two I have mentioned)[19] that the things we ordinarily say about what we can do and could have done may actually be consistent with determinism. It is hard to evade all attempt to decide whether this allegation is true – hard even for those who, like myself, are inclined to think that determinism itself is still a name for nothing clear, that has been argued for only incoherently. At least I should like to claim that the arguments considered tonight fail to show that it *is* true, and indeed in failing go some way to show that it is *not*.
>
> Determinism, whatever it may be, may yet be the case, but at least it appears not consistent with what we ordinarily say and presumably think.[20]

I am inclined to believe that Austin was right about this, but also that he was less than clear as to *why* he was right.

Go back to the case of the short putt, which I miss 'and kick myself because I could have holed it'. In that much-discussed footnote Austin says two things about this. First, 'a modern belief in science' (and I take it that he regards determinism as at least part of this belief) may make us assent to the view that 'there *must* have been *something* that caused me to fail'; but such a view 'is not in line with the traditional beliefs'. This seems to me, as I have already said, wrong, or at least extremely doubtful; I think it would be entirely natural, not particularly modern or theoretical or doctrinaire, to say 'Well, of course, I must have done *something* wrong. You don't miss an easy putt like that just for no reason. Perhaps I twitched with the bottom hand, or lifted my head.' And to say that – that there 'must have been something that caused me to fail' – is quite consistent with my remorseful conviction that I could have holed it; perhaps I lifted my head, but of course, I penitently think, I could – and should – have kept my head still. Second, a modern belief in science, Austin says, may make us suppose that something must have 'made me unable to succeed', which, again, traditional belief would not agree with. This seems to me, if anything, more clearly wrong; for whatever it may have been that caused, and would explain, my failure, it would not have to be something that made me *unable to succeed*. Not that it might not have been; if the putt was really crucial to winning an important match, and I am a prey to nerves, it might have been that I really was so shaky and tense as to be – temporarily – incapable of holing even the simplest of putts. But some more commonplace error like lifting the head does not make me unable to succeed; it simply explains why I do not succeed. 'Science' and ordinary belief need not differ about that.

So do they, in the end, differ at all? I suggest, as does Austin, not very confidently, that they do, but on a slightly different point. If, as a plain man and traditional believer, I say that I could have holed it, I do so on the basis, first, that I undoubtedly have and had 'what it takes' (fairly minimal skill) to hole a short putt like that, and second, that nothing on that particular occasion was such as to bar, block, rule out, or exclude my applying that minimal skill successfully to the task. I could have holed it, I say, in, as Austin puts it, 'conditions as they precisely were': nothing in those conditions, as I suppose, ruled out my doing so. It is on this second point, I suggest, that 'the determinist' might wish to disagree. For, he might say, in conditions as they precisely were – in *all* the conditions as *all* of them precisely were – I simply *was going to* (for example) lift my head, and so miss; in conditions as they precisely were, including states of my own muscles, nervous system, etc., no other outcome, as for instance my *not* lifting my head, was ever actually on the cards – so that, though of course I can in general hole putts like that, it was actually not possible that I should have succeeded in holing that one. I *was going to* make the mistake that caused me to fail. The conditions – *all* the conditions – really did exclude any other outcome, and my 'traditional' supposition that they did not is simply mistaken. Put generally: it is perhaps our ordinary belief that, most of the time, there are many things we can do – we have 'what it takes' to do many different things; *and* that there is often nothing in the prevailing circumstances to 'rule out' our actually doing them. 'The determinist' holds that there is – that in *exactly* those circumstances, including *all* of them and not merely those that we happen to know about and ordinarily take into account, some particular outcome *is going to* ensue, and it is not possible that things should go otherwise.

VII

Some Other Papers

There remain four papers of Austin's which have not been mentioned, or mentioned very much in passing, and these should be rounded up, if only very briefly.

First, there is a paper – not published by Austin, nor indeed written by him exactly as it now stands in his *Philosophical Papers* – on the interpretation of the Line and the Cave in Plato's *Republic*[1]. This consists in part of a paper written in the 1930s in comment on a paper by Sir David Ross, supplemented and amended, particularly in its later pages, from notes made for a class held in the late 1940s. The piece well displays Austin's characteristic care and scholarship and good sense in the interpretation of a text; but it is carefully restricted to the sole task of elucidating what Plato meant, and I think it need not be further discussed in what is not a book about Plato.

A second paper, about some issues in Aristotle's *Ethics*, is more wide-ranging.[2] This was written well before 1939, and 'takes it start', as Austin puts it, from an article by H. A. Prichard published in 1935.[3] The object of Prichard's article was to establish what he regarded as a 'heretical' account of what Aristotle meant by *agathon* – the Greek word for 'good' – in his *Nicomachean Ethics*; and Austin's paper is in part a (crunchingly effective) demonstration that Prichard's conclusion, while heretical enough, could not possibly be correct. It is not certain, however, that the demonstration, pretty overwhelming though it is, would necessarily have convinced Prichard. For against his claims that, by such-and-such a word, Aristotle 'undoubtedly' meant so-and-so, Austin proceeds, as one naturally would, by citing numerous passages in which Aristotle either says explicitly that the word in question does *not* have that meaning, or uses it in ways which clearly imply that it does not. Prichard would almost certainly have sought to brush this aside. He did not think

98

at all highly of the *Nicomachean Ethics*, and was ready and indeed eager to say that if Aristotle – who 'undoubtedly' attached a certain meaning to a given word – either said, or in what he wrote implied, that it did not have that meaning, that merely convicted him of inconsistency and confusion. There surely comes a point, however – if almost everything in an author's text implies that by x he did not mean y – at which it becomes at best quixotic to cling to the conviction that, really, he did. But apart from that, Austin's paper is not merely negative. He considered at some length what Aristotle really did mean, and issues of some interest arise from his consideration of that.

There are two key terms at issue here; one of course is *agathon*, the meaning of which was the principal topic of Prichard's article; the other is *eudaimonia* – for which, with certain not negligible reservations, Austin accepts the traditionally received translation 'happiness'. Let us take *eudaimonia* first.

Aristotle asks: what is *eudaimonia*? And Austin asks: what did he mean by that question? What sort of answer was he looking for? What seems to me interesting is that Austin brings in here – more or less following the lead of G. E. Moore – a notion that was ubiquitously current in the 1930s, but which he certainly very seldom employed anywhere else, namely the notion of 'analysis'.[4] Aristotle is not asking, he suggests, what the word *eudaimonia* means, in the sense in which any competent speaker of classical Greek presumably knew what it meant; 'some simple synonym' would not be the answer required. Nor is he asking – yet – 'for what we may call the specification' of *eudaimonia*, what happiness, the good life, 'allegedly consists in concretely'.[5] He is asking, Austin suggests, for an 'analysis' of its meaning; and 'to search thus for analysis of the meaning of *eudaimonia* does not seem to me absurd, except on the false assumption that its meaning was, and was known to be, simple and unanalysable'.[6] It is interesting too that he complains that, in Aristotle's text, 'it is hard to discover . . . where the analysis ends and the other process (viz. specification) begins' – his 'distinction between analysis and specification is most unclear'.[7] That seems plainly to imply that, in his view at that time, the line could and should have been made clear – it should have been made clear whether this or that which *eudaimonia* is said to 'be' was being offered as – in his own words – 'part of the meaning' of the expression, or as something else. That phrase – 'part of the meaning' – was one which, as we shall see, he very soon came to find objectionable, or at any rate treacherous.

Though there was, in the 1930s, a copious literature about 'analysis', Austin himself at that time seems not to have regarded the notion as very problematic.[8] With a view to its elucidation he simply draws a distinction, in support of which he cites a sentence of Aristotle's own, between 'knowing more or less *vaguely* what is meant by' an expression, and an 'attempt to *clarify* that meaning'; it is clearly implied that ordinary speakers of the relevant language share 'vague' knowledge of the meaning, but may be found to disagree when asked for clarification. It seems clear, however, that, in his opinion, 'analysis' is still concerned simply with meaning; the meaning of the expression, indeed, is *what* is to be analysed. He uses the phrase 'analysis or definition', and says at one point that analysis of the meaning of *eudaimonia* 'results, as it should, in a clear and full definition'.[9] He seems quite happy here with the notion of 'meaning' itself, and makes free use of it without discussion.

The discussion of *agathon*, 'good', is somewhat more tortuous. Prichard appears to have taken for granted that, if 'good' is not simply an ambiguous word (and no party to the argument seems to wish to say that it is), then there *must* be a 'common character' on the basis of which anything said to be good is so said; his question is what, for Aristotle, this common character must be – and he holds, incidentally, in the manner earlier referred to, that Aristotle's express denial that all things said to be good *do* have a common character 'is merely an inconsistency into which he is driven by his inability to find in these things the common character which his theory requires him to find'.[10] Austin, naturally enough, finds this way of proceeding absurd. But he seems to be himself somewhat uneasy as to how to state what Aristotle's position really was. He is happy enough to say, what is surely true, that it is at least one of Aristotle's main contentions that there is *no* 'common character' on the basis of which everything said to be good – good weather, for example, or good cheese, or a good argument – is so said; but is that to say, or not, that *agathon* has no single meaning? One might well think that it is not *necessarily* to say that, for surely there might be ways of assigning to some term a 'single meaning', otherwise than by identifying some 'common character' possessed by anything to which that term was rightly applied. But what exactly was Aristotle saying? Austin says that, in confuting 'those who had supposed that the word *agathon* always stands for a single identical predicate', Aristotle does not tell us 'what are the various meanings of *agathon*' (implying, of course, that he thought it *had* plural meanings) – he 'declines in general to discuss the meanings of *agathon* but argues that it has no single meaning'.[11] Further, when Aristotle cites examples of things 'good in themselves' of which nevertheless, he says, the 'accounts' (*logoi*) *qua agatha* are different, Austin takes him to be again denying that *agathon*, even in such cases, 'has always an identical meaning'. He seems not confident, however, that Aristotle was right in taking this position; for we still may, he says, wish to consider 'the extent to which Aristotle does in fact attach a discoverable, and even single, meaning to *agathon*', and may even hold 'that he must himself attach some meaning to it in using it throughout the *Ethics*, which we may be able to discover'.[12] What seems to me noteworthy in all this is not the evident difficulty of determining what exactly Aristotle was up to in his discussion of *agathon* – that just *is* difficult, largely because his discussion is so brief and compressed; it is rather Austin's apparent lack of much anxiety, at this stage, about the notion of meaning itself. In particular, the question whether a given expression has a single meaning, or different meanings, or meanings partly the same and partly different, appears to be taken as a perfectly good, sensible question, inviting a choice between reasonably clear alternatives – the uncertainty being only as to how Aristotle answered it, or should have answered it, in the particular case of *agathon*. It is pretty clear from passing remarks in his later writings that Austin became steadily more suspicious of the notion of meaning itself – and it is, in fact, remarkable how seldom he makes much use of it.[13]

He is already much more conscious of dangers here in another paper written, though again not published, not much later – 'The meaning of a word'[14] – which is in fact, rather surprisingly for one who has so often been called a 'linguistic philosopher', his one and only direct discussion, apart from passing remarks elsewhere, of the notion of meaning. His first point is that it of course makes perfectly good sense to ask 'what is the meaning of' some given word – 'racy', say, or 'rat'; and there are familiar ways in which we may hope to answer such a question – roughly, we may try to give an answer in other *words*, 'trying to describe what raciness is and what it is not'; or we may get the questioner to imagine, or may actually show him, actual *situations* in which 'racy' would be used, and again others in which it would not. But, being thus reasonably satisfied with the question 'what is the meaning of' some given word, we may be tempted, he says, 'being philosophers', to raise the more general-looking question 'What is the meaning of a word?'[15] That may well, and indeed should, look like a pretty nonsensical question, simply inviting the counter-question 'Of *what* word?' But it seems to be tempting, nevertheless, to 'change the hyphenation', as Austin puts it, to treat with solemnity and an air of high abstraction the question 'What is the-meaning-of-a-word?', and gravely to offer such answers as 'a universal', 'a concept', 'an idea', 'an image', or 'a class of similar sensa'. These, however, are all bogus answers to a badly misshapen question. We can of course ask what 'meaning' itself means; but there are not items or entities, whether individuals or classes or anything else, to be collectively identified as 'the meanings of words', and it is a waste of time to debate the question what 'sort of thing' the meaning-of-a-word might be.

The idea that there are items to be called 'the meanings of words' may also mislead us, Austin proceeds, into taking too seriously, or too literally, the expression 'part of the meaning of'. (We noted a moment ago

101

Austin's own use of that expression in discussing *eudaimonia*.) Not that that expression is not, often, harmless enough; it would be understandable enough to say that being male is part of the meaning of 'being a husband'. But if we allow ourselves to think, in some would-be literal sort of way, that meanings are items that quasi-literally have parts, we may come to assume that 'Is x, or is it not, part of the meaning of "y"?' is a question that always *must* have a definite answer; and that may lead us to embrace the (at that time highly popular) dogma that every proposition with a subject and predicate *must* be either 'synthetic' or 'analytic' – that is, that either the predicate is definitely *not* 'part of the meaning' of the subject-term, or it *is*. But this is to be misled by an over-simple 'model'; languages are in fact not regimented in this comprehensive way. What about, for example, 'This cat can talk'? Is it a meaning-rule of English that what can talk *may* correctly (on other grounds) be identified as a cat? Or is it a meaning-rule of English that it may *not*? The best answer, of course, is: neither. 'What the word "cat" means' is actually (and not surprisingly, after all) simply indeterminate in that respect, and there is no real basis for the supposition that 'can't talk' somehow *must* either be, or not be, 'part of' what 'cat' means. Of course, *if* an animal were to turn up, in every other respect like a cat but also able to talk, then perhaps we should have to decide what to call it; but it is not the case that, somehow, that *must* be already decided by rules of 'meaning'. The model misleads: 'we are using a working-model which fails to fit the facts that we really wish to talk about.'[16]

Finally, Austin considers the venerable question: why do we, in speaking, apply one and the same word in many (numerically different) instances? Philosophers appear historically to have favoured and fiercely debated one or other of *two* answers: either that, in such a case, there is some one thing to be found in, 'common' to, all the instances; or, that in such a case the instances are 'similar'. His wholly justified complaint is that *both* these answers – even if clear in themselves, which neither is – are grotesquely inadequate to the facts of the case. If one thinks seriously even for a moment about actual languages, it will be evident that there are enormously many *different* reasons for which we 'call different things by the same name', or otherwise use the same one word in different instances; nor, when we use the same expression, is there *necessarily* any clear or useful answer to the over-simple question whether we are using it with the 'same' meaning, or with a 'different' meaning. What about 'head' in 'head of the elephant', 'heads of discussion', and 'head of ICI'? 'On these matters, dogmatists require prodding: although history indeed suggests that it may sometimes be better to let sleeping dogmatists lie.'[17]

Finally, there is 'Pretending', published in 1958, and in fact the last paper of Austin's published in his own lifetime.[18] Though not one of his more 'important' papers – it relates to his general interest in problems about 'action', 'doing' things, but, as he concedes, only somewhat marginally – it is a splendid sample of his characteristic way of getting down to a piece of 'fieldwork' in philosophy – characteristic partly in being wonderfully funny, which he never thought inconsistent with serious philosophy. We have to consider various possible forms of expression – pretending to be angry, pretending to be an owl; pretending to sit down or to cough (but can one do that *without coughing*?); pretending to be cleaning the windows; pretending that I am cleaning the windows. We have to consider the relations between these; if I am pretending to be cleaning the windows, must I also be pretending to clean them? Probably not – for perhaps I actually do clean them, but am still only pretending to be cleaning them – I am 'really' up to some deeper game. What if, to fool the detective, I pretend to be playing golf (*not* 'pretend to play golf', which would be a different matter)? If he persists in tailing me, can I *go on* pretending to be playing golf, perhaps for a complete round? Would that perhaps (at some point?) simply amount to playing golf? What is the relation between pretending to be an owl and imitating or mimicking an owl? Pretending to be a retired colonel and posing as a retired colonel? Shamming dead and pretending to be dead? Acting (a part) and pretending? Does an actor playing Romeo pretend to be, or pretend that he is, in love? Does an 'affected' person pretend? And surely I can try to make people think that I am angry in ways that do not include, or amount to, pretending to be angry; conversely if, at a party, I pretend to be a kangaroo, I surely do not try to make you believe that I *am* a kangaroo. How do dissembling, deception, disguise, and imposture fit in here? To dress up in a full-blown, realistic gorilla outfit is scarcely – in itself – to pretend to be, or to pretend that I am, a gorilla. The general lesson which Austin seeks to inculcate here is that, in confronting a question of the form 'What is x?', we must not freeze on to, and impetuously answer in terms of, some particular case – say, pretending to be angry. We must consider whether the word occurs in other constructions. We must seriously exercise our imaginations in setting out a wide variety of well-described cases, not just one case. We should think about other words that are fairly close in meaning, but not identical in meaning, and ask ourselves when, and why, one is preferable to another. That is: we must try to be imaginative, careful, patient, and industrious. For if we are not, we are almost certain to get it wrong.

In this paper Austin does not directly answer the question what – after all that, so to speak – pretending *is*. But he certainly would not have wanted us to draw the conclusion that there would be anything pointless, or naïve, or misguided about seeking to do that – not necessarily, of course, in any short or simple way. In writing more directly about action – in 'A plea for excuses' – he says that definition, I would add, explanatory definition, should stand high among our aims: it is not enough to show how clever we are by showing how obscure everything is. Clarity, too, I know, has been said to be not enough:[19] but perhaps it will be time to go into that when we are within measurable distance of achieving clarity on some matter.[20]

VIII

Words and Deeds

The text that we now have under the title *How to Do Things with Words* is substantially that which Austin used in giving the William James Lectures at Harvard in 1955. He had lectured on the same subject-matter, from similar but not identical sets of notes, in Oxford since 1952, under the title 'Words and deeds'; and he used the Harvard text again in later lectures in Oxford, making minor corrections and additions as he went along. It is quite clear from the manuscript that he had eventual publication in mind, and was patiently and gradually making his way towards that objective – the material is quite unlike that of *Sense and Sensibilia*, no part of which had been cast by Austin himself into anything like printable form. The text remains, however, in some respects lecture-like; there is more recapitulation than one might think necessary in a printed book, more informality (though Austin's style in writing is in fact never very far from that of the speaking voice), and there are certainly brevities and baldnesses here and there, particularly towards the end, which he would certainly have expected to amplify in delivering the lectures, and may also have intended to expand for publication.

Austin said himself that the views expounded in the lectures 'were formed in 1939'. He must have meant, of course, 'began to be formed', since it would obviously be wrong to suppose that his thinking about these topics was completely static and unchanging over the following twenty years. Before 1939, he had some correspondence with H. A. Prichard about promising, and there is every reason to suppose that his interest took off, so to speak, from that. But if so, his interest in the matter was not the same as Prichard's. Prichard's perplexity was specifically about promising – how could it be that (just) *saying* something could (as in this case we are inclined to say) 'create an obligation'? Is an obligation the sort of thing that can be conjured into existence, as it were out of thin air, simply by speaking? It seems clear that Austin's interest went in another direction. He was not, I think, particularly interested in how it can be that to say something can be to 'create an obligation', or in the particular puzzle as to how, in any case, an obligation could be 'created'. What struck him, it seems – as it had also struck Prichard – was the more general point that to say 'I promise' is not (just) to *say* something, certainly not just to make an autobiographical assertion or avowal about myself, as for instance in the similar-looking 'I play cricket'. In this case to say is – essentially, primarily – to *do*; and thence – not pursuing Prichard's particular interest in how the thing done in this case could conceivably *get* done – he began to think about the general phenomenon of utterances which look on their faces *misleadingly* autobiographical, in which it appears – merely on the basis of their verbal form – that the speaker is saying of himself that he does something, whereas in fact he is – essentially, primarily – *doing* it. It was clear, of course, that saying 'I promise' was just one instance of this not at all uncommon phenomenon. The *general* topic was that of saying and doing, 'words and deeds'.

A word or two should perhaps be said about one particular feature of *How to Do Things with Words* which some have found puzzling. As a whole it is undoubtedly the most 'constructive' of Austin's writings. It is completely unlike, for example, *Sense and Sensibilia*, which consists primarily, and remorselessly, of criticism of someone else's text, his own views emerging only by implication from, or at any rate incidentally to, that critical pursuit. Here, he is not talking, except in the most indirect and general way, about the views of other people. There is certainly no particular text to be critically arraigned. His object is straightforwardly to set out and justify views of his own on questions of his own devising, introducing for that purpose some technical terminology of his own. That being so, it has seemed to some that his exposition is curiously, as it were, discontinuous, or non-linear. The sentence 'It is time then to make a fresh start on the problem' occurs rather more than *half-way through* the book[1], and it is, by and large, only in that second half that he proposes views which he seriously intends to stand by. Why, if he knew that a fresh start was going to be needed, did he spend so much time – about half the time – on what would turn out to be, if not exactly a false start, at any rate 'provisional'?[2] I think that this is not really mysterious. The main point is that the book we have contains the text of lectures; in lecturing Austin was not merely expounding, he was teaching; and to be shown alternative byways and blind alleys, how what at first sight seems hopefully luminous can turn out to be deceptive, how persistent thought about a problem can twist and turn, is more philosophically educative than to plod expositorily along an absolutely straight road. We need to understand why a fresh start is needed; and to understand that entails a certain amount of preliminary beating about the bush. I think it is true too that, at the rather late stage when Austin announces a fresh start on 'the problem', there has actually occurred in his thinking a considerable transformation in what 'the problem' *is* – his earlier chapters do not so much answer 'the question' unsatisfactorily, as trace the path – his actual, historical path – to a quite different view of what the interesting question really is. I suspect that Austin himself was not perfectly clear as to the extent to which, and the way in which, that was the case. Once he had got 'the question' in his sights in the form he really wanted, he was no longer interested enough in his earlier thoughts to want to go over them again in the helpful light of hindsight. I shall return to that briefly at the end of this chapter.

At the outset of *How to Do Things with Words* Austin introduces his topic, 'the phenomenon to be discussed', in an informal sort of way which, however, is of some importance to the way the argument develops. It is easy, he says, and has been too common, for philosophers to assume that, or at least to talk as if, the business of every 'statement' – a notion not always clearly distinguished from that of an indicative *sentence* – is, purely and simply, to state some 'fact', truly or falsely. No doubt it has usually been noted that not every sentence is of that sort – there are sentences, for example, expressing questions, exclamations, wishes, or commands; but the 'indicative' case has been accorded most of the limelight, and 'Is it true or false?' has been assumed to be the only, or at any rate the only interesting, issue. However, he says, it has come to be recognized in a groping, piecemeal sort of way, that sentences may crop up which, though impeccably indicative, may for one reason or another fail to be, or to express, 'statements'. It has been noted, for example, that there may be sentences which, while perfectly 'grammatical', are in one way or another strictly meaningless, and so fail to 'state' anything at all. It has been suggested further that there may be perfectly good indicative sentences – perhaps those expressing 'ethical propositions', or moral judgements – which are not meaningless, but are perhaps not even intended mainly, or even at all, to impart information, truly or falsely, as to matters of fact; perhaps their 'point' may rather be to evince emotion, to prescribe conduct, to influence attitudes, or something of that sort.[3] Then again there are words or phrases that may occur *in* indicative sentences that do not contribute to the 'description' of the reality reported, but rather indicate something about the circumstances in which the statement is made, how it is to be taken, or qualifications to which it may be subject. All this, Austin suggests, is highly important in its way, and has been philosophically profitable up to a point; but the topic needs further and more systematic exploration; he proposes to start with the examination – which, he emphasizes, is, to begin with, provisional – of what he calls, in his own invented and now famous word, the *performative*.

The starting-point of the investigation is not a definition of 'performative utterance' – a project which Austin would certainly have regarded as hopelessly premature at this stage. He gives instead a general description of what he is looking for. The utterances to be first investigated exhibit three features in particular – first, their form is that of impeccably correct, quite ordinary indicative sentences, containing no 'curious words' and in no problematic construction – sentences which, in fact, look grammatically just like 'statements': but second, they do not actually state (Austin uses the term 'constate') anything at all, and are not true or false:[4] and third, the uttering of such sentences is, or is a part of, *doing* something – something, further, which would not normally or naturally be described as (just) *saying* something. It is the third feature, of course, which accounts for their being called 'performative'.

That may, Austin says, sound paradoxical, but the examples he goes on to offer of utterances which fill the bill are not at all extraordinary: 'I name this ship the *Queen Elizabeth*' – as uttered when smashing the bottle against the stem; 'I give and bequeath my watch to my brother' – as occurring in a will; 'I bet you sixpence it will rain tomorrow'; 'I promise to be there'. These are all, of course, 'grammatically' quite familiar and straightforward indicative sentences; but to issue them, Austin suggests, is quite clearly not to *describe* my doing something, or to state *that* I am doing it: I am not *saying that* I name a ship, I am naming it; not saying that I bet, but making a bet; not saying that I promise, but promising.

> None of the utterances cited is either true or false: I assert this as obvious and do not argue it. When I say, before the registrar or altar, etc., 'I do', I am not reporting on a marriage: I am indulging in it.[5]

It is pertinent, I think, to raise at this early stage the question: what exactly are these examples offered as examples *of*? Part of the answer is clear: they are to be instances of saying something which is not (just) saying something, but also, preponderantly and essentially, *doing* something; that, after all, is exactly why they are called 'performative'. But what about the fact that they are all of the same grammatical form – indicative sentences, first-person singular, present tense? I think that that is a different matter. One can see why, of course, Austin chose examples of that particular sort. He began by making the quite general point that some utterances which 'look like' statements – which, going simply on their grammatical form, one would take to be statement-making – may, for one reason or another, actually not be statements at all, or not *just* statements; so that, leading on from that, he would naturally bring in examples of performatives which do have the feature of 'looking like' statements, that is, have the form of grammatically straightforward indicative sentences. But it is clear from the start, I think, that it is in a

sense accidental, or a contingent matter, that the notion of the performative was introduced and exemplified in this particular way. Austin
remarks in a footnote that he chose examples of this form – having
'humdrum verbs in the first person singular present indicative active' –
'not without design':[6] by implication he might, if his 'design' had been
different, have brought in examples of some quite different sort, or sorts;
and indeed we find him, not many pages later, admitting as performatives
– he calls them 'primitive' performatives – simple imperatives, for
instance, which have no propensity at all to 'look like' statements.[7] The
performative essentially, then, is not an utterance which *has the form of
a statement but* to issue which is typically to do something rather than
(just) to say something; it is simply an utterance to issue which is to do
something, as distinct from saying that something is done – whether or
not it 'looks' at first sight as if it might be the latter. We shall see in due
course why this is a point of some significance.

But can doing something – for example, something rather important,
like getting married – be a matter of just 'issuing an utterance', saying a
few words? Clearly not; a great deal more is involved than simply
speaking the words. If the thing in question is to get done, to be successfully 'brought off', what we may broadly call the *circumstances* must be
appropriate for the particular performance; if they are not, then, even if
the utterance itself is duly issued, the intended or purported performance
will be in some way and degree vitiated or flawed, perhaps even completely void and ineffectual. To take the case of getting married: if the
utterance 'I will' is to take effect, to *be* to get married, it must be
issued at the right point of a correctly conducted ceremony; the person
conducting it must be duly licensed or qualified to do so; neither the
speaker nor his or her 'intended' must be already married at the time;
the two principals must not be of the same sex; and no doubt one could
go on. If things are wrong, or go wrong, in such ways as these we have
what Austin chooses to call a 'misfire':[8] the utterance itself may be issued
all right, but not 'happily', not effectually – the act, getting married, in
which it is to be used, is simply not thereby achieved. It is not, of
course, that the speaker will not have done anything at all – he may, for
example, have committed bigamy, which is no light matter – but he will
not have *got married*, which was the at least ostensible object of the
exercise. Importantly different from this are what Austin calls 'abuses'
of the procedure. If, for instance, I promise you to do something, the
supposition is that I at least believe that I can actually do it; that I fully
intend to do it; and also, perhaps, that I believe my doing it will be in
some way welcome or beneficial to you. If, when I say 'I promise', these
conditions are not fulfilled, we have, not indeed a misfire – for I *have*
promised, after all – but an abuse of the procedure; I had no business

to make such a promise, ought not to have made it. To these sorts of ways in which 'the circumstances' may be inappropriate for the performance of these sorts of doings, and may accordingly – even notwithstanding correct issuing of the utterance in the case itself – vitiate or make void the purported doing, Austin gives the general name 'infelicities';[9] just as, or at any rate somewhat as, a statement or 'constative' may be true or false, a performative utterance may be, *not* true or false, but happy or unhappy.

I have deliberately not mentioned so far, or not mentioned explicitly, the first and most important 'circumstance' which Austin stipulates as necessary to the 'happy' execution of these performances; and we must now look rather closely at that, since it raises a problem. The very first necessary condition to be satisfied, as Austin states it, is that 'there must exist an accepted conventional procedure having a certain conventional effect, that procedure to include the uttering of certain words by certain persons in certain circumstances'. [10] Austin hopes that this will strike us as 'obvious'; and up to a point it does indeed seem unproblematic. If, for example, I am to succeed in getting married, perhaps even to intend or aspire to get married, by saying the words required, there must obviously *be* a recognized, validated form of ceremony or procedure - recognized as a valid way of achieving that 'conventional', in this case among other things legal, 'effect' – *in* which the uttering of those words has its recognized place. For suppose that, by contrast, having got married, I decide to divorce my wife, and purport to do so by saying to her publicly, solemnly, and loudly 'I divorce you'; clearly, whatever my intention may be, I do not thereby divorce her, since, at any rate in the relevant – that is, our – society and legal system, that is not a recognized, accepted way of doing it: there *is* a recognized 'conventional procedure' for getting divorced, but that is not it.[11] Rather similarly, though slightly less clearly and of course less formally, there is, we may say, a recognized procedure or 'drill' for the naming of ships; a properly invited person, at the right point in the drill, says 'I name this ship the *Queen Elizabeth*', and in virtue of that 'the Queen Elizabeth' *is* its name henceforward. And of course one could think of innumerable other such cases – though, also of course, some will be much less strict and formalized than others, and it may sometimes be rather uncertain, or left rather vague, what exactly the 'proper' conventional procedure is.

So what is the problem here? One might put it, rather fittingly, by saying that while it is clear enough what Austin is saying at this point, it is rather importantly *not* clear what he is doing in saying it, or what is the underlying course or mechanism of his argument. One way of looking at it might be this: we note, to begin with, that there are cases in which to say something is not (just) to *say* something, certainly not (just) to say something true or false, but is rather to *do* something; and we call utterances of which this is true 'performative' utterances. We then go on to ask: how can that be? How does it come about, what makes it the case, that sometimes to say something is also, is even primarily and essentially, to *do* something? And then we may offer as an explanation that there are (various sorts of) conventional procedures for doing (various sorts of) things – having, that is, certain recognized conventional 'effects' – some of which 'include the uttering of certain words by certain persons in certain circumstances'; and that, we suggest, is the explanation - to say certain words can be to do something, to perform an act, *because* and just in so far as the words are a prescribed component of an established conventional procedure. Well, if that is what is going on, it would clearly be pertinent for a reader to ask: is the explanation correct? Is it, that is to say, really the case that, when we have an instance of performative utterance, an instance in which to say something is to do something, we always have a case of words that are included in, are part of, some 'conventional procedure'? Or does that perhaps fit only some of the cases, leaving others in need of explanation in some different way?

But one might look at it differently. It might be that, when Austin brings in 'conventional procedures', he is not offering an *explanation* of the phenomenon of performative utterance, but rather spelling out in more detail what, at any rate at this stage, he *means* by 'performative utterance'. That would obviously make an important dialectical difference. For now, if one were to come up with some specimen of a saying which appeared to be a doing but *not* to be an element in any 'conventional procedure', that would not raise the question whether Austin's 'explanation' is correct; it would simply not be a specimen of what he is talking about, not in his present sense a performative utterance at all. Briefly, the question is: when Austin says that, for there to be the possibility of 'happy' (or indeed unhappy) performative utterance, there has to be an accepted conventional procedure, is it to the point, or not, to look about for counter-examples? Might there be a performative utterance of which that was not true? Or is anything, of which that is not true, not a performative utterance? I would not claim with any confidence to know the proper answers to those questions; I am not even sure that they *have* 'proper' answers; but it will not be fatal, I hope, to leave the issue afloat and unresolved at this stage – if only because Austin is, after all, at pains to stress that 'everything said in these sections is provisional, and subject to revision in the light of later sections'. Let us, for the time being, simply see how things go.

So far, we have marked off the issuing of a performative utterance as, first, a case of doing something – for example, naming a ship – rather than of (just) saying something; and, second, specifically *not* a case of saying something true or false. The performative has been introduced by

way of contrast with the 'constative' – with some emphasis on the point
that this contrast holds even when, to the eye of grammar, the sentence
uttered looks just like those sorts of sentences in which statements are
made. But of course, as Austin now stresses, to say that the performative
is thus contrasted with the constative does not mean that the performative
has nothing at all to do with any questions of truth or falsity; on the
contrary, we noted right at the beginning that to issue, for example, the
utterance 'I promise' is at least to *imply* that I do in fact fully intend to
perform and believe I can, and the performance is vitiated (in this case,
abused) if that is not *true*. We can, in fact, now say more generally –
having seen that the issuing of performative utterances is liable to a
variety of 'infelicities' – that to issue any performative utterance is to
imply that the circumstances necessary to its 'happiness' do in fact obtain.
But what now begins to worry us is this: we seem to have been suggesting, so far, that whereas the constative is (just) true or false, the performative is by contrast happy or unhappy, and *not* true or false; but
now, if we note that to issue a performative utterance is nevertheless to
imply that certain other things are true and not false, we may observe
that the same goes for constatives too. May *they* not be happy or
unhappy? Is our contrast here tenable? We need to look more closely –
though not, Austin says, 'too technically' – at implication.[12]

One thing – no doubt the most anciently and comprehensively studied
thing – that is often called 'implication' need not, we may think, too
much worry us, namely, entailment. That all men blush entails that some
men blush; it is inconsistent with, contradicted by, the proposition that
some men do not blush. But surely we are not to say that, if some men
do not blush, the constative that all men blush is thereby 'unhappy'; we
can say straight out that, in that case, it is *not true*, and anyone who
constates it therein simply makes a false statement. However, there are
cases of implication which are not of that kind. My saying that all men
blush implies that I believe they do. (At any rate let us take that to be
so, though Austin suggests that the connection here is really stronger
and closer than an implication, as ordinarily understood.[13]) But this is
not entailment. It could perfectly well be the case both that all men blush
and that I do *not* believe that they do; and if I do not believe that they
do but say nevertheless that all men blush, it does not follow that I have
made a false statement – my belief may be mistaken. What *can* be said
is that, if I do not believe that all men blush, then I 'have no business'
to say that they all do. But that looks at least exceedingly like one of
the infelicities: if I do not intend to do something, though I may promise
to do it, I have no business to promise, that is an 'abuse' of the procedure;
is it not a very similar sort of abuse for me, if I do not believe that
something is the case, to state that it is? Or consider a rather different
case: to say that the King of Italy has grey hair is to imply that Italy has

a King; but it is at any rate not obviously true that it *entails* that, since, if Italy has no king, we should not necessarily want to say that the statement is false. Rather than saying that it is false – which would suggest that there is a King of Italy who has *not* got grey hair – we might say that the question of its truth or falsity 'does not arise'; to refer to something by such a phrase as 'the King of Italy' *presupposes* – and therein 'implies' – that there is such a thing, but the purported statement is, say, void, rather than false, if in fact there is not. But that too looks exceedingly like a case of 'unhappiness'; is it not very like the case of my bequeathing to my brother a gold watch which, in fact, I have not got? A bequest of property *presupposes* that the property is there, and is 'void' if it is not. Finally, Austin suggests, it is by no means clear that even entailment – which one might think to be tidily confined to the relations of truth-value between constatives – does not come in at all in the performative case. To say 'All men blush and some do not' is a self-stultifying procedure which defeats the purpose of assertion; that looks exceedingly like saying 'I promise but I am not bound to perform', which defeats the purpose of promising, of making a contract.[14] Perhaps 'I promise' could be said to *entail* that I am bound to perform.

Austin's point here is this. So long as we look at 'the constative' and 'the performative' in a wholly unparticularized, contextless sort of way, we may well be tempted to regard them as *completely* different. What is there to be said about 'The cat is on the mat' except that it is either true or false? What is there to be said about 'I promise' except that, in saying that, the speaker promises? His performance may be happy or unhappy, but he says nothing either true or false. But then, if we imagine these utterances in some sort of context, if we consider 'the total speech-act in the total speech-situation',[15] things look a great deal less black and white. To say, in an actual case, that the cat is on the mat will indeed be to say something false if the cat referred to is *not* on the mat in question; but what if there is no cat in the room, or two or more cats – or several mats? In the actual making of real statements in real situations there are certainly issues that may arise quite other than those of truth and falsehood – issues to do with, for example, the felicity or otherwise of the speaker's total performance. On the other side, while the issuing of a performative utterance may not itself be to say anything true or false, it will certainly *imply* in one way or another – just as making a statement does – that this or that is the case, is true and not false. So the two cases seem in reality not, after all, to be *completely* different; and considerations of this sort may even, Austin thinks, 'suggest that at least in some ways there is danger of our initial and tentative distinction between constative and performative utterances breaking down'.[16]

He proceeds thus:

We have then to take a further step out into the desert of comparative precision. We must ask: is there some precise way in which we can definitely distinguish the performative from the constative utterance? And in particular we should naturally ask first whether there is some *grammatical* (or lexicographical) criterion for distinguishing the performative utterance.[17]

Now, I believe that we ought to be astonished, and even disquieted, by this last observation. It is surely very puzzling indeed. Whatever Austin's answer may turn out to be to the question he raises, why should it seem to him 'natural' to ask it? For one might think – and I believe one *ought* to think – that what we have learned so far about the performative utterance suffices to make clear that instances could, in principle, not possibly be distinguished in that way, and so that it is very far from 'natural' to entertain the idea that they might be. There are at least two reasons for that. First, we remember, if we go back right to the beginning, that the whole point, the noteworthy feature, of the utterances originally brought in as instances of performatives was that they were *not* 'grammatically', formally or verbally, distinguishable from statements; the very point that we were asked to attend to was that although they obviously were not – or, at least, were obviously not *just* – statements, they looked 'grammatically' just as if they were. It is true that we noted that Austin's original examples were hand-picked for this very purpose, and that he presumably did not mean us to conclude that *every* performative, as such, must exhibit this deceptive statement-like look; still, it must seem extraordinary for him to put forward, as a 'natural' question, whether performatives are 'grammatically' identifiable as such, when he has himself insisted that at least many of them are not. But second, moving on to his initial general account of the necessary conditions for the 'happy' issuing of a performative, we remember that, at any rate in the cases to which he gave prominence, such issuing was to be 'the uttering of certain words by certain persons in certain circumstances' as part of 'an accepted conventional procedure having a certain conventional effect'; and nothing was there said in general – and obviously nothing could or should have been said – as to what the 'certain words' in such cases must 'grammatically' or lexicographically be like. For it seems obvious that, in general, any sort or concatenation of words at all – questions, single words, mere phrases, imperatives, exclamations, or, come to that, statements – *could* have a performative role as part of 'an accepted conventional procedure'. Surely there can be no question there of any grammatical – or lexicographical – constraint; it is just a question of what the relevant conventional procedure prescribes should be said; and, grammatically speaking, that might be just anything.

Before taking that point any further I want to bring in another one, which also suggests – as I think the last point does – that at this stage it is pretty unclear what is really going on. Suppose that we ask: what is Austin now worrying about? He is asking whether there is 'some precise way' of distinguishing the performative from the constative utterance, evidently on the ground that some risk has come to light of the distinction's 'breaking down'. But I believe, again, that that worry should strike us as surprising. It was generated by the realization, correct and indeed valuable in itself, that the performative and the constative are not so different, not so *completely* different, as one might be tempted to suppose. In particular, statement-making, like performative utterance, may be happy or unhappy; 'true or false?' is not the *only* question that arises, and sometimes perhaps it does not arise at all. Similarly, performative utterance, even if not true or false, may certainly *imply* truths or falsehoods, just as statement-making does. But why is all that worrying, rather than just an interesting point? Does it suggest that there may really be no distinction after all? Surely not, we may think. For a typical performative utterance, after all, we have been told, is something said, having a certain 'conventional effect', in the course of carrying through a certain 'accepted conventional procedure'; and it seems unproblematically obvious that at any rate most statement-making is nothing of *that* sort. If I remark at the breakfast-table 'Here's a letter from Aunt Mabel', what I say may indeed be 'unhappy' (perhaps I have no Aunt Mabel); but it does not look in the least like a ritual or conventional formula, uttered as part of an accepted conventional procedure. (My wife and I do not play games at the breakfast-table.) The case of utterances that occur ritually, ceremonially, 'operatively' as prescribed parts of conventional procedures still looks like a perfectly good, distinguishable case, in principle readily distinguishable from, even if not in absolutely every respect different from, that of 'ordinary' talk, including 'ordinary' statement-making.

But let us go back for the time being to Austin's question, astonished though we well may be that he should think it 'natural' to ask it: is there 'some *grammatical* (or lexicographical) criterion for distinguishing the performative utterance'? It takes him little time, as indeed it should, to find that the answer is negative. The examples he has so far cited of performative utterance have, as it happens, been of a particular form – first-person singular, present indicative active, as in 'I name this ship . . .', 'I bet you sixpence . . .', 'I promise . . .'. That, however, clearly affords no sort of general criterion. For an utterance, he remarks, may be performative but not in that form: instead of 'I give you permission to go' I may say simply 'You may go';[18] and an utterance may be in that form but not performative: 'I vote for the Liberal' may be, not voting for the Liberal, but simply stating what I habitually do when I vote. (This, of course, was the very first point that Austin made – a performative utterance may be 'formally' exactly like a constative.) Even more obviously, there is no help to be found in individual *words* – 'I promise', 'I bet' may be performative, but certainly not just because of the occurrence of 'promise' and 'bet'; for 'He promises', 'They bet' are very clearly *not* performative in the way that the first-person utterances are.

Nevertheless, Austin suggests, there does seem to be something special, something pre-eminently and specially clearly performative, about the sorts of examples with which we began. A speaker who says 'I promise' or 'I bet' not only makes a promise or a bet, but in a particular way makes it explicity clear that he is doing exactly that: namely, the *word for* what he is doing makes an overt appearance *in* what he says, and the first-person present indicative shows that the speaker himself here and now does that very thing. Might it be said, then, Austin asks, that any genuine performative utterance, whatever its original form, could in principle be put into *that* form?[19] It certainly looks as if that ought to be so. For if a speaker really is issuing a performative utterance – is *doing* this or that in saying what it is that he says – it surely must be possible in principle to 'show' what he is doing, to make that explicitly clear, *in* what he says; and the explicit performative form does that very thing.

But that suggestion, even if correct, now seems for our purpose to run head-on into a fatal difficulty. What we were trying to do, we remember, in taking this 'further step into the desert of comparative precision', was to find some way of definitely identifying the performative utterance as *distinct from*, contrasted with, the constative utterance. We now suggest that an utterance is performative if it is either in, or could in principle readily be put into, the particular form 'I X', in issuing which the speaker (explicitly) X-es. But it seems, fatally, that *every constative* fulfils that condition; for surely any speaker who makes the statement that p could in principle do so in the form 'I state that p', in saying which he makes it explicitly clear that he is making a statement. So it seems that whatever doubts we may have previously entertained, the putative distinction, if we seek to draw it in *this* way, has now *completely* 'broken down'.[20]

At this point in his argument Austin makes, in effect, a completely new start, and it will be timely to reassess for a moment what has been going on so far. It has often been said, and it is, I think, more or less the received view, that he starts all over again for the reason that his initial, provisional project of identifying and isolating 'the performative' now turns out to have got nowhere, to have 'broken down'; he has been attempting to make a distinction which, at this point, he decides simply to 'abandon' as untenable. I believe that the position is really much less clear than that – that it is, indeed, not really *clear* at all. The reason for perplexity is, as I would argue, that it has never been really clear, from the very beginning, *what* distinction Austin was trying to make, what line it was even his 'provisional' intention to draw; and in so far as it is unclear what 'the distinction' was supposed to be, it can scarcely be clear that the distinction is now to be abandoned, or that the attempt to draw the line has broken down.

When we were first introduced to the idea of 'performative utterance', it appeared that Austin had this in mind: there are certain cases, quite special though not at all uncommon or peculiar cases, in which something is said as the – or at any rate as an – 'operative' element in a conventional, ritual, or ceremonial procedure. There are prescribed rituals for marrying, divorcing, betting, bequeathing or giving property, naming ships (important, expensive ships anyway), baptizing babies, making contracts, conducting games, and so on. In such cases – and of course assuming that 'the circumstances' are right – to utter the key words is not *just* to *say* whatever it may be; it is actually, or also, to *do* the thing in question. For a player (in cricket) to say 'How's that?' to an umpire is not just for him to enquire whether the batsman is out, as a spectator might do (and might merely be ignored if he did); it is – because of a convention (rule) of cricket – to *appeal for a decision* as to whether the batsman is out, and the rules further oblige the umpire to give a decision. In such cases convention prescribes that for a player to *say* the appropriate words *is* – constitutes, counts as – *doing* the thing in question; and, as Austin noted, to do the thing in such cases will usually have some further conventional 'effect' – as, for instance, the ritual of appealing touches off, so to speak, the further ritual of the umpire's deciding. I believe that there is nothing whatever wrong with this. No doubt, as we remarked earlier, there will be a good many more or less marginal or unclear cases. There will be cases, for instance, in which it is left rather vague and indeterminate just what 'the convention' prescribes; law, in particular, and to a considerable extent the conduct of competitive games, aim at completeness and exactitude in that respect, but no doubt there are many less full-blown, formal proceedings in which both the 'procedure' is left much looser, and perhaps also its conventional 'effect' is less sharply defined. There will be cases, too, in which it may be unclear whether there really is a convention at all; is it an 'accepted convention' that, say, a pet animal is to be given a name only by its owner, or is that merely something that usually happens? Is an owner's whim conventionally *effective*, or just normally indulged? But the central idea is, I think, clear enough; there are undoubted cases of conventional, ceremonial procedures in which to *say* (happily) this or that is to *do* whatever it may be – to name, to appeal, to marry, to bequeath, and so on; and if that is what it is to 'issue a performative utterance', we have a notion no doubt susceptible of much elaboration and development, but surely not in danger of having ultimately to be 'abandoned'.

Now, there is in fact a special and peculiar reason, to which we shall have to return in due course, why this particular way of defending or justifying 'the distinction', however natural and indeed comparatively simple it may look, is one that Austin himself could not quite happily have adopted. But there are other reasons too, some of which have already been glanced at. The way I would put it is this (and we shall see again, in due course, that this is *not* how Austin would put it himself); although his formal statement, early on, of the 'necessary conditions' for performative utterance does give great prominence to – mentions first and emphatically – the condition that there be 'an accepted conventional procedure' *in* which the utterance is conventionally to be issued, he appears in fact not to be exclusively, perhaps not even particularly, interested in these particular cases. Notwithstanding the rather formal way in which these 'necessary conditions' are set out, which would suggest that he is telling us what 'performative utterance' *means*, it seems that we cannot really take it that that is what he is doing; at any rate, in even the early stages of his text, 'performative utterance' clearly does *not* just 'mean' that, whether or not he himself clearly realized that that was so. He suggests, for example, that one might say – and seems to imply that it would be all right to say, so far as it goes – that 'everything with the verb in the imperative mood is performative';[21] and while of course it looks natural enough to say that someone who speaks in the imperative mood is always 'doing' something – 'telling' some person or persons to . . . – it would seem fantastic to suggest that every utterance in the imperative mood occurs as part of an 'accepted conventional procedure'. A more important point is, I think, that from the earliest stage he was much interested in something quite different from 'conventional procedures' – whether or not, again, he clearly realized that that was so: namely, the case in which what the speaker says *makes explicit* what he is doing in saying it. Rather confusingly, I think, his early examples of utterances occurring as 'operative' items in conventional procedures were *also* of this explicit-making sort; 'I name this ship the *Queen Elizabeth*' is not only a key element in the drill for naming a ship, but also makes it explicit, in the utterance itself, that naming a ship is what the speaker is doing. (By contrast, the prescribed way to appeal, in cricket, contains no explicit indicator that the speaker is appealing.) But Austin is much interested in this explicit-making function even when the feature of 'conventional procedure' is absent; he mentions 'I advise you to do X' as a performative utterance, no doubt for the reason that to say that is to advise you, and furthermore to make it explicitly clear that I do; but giving advice is surely not a formal, conventional pro-

118

cedure, ritual, or drill. (If told to advise my daughter to give up smoking, I could scarcely enquire 'How is advising done?')

So the question whether the 'initial distinction' has 'broken down' can clearly be given no simple answer. The fact of the matter is that in roughly the first half of his book Austin has been operating with – and, I fear, sliding to and fro between – at least three distinct notions of what 'performative utterance' might be; and 'the distinction' fares differently, depending on which of the three notions one looks at. In some ways the most prominent – and also, I think, the one that was in Austin's mind from the very start – has been that of 'conventional' utterance as part of a conventional procedure, ritual, drill, or ceremony – utterance which, in virtue of the convention, counts as, or constitutes, *doing* whatever it is that the conventional procedure is specifically designed for getting done. That *that* sort of utterance is distinguishable from 'ordinary' saying, and in particular from everyday statement-making, seems to me clear and not seriously contestable, so that *that* distinction has not broken down at all. But there has also featured quite prominently the different case of utterances whose special feature is that they make explicitly clear what the speaker is doing in speaking – most notably, by including as the main verb of the sentence the *word for* what he is therein doing; and although in a way this distinction does not 'break down' either – in that such utterances do seem to form a fairly readily distinguishable class - it does not draw a line in the same place as the former distinction, and in particular it does *not* of course, as we have seen, distinguish performative utterance *from* statement-making since, in making a statement, I may in this way make it explicitly clear that that is what I am doing. And third, there has come in from time to time the again different, quite general idea of performative utterance as that in which, whatever its form may be, the speaker *does* something; and desperately vague though that may be as it stands, rather clearly we have there simply no distinction at all – for surely every speaker does *something*, in saying absolutely *anything*.

It is in fact from this last point that Austin makes his fresh start. Remarking – with, I think, considerable understatement – that so far it has 'seemed that we were going to find it not always easy to distinguish performative utterances from constative', he now decides 'to consider from the ground up how many senses there are in which to say something *is* to do something, or *in* saying something we do something, and even *by* saying something we do something'.[22] We are now to consider, as one might put it, the performative dimension of utterance in general.

A speaker speaks: what does he *do*?

Well, first (if we confine ourselves to literal speaking) he makes certain noises. Austin calls this a 'phonetic act', and has little more to say about it. One might ask, as one always can in such cases, just how closely alike two phonetic performances must be for them to be counted as instances of 'the same' phonetic act, but there would be little profit in pursuing that, at least for our purpose.

Second, a speaker normally speaks in a *language*. The existence and availability of languages is something that Austin simply takes as given; without attempting to define either 'language', or 'a language', in general he assumes that we have to hand and within our competence a vocabulary – words and phrases – and a 'grammar' that determines what ordered sequences of words and phrases are admissible as 'sentences'. Thus, given that apparatus, we can say that a speaker's phonetic act is normally also the uttering of noises *as* words belonging to a certain language's vocabulary, ordered *as* conforming to that language's grammar – and, he adds, 'with a certain intonation, etc.'[23] This he calls a 'phatic act'. Clearly, there will be two different ways in which a purported phatic act may be, so to speak, misperformed: besides the possibility of its being phonetically 'wrong', that is mispronounced, it may employ 'words' that are actually not included in the language's vocabulary, or it may put words together in some grammatically inadmissible way; in either case, as Austin says, 'its typical fault is to be nonsense – meaningless'. (Those are not, of course, the *only* ways of producing meaningless sentences – nor, as a matter of fact, is an ungrammatical sentence always completely unintelligible). He clearly intends, however, that even an impeccably performed, non-meaningless phatic act may yet be *ambiguous*; for the notion of 'what he means' is not brought in at this stage. That is: if one speaker says 'The case is closed', meaning that the lid of an item of luggage is fastened down, and another speaker says 'The case is closed', meaning that some legal proceeding has come to an end, I think that Austin would want to say that they perform the same phatic act – they utter the same words in the same construction, notwithstanding that what they mean by 'case' and 'closed' is quite different. But this is perhaps not absolutely clear; Austin certainly allows in general that a 'pheme' – that which is uttered in performing a phatic act – 'may be used on different occasions of utterance with a different sense', that is may be in itself ambiguous;[24] but I do not know whether, in the particular example I have given, he would have allowed that the first 'case' is really the *same word* as the second (the two differ not only in sense, but in etymology). But nothing much turns, I think, for present purposes on deciding this sort of question. (Nor the question, for instance, whether word-*order* is crucial – is 'Habemus Papam' the same sentence, or not, as 'Papam habemus'?) What Austin wants to say here is that a speaker, in speaking (and in performing a phonetic act), typically produces a *sentence* of a language – words of a language in a certain sort of grammatical construction; refinements on the theme of 'same word' and 'same sentence', though by no means without interest, are I think immaterial to his purpose. To utter a sentence of a language – not merely phonetically as a parrot might, but *as* a sentence of a language – is to perform a phatic act. We report what phatic act is performed by simply reproducing – mimicking, or in writing within quotation marks – the sentence uttered.

But next, in the ordinary way a speaker does not *just* utter a sentence of a language. He utters it in *saying*, or in order to *say*, something or other; and Austin calls this the performance of a 'rhetic' act.[25] To get from the phatic to the rhetic act, so to speak, we need to determine two things, which Austin calls 'sense' and 'reference'. As to 'sense', we need to grasp not only what the words used mean – or the several things they *could* mean – in the language; we need to grasp what the speaker meant by those words (what he used them *as* meaning) in the particular case. Of course, what a speaker uses words as meaning will very often, indeed normally, be exactly the same as what the words mean in the language. But, as we have seen, a phatic act – or, more strictly, a pheme – may be ambiguous; and if so we need, in identifying the rhetic act, to 'disambiguate' the pheme: in saying 'The case is closed' (phatic act) he said (rhetic act) that a certain item of luggage had its lid fastened down. How is that done? Well, usually the circumstances in which he speaks will make it clear (if the question arises) what he means by the words uttered – that he is, for instance, talking about luggage rather than legal proceedings; but sometimes we may simply have to ask the speaker to explain.

As to 'reference', I take it that Austin has in mind here – though he says very little about it – the sort of considerations he dealt with at more length in 'Truth'. In order to know 'what he said' in saying that the case was closed, we need to know not only what he meant by 'case' and 'closed', and not only what case, or which case, he was referring to, but, rather roughly, which case *when*: we need to identify the 'historic situation' which, in speaking as he did, he intended to report or describe. (We may note, looking back to the paper on 'Truth', that Austin understandably mentions there as a 'puzzling case' that of general non-contingent propositions, which seem not to refer to 'historic situations' at all. But here he is quite content that the case should remain puzzling.[26])

It is rather surprising, though I think not particularly important, that he remarks in passing that to utter words 'with a more-or-less definite sense and reference' is to utter them with a certain *meaning*, 'in the favourite philosophical sense of that word'.[27] This is surprising simply because this sense of 'meaning' is *not*, I would have thought, that particularly favoured by philosophers, who appear, on the contrary, much more typically inclined to insist that reference is one thing and meaning is another: we can ask and answer the question what 'The cat is on the mat' means, without even raising the question what in particular, in this case or that, is referred to by its utterance. I would have thought that the favourite philosophical sense of 'meaning', was that in which words and sentences have meanings; whereas, of course, Austin's 'sense and reference' both have to do, not with what certain words or sentences mean (in the language), but with what particular speakers mean in particular cases by the words they utter. That is to say, I think, that, contrary to Austin's passing remark, the 'favourite' sense of meaning would come in at the level of phatic rather than of rhetic acts. But I think also that nothing of much relevance turns on this.[28]

So far, then, we have three distinguishable sorts of things which, in any ordinary sort of case, a speaker could be said to 'do' in speaking. He makes certain noises: he utters a sentence of a language: he 'says' some particular thing. Clearly these 'acts' are, in a sense, separable as well as distinguishable. It is possible to perform a phonetic act parrot-wise (perhaps actually being a parrot) without producing the sounds as – perhaps being unaware that they are – a sentence of a language. It is possible to produce – perhaps to mimic, or quote – a sentence of a language, not therein (for one's own part or on one's own account) 'saying' anything. But more ordinarily, of course, the three acts go together: I make the noises 'The cat is on the mat' as the sentence 'The cat is on the mat', to say, or in saying, that the cat is on the mat. 'The act of saying something in this full normal sense I call, i.e. dub, the performance of a locutionary act.'[29]

We may wish to ask: is 'the act of saying something in this full normal sense' a *single kind* of act? Austin says almost nothing explicitly about that, but from what he does say it seems that the answer must be that it is not – that, even at this level, locutionary acts fall into distinguishable classes. From examples he gives it appears that there will be at least three very general sorts of locutionary acts, namely '. . . said that . . .', '. . . told to . . .', and '. . . asked . . .'.[30] It is pretty obviously not accidental that this trinity mirrors another: that of the indicative, imperative, and interrogative 'moods' of sentences. If my sentence (pheme) is an indicative, my locutionary act is (necessarily?) of the 'said-that' sort; if an imperative, 'told-to'; if an interrogative, 'asked'. Some possible questions arise here, obviously enough. Are there perhaps other kinds of locutionary act besides these three – what about 'optatives', for example? ('Would it were day!') Might it be that some of these are in some sense (and possibly in some languages) 'reducible' to others – asking you what time it is to, perhaps, an instruction to you to tell me what time it is?[31] (Surely a question, like an instruction, is normally 'meant' to elicit an active response.) Might not being told, perhaps in a certain tone of voice, that I shall do something come in suitable circumstances to much the same as my being told to do it?[32] Would it in fact be possible to hold that '. . . said that . . .' was *the* basic locutionary act, 'asking' being reducible to 'telling to', and 'telling to' to 'saying that' in an appropriately phrased future tense? But these – apart from being, I am sure, not the sort of questions that Austin liked (too speculative) – are not questions that he chose to pursue. It is of some importance to note, though, that in Austin's scheme, when we have before us the locutionary act which a speaker performs, we are in a position to say at least *something* more specific about what he therein does – he says that so-and-so, *or* tells someone to such-and-such, *or* asks whether this-or-that.

However – and here we get on to what Austin is more seriously interested in – although in identifying the locutionary act we thus identify in some very general way what the speaker does – for example, he *says that* the cat is on the mat – there will normally arise other, and further, questions. Let us deal first with the least problematic case, which he calls that of 'perlocutions'. The notion here is that saying something will 'often, or even normally, produce certain consequential effects upon the feelings, thoughts, or actions of the audience, or of the speaker, or of other persons'.[33] Thus, by telling someone something I may, for example, change his opinion on some matter; or mislead him; or surprise him; or alarm him; or induce him not to do something. And, whether or not I intended to produce such effects, they may be incorporated in the designation of 'what I did'. By telling him that my horse was not fully fit, I changed his view as to the likely winner of the race, perhaps thereby deterred him from betting on my horse. I alarmed him by saying that it looked like rain – he had just hung the washing out on the line. And so on. It is a pervasive and important truth that, in saying what some person did, we may incorporate *in* the designation of what he did a larger or smaller slice of what might also be regarded as 'effects' or 'consequences' of 'what he did' when that is identified in some other way. To pull the trigger with the effect that the gun goes off is to shoot; to shoot with the consequence that someone is injured is to wound; to wound with the result that the person dies is to kill. Just so, to tell you something that surprises you is to surprise you, or something that causes annoyance is to annoy. To produce by saying something effects or consequences or results of that sort is to perform what Austin calls 'perlocutionary' acts. Let us note three points here. First, it is, as we shall see, important that the production of such effects may or may not be intended by the performer, and may not occur even if he intends that it should – I may perlocutionarily shock you unintentionally by making what I take to be some quite innocent remark, or alternatively may fail to shock you when that is my intention. Second, the perlocutionary effect in question will very often be producible also in some completely non-verbal way – I may deter you from betting on my horse not by saying anything but by knocking you down, or may shock you by lighting a cigarette in church, but it is clearly intended that such effects come into – or can be said to *be* – the performance of 'real' perlocutionary acts only when they *are* brought about by *saying* something. And third, it is I think at least implicit in what Austin says that, for a perlocutionary act to be performed, the effects in question must be effects of (at least) a full *locutionary* act. I might startle you, for example, by the phonetic act of speaking loudly in your ear, or (if I have been thought hitherto to be a hopeless aphasic) by the phatic act of saying anything at all; but it seems to be part of the notion of a perlocutionary act that the effect in question is brought about by my *saying what I say*, not merely by my speaking at all, or saying anything at all. It is a perlocutionary act to cause panic by shouting 'Fire!', but probably not by simply shouting, even if that too should for some reason or other cause panic.

How then, we may ask, do perlocutionary acts 'get done'? What makes it possible for us to perform acts of that sort? The answer seems, and I believe actually is, reasonably clear. It is simply that we are able as language-speakers to perform locutionary acts, and that locutionary acts do as a matter of fact have certain effects, results, or consequences. It may be made a question *how much* of what ensued upon my saying what I said can properly or justifiably be said to be an effect, result, or consequence of my locutionary act; but that is a quite general (perfectly proper) question about the notion of an effect (etc.) rather than an issue that arises particularly here. Again, it may be made a question how far the effects (etc.) of my saying what I said can properly – including, importantly, *fairly* – be incorporated succinctly in an acceptable designation of 'what I did'. But it is at any rate clear, and a point of some importance, that when we have established what locutionary act a speaker performed, it will always be a *further question* what perlocutionary act (if indeed any) he performed thereby; for that is fundamentally, at least in part, just the question 'And what actually happened as a result?' And clearly we shall in no case be in a position to answer that question simply by perusing the locutionary act itself. We cannot answer it either, as we have already noted, by investigating what the speaker intended. I may intend to amuse my audience when in fact it does not come about that my audience is amused; I may annoy you by saying what I say without intending to do so. A further question, then; and the question is essentially: 'What actually ensued?'

Let us take it, then, that we have a reasonably clear notion of those two sorts of things that a speaker (any speaker in any ordinary case) will be 'doing' in speaking, for instance in issuing the utterance 'The cat is on the mat': first, the locutionary act of *saying that* the cat is on the mat, and second, perhaps the perlocutionary act of reassuring you *by* saying that the cat is on the mat. We must now bring in the further, and

I think the most interesting and arguable, issue of what a speaker does, not *by* saying what he says, but *in* saying it – what Austin calls the 'illocutionary' act.[34] This species of act comes between, as it were, the two classes of speech-acts that we have so far considered; how is it to be distinguished from its neighbours on either side? I say that my horse is not fully fit (locutionary act); *in* saying that, I give you a warning (illocutionary act); and *by* saying that, I perhaps deter you from betting on my horse (perlocutionary act). What distinctions are to be drawn?

Well, the terms 'illocutionary act' and 'perlocutionary act' were actually invented (by Austin) with an eye on this distinction between 'in' and 'by' – what I do *in* saying something, and what I do *by* saying it. However, although the difference of use between these two formulae does offer some sort of clue to what Austin has in mind, he insists that it does not by itself, if mechanically applied, provide a generally reliable way of drawing his distinction. To abbreviate his argument: first, the 'In saying . . .' formula does not always pick out the performance of an illocutionary act – forgetting, for example, is patently not an illocutionary act (nor any other kind of speech-act), but we would happily say 'In saying he was in London, I was forgetting that he might be away on holiday', or simply 'In saying that he was in London I was, I'm afraid, mistaken'. Equally, the 'by' formula does not always pick out perlocutionary acts: 'By saying that the case was closed, I meant that there was nothing more we could do'. 'The general conclusion must be . . . that these formulas are at best very slippery tests for deciding whether an expression is an illocution as distinct from a perlocution or neither.'[35] So what *can* be said as to the basis of this distinction?

We may start with a relatively uncontroversial negative point. Whereas the perlocutionary act that I perform in speaking is essentially just a matter of what 'effect' is thereby brought about, of what actually happens, that is *not* the case with the illocutionary act. If I deter you from betting on my horse by saying that it is not fully fit, your being deterred is simply the effect or consequence (whether or not intended) of my saying that. But if in saying that my horse is not fully fit I warn you not to bet on my horse, my warning you seems clearly not to be just an effect – and certainly it could not be an *unintended* effect – of my saying that; it is not something that is in fact brought about by what I say, but something that I do in saying it – akin rather to 'what I mean' than to anything that may happen as a result of my utterance. If in saying 'I should resign' I advise you to resign, I may or may not bring it about that you actually do resign – that is a question of 'what happens next'; but that in so speaking I give you my advice is not a matter of what happens *as a result* of my utterance: it is a matter of what, *in* issuing that utterance, I was doing – of how I meant it to be 'taken',

125

what I meant my remark 'as', whatever the effect of my so speaking may actually turn out to be.

A further point is also, I think, uncontroversial. We noted earlier that when it is established what locutionary act a speaker performed, it will always be a further question what perlocutionary act, if any, he performed thereby; for that brings in the question 'What actually ensued?', and clearly that question cannot be answered by contemplation of the locutionary act itself. Illocutionary acts differ in this respect; given the locutionary act, it will indeed often, perhaps usually, but certainly not always, be a further question what illocutionary act was performed; and when that *is* a further question, it is so for a different reason. If someone says (locutionary act) that the horse is not fully fit, it will be a further question what illocutionary act he performs – not, however, because we do not yet know what happened as a result, but because that locution *could* be meant, and taken, in several different ways. Was he warning unwary punters? Was he giving his appraisal of the animal's condition? Or voicing a suspicion? Or just giving information to those who might be interested? And so on. We see also that this will not *always* be a further question; for although what a speaker is doing in speaking is often, even usually, not made fully, or even at all, explicit in what he says, that of course *can* be made explicitly quite clear, and sometimes is. If I say 'I warn you that the horse isn't fully fit', my so speaking must be taken, can only be taken, as the giving of a warning; and it seems right to say in such a case that the locutionary act itself 'tells' us also what illocutionary act is performed, and so leaves no room for that issue to be raised as a further question. To make the illocutionary force of an utterance fully explicit – as of course we very often, even usually, do *not* do – is precisely, I think, to take the illocutionary force into the locution itself. To say 'I advise you to resign' not only *is* to give you advice; it *means* that I do. Austin insists, correctly, that the notion of illocutionary force should be distinguished from that of meaning,[36] but I see no reason why he should have wished to deny that the meaning of an utterance can sometimes uniquely determine its illocutionary force; it seems natural, in fact, to say that this is exactly what the use of his 'explicit performative formulas' aims at. It is obvious, by contrast, that the meaning of an utterance can *never* determine its perlocutionary effect; for, whatever my intention may be, I cannot in fact convince you, or shock you, or frighten or reassure you, *simply* by saying (something which means) that I do. In such a case it is, as one might put it, not for me to say; I must wait and see.

Of course we should notice here that, with illocutionary acts too, it is not entirely for me (just) to *say*. If I mean to warn you in saying that my horse is not fully fit, I do not actually do so simply in *saying* that; you may hear and understand what I say but fail to grasp the way I mean it; and even if I explicitly say that I warn you, you may not hear what I say or may not understand it. 'The performance of an illocutionary act involves the securing of *uptake*.'[37] To speak with a certain illocutionary force is not quite *eo ipso* to perform an illocutionary act, since what is said may not be taken in (or up), in which case the act is not 'happily' brought off. It is a rather different point, I think, that, say, a promise or a bet needs not only to be taken in as so intended, but actually taken up, accepted, as a two-party agreement; taking up, in that sense, is something more than uptake.

But now – still on this question of how to distinguish illocutionary from perlocutionary acts – we must consider something else that Austin says, without much argument or explanation, but repeatedly and rather emphatically. For example: 'illocutionary acts are conventional acts: perlocutionary acts are *not* conventional.'[38] 'Strictly speaking, there cannot be an illocutionary act unless the means employed are conventional.'[39]

> Speaking of the 'use of "language" for arguing or warning' looks just like speaking of 'the use of "language" for persuading, rousing, alarming', yet the former may, for rough contrast, be said to be *conventional* . . . but the latter could not.[40]

'We must notice that the illocutionary act is a conventional act: an act done as conforming to a convention.'[41] And: 'we also perform *illocutionary acts* such as informing, ordering, warning, undertaking, etc., i.e. utterances which have a certain (conventional) force.'[42] What does all this mean?

I think we can fairly easily get out of the way one thing that Austin clearly does *not* mean. When he says that for the performance of an illocutionary act, 'strictly speaking' the means employed must be 'conventional', he surely does not mean merely that the doing of the act involves or includes some use of language. It would be understandable enough to describe the use of language as a conventional, convention-employing means of getting things done, as contrasted with such causally efficacious means as pushing or pulling, hitting things or blowing things up; means that 'work' by way of meaning and understanding could in general be acceptably said to be 'conventional'. However, when Austin says that the illocutionary act is conventional, he plainly does not mean simply that it is an act of speaking, making use of language. For one thing, he holds that that is actually not always true: although 'many illocutionary acts cannot be performed except by saying something', some 'can be brought off non-verbally; but even then to deserve the name of an illocutionary act, for example a warning, it must be a *conventional* non-verbal act'.[43] Also, the performance of perlocutionary acts typically – though perhaps, again, not always – involves the use of language; but he insists that such acts are *not* conventional; 'though conventional acts may be made use of in order to bring off the perlocutionary act',[44] an act of that sort nevertheless is not itself conventional, in the sense in which, as he says, the illocutionary act always is, whether or not it is an act of literally *saying* something.

I believe that the question which Austin is offering to answer here is this: what is it that gives a locutionary act the illocutionary force that, in a particular case, it has? How does it come about, or what makes it the case, that in saying something I *eo ipso*, or therein, perform a specific illocutionary act? We have already seen that, given a certain locutionary act, it will usually be a further question what illocutionary act was performed therein; if you say that there is a bull in the next field, we can say indeed that you have (presumably) made an assertion, said that something is the case; but that is to answer only in the broadest, minimally informative terms the question what illocutionary act you performed; and further questions arise. Were you warning me to keep out? Or drawing my attention to an interesting phenomenon? Or controverting the view that there are no bulls in Wiltshire? And so on. The question is, then: how do these 'further questions' get answered? What *makes* your act of speaking an act of, say, warning? Or in virtue of what are you able, in speaking as you do, to warn? 'Convention', Austin says: the specific illocutionary act is an act 'done as conforming to a convention'; that is how it 'works', and how it is to be identified as the particular act that it is.

At an earlier stage, when we were considering whether or not the 'initial distinction' had 'broken down', I suggested that, on at least one view of what 'the distinction' was intended to be, it had not broken down at all, but was on the contrary at least reasonably firm and clear. Namely, *if* the performative utterance was to be a ritual, conventional affair, issued as an operative element in an accepted conventional procedure for doing this or that, then it seemed a perfectly reasonable project to distinguish, as 'performative', utterances of that sort from cases of what I called 'ordinary' saying. 'I name this ship the *Queen Elizabeth*' would be performative, a key element in the ritual of naming the ship; the ordinary conversational remark 'That's the *Queen Elizabeth*', made while strolling round the docks, would not be performative (but constative), as not occurring as an element in any conventional procedure. Similarly, we contrasted the bowler's performative 'How's that?' – *appealing*, in virtue of and in accordance with the rules of cricket – with the spectator's 'ordinary' interrogative, just asking a question. I mentioned, however, at that earlier stage that Austin himself could not happily have defended the 'initial distinction' in that way; and we can now see why not. He holds, of course, that 'to perform a locutionary act is in general . . . also and *eo ipso* to perform an illocutionary act':[45]

a speaker, that is, typically performs *some* illocutionary act in saying anything at all. But if we now say, as it seems pretty clear that he does, that every illocutionary act is a conventional act, 'done as conforming to a convention', then there will evidently be *no difference* between what – in offering to defend the 'initial distinction' – I called performative utterance, as supposedly contrasted with 'ordinary' saying. To appeal in a cricket match, or to name a ship, is a conventional act having a certain conventional effect; but so also, he seems now to be saying, is every ordinary act of saying anything at all – for (ordinarily) every such saying has a certain illocutionary force, and that is, he seems to say, precisely *because* it is always a conventional act, done as conforming to an accepted conventional procedure. Austin himself, at any rate, could not have attempted to rope off any *sub-class* of utterances as being conventional acts, since he attributes that characteristic to every utterance.

But surely this must be wrong (at least in some cases – we shall come back to that). Suppose that, sitting in my deck-chair on the beach, I see some children evidently shaping up to go for a swim; it occurs to me that I ought to warn them of the strong current just beyond the rocks. Accordingly I go over and say, 'There's a strong current just beyond those rocks'; they are duly grateful, and confine their swimming to waters close inshore. What makes it the case that, speaking as I did, I warned them? It is clearly not a *convention* that a person who so speaks is issuing a warning; indeed, so far as 'what I said' goes. I might well not have been – I might have been explaining the curious configuration of the sand-banks, or simply passing the time of day. Surely I was, in this case, warning those children if, in mentioning the strong current beyond those rocks, my *intention* was to make them aware of a potential danger to swimmers. And how did they grasp, as we assume they did, that I *was* giving them a warning? Not by recognizing some conventional drill which I was carrying out, but, surely, by realizing that that was my intention in speaking. Given the familiar fact that strong currents may be a danger to swimmers, a person who, addressing some people preparing to swim, tells them of a strong current in the vicinity can safely be assumed to be warning them – drawing their attention, that is, to a certain risk in their envisaged course of action. I exploit, in speaking as I did, not a convention for warning – there is, in general, no such convention – but their safely assumed ability, in the circumstances of the case, to recognize with what intention I said what I said.

But we must say something more than this. To warn, we say, is to speak with a certain intention – the intention, that is, of bringing to an addressee's notice a certain danger, perhaps impending ('That bull's going to charge') or liable to impend if he acts in some envisaged way. But that does not, by itself, constitute warning an illocutionary act; for very probably, in the case just given, I said 'There's a strong current just beyond those rocks' with the intention of *deterring* the children from swimming out that way; but to deter them from doing that (if I do) is a perlocutionary act, notwithstanding that that is the intention with which I speak. Why then is warning them an illocution, and deterring them not? There are two points to be made. First, the perlocutionary act – any such act – may be performed *un*intentionally; if you are a weak or nervous swimmer, I may deter you from venturing into the current I mention even if I intended only to tell you it was there, or even was offering it as an extra, amusing thrill for bathers. It seems right to say, by contrast, that the illocutionary act cannot be unintentionally performed. I may indeed, in making some casual remark, unintentionally – inadvertently, unwittingly – alert you to, or apprise you of, some impending danger; but I do not, I think, *warn* you of it unless I speak – and speak, furthermore, *to you* – with that intention. But second, it is I think a more substantial point that the illocutionary intention, if we may call it that, unlike the perlocutionary intention, is actually *fulfilled* on the sole condition that it is *recognized*. You may know quite well that I intended to stop you swimming beyond those rocks, but if you think the risk is not serious or do not mind taking risks, my perlocutionary intention may be unfulfilled. By contrast, whatever you may think of what I say and whatever you may choose to do, I have (successfully) *warned* you if you have grasped what my intention was. If you realize that I spoke with the intention of bringing a potential danger to your notice, then at any rate you cannot subsequently deny that you were warned.

This last point gives us, I think, the real reason why, in the performance of this sort of illocutionary act, the explicit-performative formula is particularly well in place – both why its employment is possible, and why it is (so far as it is) often helpful and desirable. If the essential thing, for the successful performance of the illocutionary act, is that the speaker's intention in speaking should be grasped by the addressee, then it will often be desirable and helpful that his intention should be made as fully manifest as possible. Particularly if the circumstances are such that his intention may not be immediately clear – that he might 'just as well' be stating an interesting fact as giving a warning – it will improve things if his particular intention is made quite manifest; and the ideal, as well as very natural, way to do that is for him to include *in* what he says an explicit indicator of his intention in speaking. If I think that when I say 'He's a Roman Catholic', you may take me to be just chatting rather than apprising you of hazards in discussing the news from Northern Ireland, I would do well to say 'I warn you that he's a Roman Catholic'. It is, I believe, the very same consideration that makes employment of the explicit-performative formula 'possible'. I *can* properly say 'I warn . . .', 'I advise . . .', 'I suggest . . .', and so on, just because in such cases it is a matter of what I mean, what I intend, and so it is *for me to say*; if success in the performance requires that my intention be grasped, I can most effectively ensure that I succeed (in warning, etc.) by explicitly saying – or, rather better, by explicitly manifesting in what I say – that that *is* my intention; and as to that I could not, at least in any non-convoluted way, be making a mistake. Thus if I say 'I warn you that it's highly inflammable', you might perfectly naturally respond by saying 'No, it isn't' – for my belief that it is, and hence that danger impends, could indeed be mistaken, and if so, quite properly contradicted by you. But you could *not* naturally respond by saying 'No, you don't'; for what my intention is in mentioning the stuff's inflammability is simply for me to say, and you are equally simply 'in no position' to controvert me on *that* point. (Perhaps you might, rather oddly and perhaps facetiously, say 'No, you don't' by way, not of suggesting that I am mistaken, but of questioning my sincerity; for indeed I may insincerely profess an intention I do not really have. 'I hereby resolve to give up smoking': 'No, you don't,') Perlocutionary acts are obviously quite different in this respect; for here success is a matter not of making manifest what the speaker intends, but of whether the outcome in fact accords with his intention. If I were to say, rather absurdly, 'I convince you that it's going to stay fine', you could very properly – and with some surprise – respond with 'No, you don't', for perhaps you are, as a matter of fact, unconvinced, and that is for *you*, not me, to say; for that reason, 'I convince you . . .' is an intrinsically absurd form of words. Even Dr Johnson's 'Sir, I refute it *thus*' – striking his foot against a stone 'till he rebounded from it' – is, if not in itself objectionable as a form of words, at any rate not a case of the explicit performative; for, while no doubt he meant his performance *to be* a refutation of Berkeley, we are by no means obliged to concede that he did thereby refute him. You do not refute a philosophical doctrine just by saying that you do. ('I refute . . .' is, alas, now commonly used as if it *were* a performative formula, synonymous with 'I deny . . .', but that is attributable to mere ignorance of what the word means.) I think it is for the same reason that 'I insult you' is not a performative formula. Austin, who considered the question very briefly, suggests that we perhaps disapprove of, and therefore do not countenance and employ, a means of handily facilitating the insulting of people; this is a performance that we do not wish to encourage.[46] There may be some truth in that, but I suspect that it is a more pertinent point that the manifest intention to insult does not ensure success; I may not *be* insulted by your calling me a typical Wykehamist, may not 'take it as' an insult, even if your intention to be insulting is absolutely clear – accordingly it is not (simply) for you to say. I have seen well-intentioned notices headed 'Polite Notice', which seem rather odd for the same reason again; the avowed intention to be polite does not guarantee politeness – I want to read the notice to find out whether it actually *is* polite, a point on which my opinion is at least as pertinent as that of its composer.

If, then, a great many illocutionary acts (of which we have taken *warning* as an example – others might have been advising, requesting, objecting, suggesting) are not 'conventional' acts, not acts done as conforming to or as part of any prescribed conventional procedure or ritual, what about those illocutionary acts that *are* conventional – 'I, the Returning Officer, declare the said Herbert Stiggins duly elected', and so forth? There are different cases here. There are a great many conventional acts which are, so to speak, *essentially* conventional: acts such as appealing (in cricket), bidding (in bridge), or acquitting (in the law), which cannot be done at all except in virtue of the existence of, and in pursuance of, the relevant 'conventions' – rules or laws. There are a great many others which, while they can be done non-conventionally, in a more or less *ad hoc*, informal way, may *become* conventionalized. I may give away a pair of old shoes without formality, but if I wish to give you my house I must go through the proper forms; I name the family car 'Fred' without ceremony ('Let's call it Fred'), but naming the *Queen Elizabeth* is a different matter. But in either case the purpose, or object, of the convention is to enable the thing in question to *get done* – either done at all, or done clearly, definitely, and beyond dispute. Thus, it is to be presumed that the speaker of the prescribed words in such a case intends to get done – to do, or to assist and further the doing of – whatever it may be: that the Returning Officer who says 'I declare the said Herbert Stiggins duly elected' speaks with the intention of formally consummating the election of Stiggins. But it seems right to say that in cases of this sort it is actually not all that important what the speaker's intentions are; it is just as important, and will often be much more important, simply whether he did speak the words conventionally prescribed. To warn you, I do not have to say 'I warn you': there is nothing in particular I *have* to say; I need to get you to recognize my intention of bringing to your notice a possible or impending danger. But to get Stiggins elected, I *do* have to say (being the Returning Officer) 'I declare the said Herbert Stiggins . . .'; if I say instead 'So Stiggins is the winner' or 'Three cheers for Stiggins!', while you may see that my intention is to declare him elected, you could and probably should deny that I have actually done so, for here there *is* a conventional procedure, and I have not complied with it.

I believe that this point bears rather interestingly on the matter of the explicit performative form. We said earlier that this form comes in very naturally in the performance of many illocutionary acts, since it serves to make manifest, overt, explicit the speaker's intention in speaking, and that that is what performance of the act essentially consists in (*plus* 'uptake'); the very best way of getting you to recognize my intention to warn is to say 'I warn . . .', and furthermore that I *do* warn is for me to *say*. We clearly cannot say just this about *conventional* acts; for here, while the speaker in any given case presumably has the appropriate intention, it is not the sole crux of the matter that he has it, nor can he 'bring off' his act (merely) by making his intention fully clear. He has (also) to say the right thing; and it seems in general that the right thing to say in such cases simply *may or may not* be in the explicitly performative form. It seems natural enough, of course, that it often will be; it is understandable enough that, in prescribing or evolving the proper form for declaring a candidate elected, we should require the proper person formally to say 'I declare . . .'. But that is quite often not the way it goes. A bowler who appeals to the umpire is not required to say 'I appeal', the foreman of a jury, in announcing the verdict, is not required to say either 'I announce . . .', nor yet 'We acquit' or 'We convict', and an umpire in giving a batsman out is not required to *say* anything at all (he makes a conventional gesture). The principal reason for this seems to be that in these genuinely 'conventional' cases what the speaker is doing in speaking (or in the case of the umpire, gesturing) is already made wholly clear and manifest, in the circumstances, by the conventional procedure itself. We already *know* that at this stage of the formal proceedings in court, the foreman of the jury is announcing their verdict; so there is simply no need for him to say overtly that he is doing so, or in any way to indicate that he is doing so *in* what he says. What he needs to say is only what the verdict is; the rest is already clear, in the nature of the case.

It would be possible, I suppose, to say nevertheless that the prescribed form of words in a conventional illocutionary act, in which the speaker X-es, might 'in principle' invariably have been, or could be imagined as being, of the explicit performative form, 'I X'; but I can actually see no great point in saying that, true though it probably is, for it is equally possible, in principle, that the conventions should *never* prescribe words of that form. To *say that* I warn, or advise, or suggest is peculiarly appropriate just because there is no prescribed form for warning, or giving advice, or making a suggestion; but if there were, it might well be unnecessary, or even impermissible, to say that I do. If the words are not required, so to speak, to carry on their face an indication of what the speaker is doing in speaking – since that is already settled by the convention itself – then it becomes a really entirely open question what the proper, conventional form of words should be.

In his penultimate chapter Austin takes up once again the question whether the initial distinction, the 'original contrast', is tenable. Can we say that there is a special class of utterances, to be called 'performative', to issue which is to *do* something as opposed to the constative, just *saying* something, and which are happy or unhappy as opposed to being true or false? He suggests, not in the least surprisingly by this time, that the contrast, at any rate as baldly and briefly propounded in that way, looks precarious indeed.

It looks precarious on both counts. First, as we have by now abundantly seen, there is no opposition, no tenable line to be drawn, between saying something and doing something. To say something, anything, is always to do *something* – certainly to perform a phonetic act, and in any normal case to perform a locutionary, illocutionary, and probably a perlocutionary act as well: the question what a speaker *does* always arises, and can be answered in a rich and interesting variety of ways. In particular, there is no line to be drawn between doing something in speaking and 'the constative', stating; for 'to state is every bit as much to perform an illocutionary act as, say, to warn or to pronounce . . . "Stating" seems to meet all the criteria we had for distinguishing the illocutionary act.' It can be 'put absolutely on a level with arguing, betting, and warning':[47] I may say 'In saying that it was raining, I was not betting or arguing or warning: I was simply stating it as a fact'; and I may say 'I state that he did not do it' just as I may say 'I argue', or 'I suggest that he did not do it', therein specifying the illocutionary force of my utterance. Furthermore, while stating is 'doing', that does not rule the question 'true or false?' out of order; for if I state that it is raining, of course the question arises whether my statement is or is not true.

Second, there is no exclusive opposition between 'happy or unhappy' and 'true or false'. A statement of course can, in general, be true or false. But it may also, in various ways, be 'unhappy': an 'abuse', for example, when I state something that I do not believe, or 'void' when I state that my car is in the garage, having no car and perhaps no garage either. There seem also to be statements that one cannot 'happily' or properly make, because for one reason or another one is 'not in a position' to (rather as you may not be 'in a position' to give me an order): where I have no knowledge, for example; or *could* have no knowledge (and so can only guess, or conjecture); or where the statement has already been made by someone else (and I can only confirm it). That all seems very clear.

But Austin's next point is, I think, considerably, and indeed importantly, understated. Although we have to concede, he says, that stating is an illocutionary act 'on a level' with others, and may, like other illocutionary acts, be happy or unhappy, we may still have the feeling that statements are somehow a special case – namely in this respect, that the other cases

> are not essentially true or false as statements are. We may feel that there is here a dimension in which we judge, assess, or appraise the

constative utterance (granting as a preliminary that it is felicitous) which does not arise with non-constative or performative utterances.[48]

But, he says, this feeling should not be indulged – for after all the other cases (some other cases) are not as different as all that; 'there is an obvious slide towards truth or falsity in the case of, for example . . . estimating, finding, and pronouncing'.[49] I may estimate that it is half past two *rightly or wrongly*, find that he is guilty or pronounce the service a fault *correctly or incorrectly*, and that is surely 'sliding towards' truth or falsity. My reason for saying that the point is understated is this: that in these other cases we surely have, not really a 'slide towards' truth or falsity, but involvement of the very *same* notion of truth and falsity as in the case of statements.

We must go back a little. Recall the example: 'In saying that it was raining, I was not betting or arguing or warning: I was simply stating it as a fact.' We said, or rather Austin said, that 'here "stating" is put absolutely on a level with arguing, betting, and warning'. Well, if so, 'In saying that it was raining, I was (simply) stating that it was raining' is not a tautology – in saying that, I might *not* have been 'stating' but arguing, or perhaps betting or warning. But what is common to all these cases is my (locutionarily) *saying that* it was raining; and while it is a *further question* – a question about illocutionary force – whether I was therein betting, arguing, warning, or simply stating (as a fact) that it was raining, surely the question 'true or false?' can be raised *in each case*, with respect to 'what I said'. *In each case* I said that it was raining – so the question can be raised: whatever I was *doing* in saying that, *was* it raining? To turn to the other examples: I say that it is half past two; if that is true, then, if I am making an estimate, my estimate is exactly right. I say that he is guilty; if that is true, then, if I am giving a verdict, my verdict is the correct one. I say that the service was a fault; if that is true, then, if I am deciding (as an umpire), that is a correct decision. And: I say that it is raining; if that is true, then, if I am stating it 'as a fact', my statement is factually correct. The cases of a correct verdict or decision, or a right estimate, do not bring in something like, or something 'sliding towards', the notion of truth or falsity; they surely bring in that very notion itself, as the case of stating does. (Austin, in fact, at one point seems to say this himself: we probably shall not, he says, use the word 'true' of estimates, verdicts, and so on; but 'we shall certainly address ourselves to the same question.'[50] My submission is that it really is *just* the same question, namely whether 'what I said' was true or false.)

If that is right, then it would seem that Austin might have put his point, indeed should have put his point, in a much stronger way. Instead of saying that 'something like' the question 'true or false?' may arise with at least some illocutionary acts other than stating, could he not have said that that very question itself may arise with any illocutionary act – of course *including* stating – in which the *locutionary* act is an act of 'saying that . . .'? For, mostly at any rate, when one says that p, the question 'Is it true or false that p?' at least may arise, whatever, *in* saying that p, one may be doing. The only cases in which that question quite clearly could not arise at all would be those in which the speaker does not 'say that' anything – in which for instance, to use Austin's own terms, the locutionary act is not 'says that', but 'tells to', or 'asks'. But of course we must make a distinction here; we must be careful to add that, though the question 'true or false?' may *arise* in most 'says that . . .' cases, its significance or interest, with respect to appraisal of the speaker's total performance, will still depend crucially on what his (illocutionary) performance was. If he states as a fact that p, then he is thereby strongly committed to its being the case that p, and his statement is wrong, and his credit to that extent impugned, if it is *not* the case that p. Similarly, if he estimates or pronounces or declares that p, he presumably wishes, and can presumably be expected or required, to estimate or pronounce or declare *correctly* or as nearly so as possible, so whether it is true or not that p will be a matter of significance. But if he merely suggests that p, p's not being the case will not be a very bad thing ('It was only a suggestion'). If he guesses that p, p's not being the case perhaps need not count against him at all – he guessed wrong, but what of that? It was just a guess, after all. And – a different sort of case – if he says that he is glad to welcome . . . , while the question could indeed be raised whether he *was* glad to welcome . . . , we are not going to take that question very seriously; for in such a case the speaker's business is to speak politely, not to inform the audience what his real feelings are; and we all understand that perfectly well. But this is to say that, when a speaker says that p, the question whether it is true or false that p will not always (in critical assessment of his *performance*) *matter* very much, though of course sometimes it will: how far and in what exact way it matters will depend on how far and in what way, and how 'seriously', the particular performance committed the speaker to p's being true; but to say that the answer to the question will not always matter much is not to say that it may not always arise.

I have been saying so far that where a speaker's locutionary act is one of 'saying that . . .', the question 'true or false?' may always arise. Could one not say simply that it *does* always arise? It would surely be injudicious to go as far as that. I suppose it always does arise at least in this sense, that when a speaker says that p, the question 'Is it true or false that p?' at least makes some sort of sense, can intelligibly be asked; but of course it cannot be presumed that it must always have an answer, or even be a 'proper question'. We have seen that, in Austin's view, some 'sayings that' are neither true nor false, are for example 'void', on account of infelicity. Some would say, for completely different reasons, that 'Is it true or false that p?' has no proper answer when 'p' expresses an ethical proposition, or moral judgment.[51] And of course Austin himself holds that when a speaker says that he promises – or anything else in the explicit performative mode – 'what he says' is neither true nor false.[52] Without taking sides on such particular issues as these (and there are other cases), no doubt we should recognize that when a speaker says that p, although it probably always makes some sort of sense to *ask* whether it is true or false that p, there may sometimes be reasons for holding that the question has no answer in those terms.

It is difficult to be quite sure where Austin himself stands on these matters, partly because his discussion of them in *How to Do Things with Words* is extremely brief. I am fairly certain, however, that his remarks in the lectures are intended to convey that much of what I have been suggesting in the last four paragraphs is objectionable; and I must now try to explain why he would have so held. It comes, I think, to this: we began from the point – in throwing cold water on the supposed contrast between 'performative' and 'constative' – that to be true or false is not something specially and exclusively peculiar to 'stating'; there was said to be a 'slide towards' truth and falsity in some other performative cases, such as estimating, warning, and pronouncing, or, as he had put it much earlier, considerations 'of the type' of truth and falsity may 'infect performatives (or some performatives).'[53] My suggestion was – and we noted that at one point Austin seemed to agree – that this understated the case; for if 'stating' that p is, as he holds that it is, just one illocutionary mode of (locutionarily) saying that p, then it would seem that with very *many* illocutionary acts other than stating 'we shall certainly address ourselves to the same question' – that is, is 'what he said', namely that p, true or false? This is to say that the question 'true or false?' arises (may arise) at the level of *locutions*, and so of course may be involved, in one way or another, in very *many* illocutionary performances in which the locutionary act is of the 'said that' sort. I think it is quite clear that Austin did not just overlook this. It is not that he had forgotten, or failed to appreciate, that on his own showing 'saying that p' is one kind of *locutionary* act. On the contrary: he says that 'with the constative utterance' – when 'true or false?' is at the forefront of our minds – 'we abstract from the illocutionary . . . aspects of the speech-act, and we concentrate on the locutionary'.[54] But this, he clearly means, is a natural *temptation* that ought to be resisted; the abstraction is illegitimate, or at any rate an over-simplification; for it is his contention that, in fact, truth 'essentially . . . brings in the illocutionary aspect'.[55] 'The truth or falsity of a statement depends not merely on the meanings of words but on what act you were performing in what circumstances.'[56]

I believe that he is at least partly wrong about this. Let us take a closer look. He says:

> It is essential to realise that 'true' and 'false' do not stand for anything simple at all; but only for a general dimension of being a right or proper thing to say as opposed to a wrong thing, in these circumstances, to this audience, for these purposes and with these intentions.[57]

At first sight this remark may well look *completely* wrong. For of course, one will object, to say that what someone said was true is very far indeed from comprehensively pronouncing it to be 'a right or proper thing to say . . . in these circumstances', etc. What he said might be true, but at the same time tactless, misleading, irrelevant, pointless, unfounded, embarrassing, inopportune, offensive, uninteresting, rude: true, but far indeed from a right or proper thing to say; and if we wish to say that what someone said was *not* a right or proper thing to say ('in these circumstances', etc.), we may have in mind any of a very wide range of failings other than falsehood. But surely Austin did not really mean to say, what would indeed quite clearly be wrong, that 'true' and 'false' are just general labels for (*all* kinds of) satisfactoriness or otherwise in things that people say.[58] I think what he meant was that, while of course there are many quite different ways of being (or not) a right and proper thing to say, ways that have little or nothing to do with truth, the question 'true or false?' itself cannot be answered without at least some reference to the circumstances, the audience, and the speaker's purposes and intentions.

Well, there are cases of this sort – no doubt a great many cases – and Austin from time to time, from 'Truth' onwards, mentions several of them. There are innumerable cases in which 'what is said', when confronted with 'the facts', can be seen neither to 'fit the facts' exactly, nor yet to be completely wide of the mark. Neither 'true' nor 'untrue', just like that, seems appropriate. Is it true or false that France is hexagonal? that Italy is boot-shaped? that Stiggins is bald? There are rather different issues here. 'Hexagonal' is a precise enough term, but still, is it true or false that *France* is hexagonal? 'Boot-shaped' is pretty vague, which befogs still further the question whether Italy is boot-shaped. And is it fair (perhaps to Stiggins) or unfair to say (baldly) that Stiggins is bald? It seems right enough to say that, in cases such as these, it is idle, perhaps impossible, doggedly to press the bare question 'true or false?' We would not be happy, and it would not be sensible, to say baldly, just like that, either one or the other. The question that arises in such cases is something like: will it do? Does it get by? Is it fair? Is it good *enough*? And of course that raises the question: good enough for what, or for whom? It will do in some circumstances, for some intents and purposes, but for others not. Sometimes we shall be happy to say 'true', but sometimes we shall not. Nevertheless, that being fully granted, it still seems to me that Austin is wrong here – in two ways. The first is that he is surely wrong in suggesting, as he seems to do, that the case in which such questions arise is the absolutely typical, perhaps universal case. For surely there are also innumerable things that people say, or could say, of which we could say – without knowing of any circumstances in which they were said, by whom, to whom, or for what purpose – 'Well, anyway, it's *true*'. It is true that Marcus Aurelius was a Roman emperor, that 19 December 1987 was a Saturday, and that France is part of Europe; surely anyone who says, to anyone or in any circumstances or for any purpose, that Marcus Aurelius was a Roman emperor says something *true*. It is true, furthermore, even if, for any of a wide variety of possible reasons, he ought not to have *said* it. Here we can – and surely we *very often* can – quite legitimately 'abstract from' any questions about the circumstances of utterance, noting just that it was (locutionarily) said that p, and that p is true. Austin mentions as a pretty bogus, visionary ideal the notion of 'what would be right to say in all circumstances, for any purpose, to any audience, etc.'[59] Perhaps that is bogusly visionary, indeed. But if we replace here, as of course we should for the purpose of this argument, the word 'right' by 'true', we have something not bogus or visionary in the least. 'The United Kingdom has a Queen' would be an example (remembering that the *locutionary* act has 'sense and reference', so that we know from that act what, *and when*, we are referring to). It might well not be *right* to say this in all circumstances, etc.; but unquestionably it would be true.

The second point is this. Austin says that, if we are not to fall into culpable over-simplification, we have to bring in 'the illocutionary aspect': 'the truth or falsity of a statement depends not merely on the meanings of words but on what act you were performing in what circumstances.' Well, he has, I think, shown, and we have agreed, that whether we are happy to say 'true' or 'false' will indeed often depend on 'the circumstances' – is it good *enough*? But I do not see that he really does anything to show that it 'depends . . . on what act you were performing', that is on 'the illocutionary aspect'. For if I say that it is raining, and it is raining, then what I say is true, whether I am betting that it is, warning you that it is, guessing or suggesting that it is – or even if I intend to lie and believe myself to be lying. It seems to me that in bringing in the question of 'what act you were performing in what circumstances', he has actually brought in two very *different* questions, and that while the second ('what circumstances?') is indeed sometimes relevant to the question of truth, the first ('what act?') is not. It is only fair to add that at the beginning of his next lecture, Austin himself seems to back away to some extent from his more extreme position. There, in summing up what he had previously said, he says that his contention has been that truth and falsity are 'names for . . . a dimension of assessment – how the words stand in respect of satisfactoriness to the facts, events, situations, etc., to which they refer'.[60] It is noteworthy that that summary *omits*, and in my submission beneficially omits, his earlier references to satisfactoriness 'in these circumstances, to this audience, for these purposes and with these intentions'. Those latter questions of satisfactoriness will usually raise the question whether what the speaker said was the right, or a proper, thing to say, not (usually) the question whether what he said was true; and I believe that Austin's tacit amendment, in his recapitulation, shows that he may really have been aware of that.

However, we have not yet quite done with these matters; the same problems and perplexities recur in one further connection. In his final lecture (we shall return briefly to the rest of this in a moment) Austin distinguishes and invents names for 'five very general classes' of speech-acts, or of verbs for species of illocutionary performance. He does so without much enthusiasm and he is not, he says, equally happy about all of them, but he adds: 'they are, however, quite enough to play Old Harry with two fetishes which I admit to an inclination to play Old Harry with, viz. (1) the true/false fetish, (2) the value/fact fetish'[61] How are we to unravel this decidedly cryptic remark?

As to 'the true/false fetish' I would like to say – without, I hope, too much repetition – three things. First, I believe, and have conceded, that Austin has indeed played a fair amount of Old Harry with that – or has supplied us with ammunition to do so – *if* the fetish is to the effect that, for just any 'statement' or 'proposition' that p, there is always, must be a yes-or-no answer to the question 'Is it true that p?' We remember that years earlier, in 'Truth', he had correctly pointed out, and we have seen that he repeats in these lectures, that in vastly many instances 'what is said' is neither exactly, flatly, incontestably 'right' for the facts of the case in question, nor completely, flatly, unarguably 'wrong'. There may be much to be said for the principle in a logic textbook that 'every proposition must be true or false'; but if we turn that into 'everything said (asserted) in ordinary discourse must be (capable of being definitely and sensibly said to be) true or false', we are in the realm of fantasy. That is surely clear enough.

Second, however, I would repeat that Austin seems persistently to underplay the incidence of cases which do *not* raise troubles of that sort. The English town of Marlborough, for example, is in Wiltshire; that is not 'fair', or 'good enough', or 'roughly true', or 'acceptable', or anything of that sort; it is simply *true*. It is surely not a 'fetish' to believe that we are not *always*, in considering these issues, making some more or less arguable 'appraisal' along some scale or dimension of assessment; very often, black-and-white 'true or false?' *is* quite properly, and often easily, answerable. Austin said, in 'Truth': 'the statements fit the facts always more or less loosely.'[62] *Always*? It is, I think, the intrusion of that 'always' that I really object to.

But probably the most important point, already hinted at, is this: that, however much Old Harry Austin may or may not have played with the true/false distinction, I cannot for my part see that his lists of illocutionary acts (forthcoming in the following pages), or of verbs of illocutionary force, are, as he says, 'quite enough' to put him into a position to do so. Indeed, as I have already said, I cannot see that they are really relevant at all – I mean, of course, to that particular question. Of course, if I have 'said that' p, it *will* be crucially relevant, as we have seen, to the appraisal of *my performance* what I was doing in saying so, and even perhaps to whom and in what circumstances I said it – it may have been a wild guess on my part, a foolish suggestion, a well-founded estimate, a plausible conclusion, an acceptable assessment, a helpful piece of information, and so on. Certainly we shall need to know, among other things, what I was doing, what my illocutionary performance was, if we are to assess that *performance* along some dimension of appraisal, of 'satisfactoriness' *as* a performance. But we usually do *not* need to know all that, in addressing the straight question: is it *true* (as I said) that p? If Marlborough is in Wiltshire, then anyone who performs the locutionary act of saying that Marlborough is in Wiltshire says something true; and having settled that as we easily can, we may if we wish go on to such quite *different* questions as: was he making an intelligent guess? or a confident assertion? or an ill-mannered denial? or an irrelevant objection? and so on. As we have seen, there may sometimes be all sorts of difficulties with the question: is it true or false that p? Those difficulties, however, when and in so far as they arise, are to my eye neither aggravated nor alleviated by raising the quite different question, what one who says that p is or was doing, might do or have been doing, in saying so.

So what about the 'value/fact fetish'? I proceed with diffidence here since, although it is of course clear enough that Austin felt a highly characteristic distaste for this supposed dichotomy, and also believed that his doctrine of illocutionary forces was 'quite enough' to undermine it, I am not clear as to why he believed that; and he does not explain.

It depends, of course, crucially on what one takes the 'fetish' to be. A possible version, which would indeed be highly fetishy and hopelessly vulnerable, would be the idea that in discourse – it would probably be necessary to say, in indicative discourse – we can be seen from time to time to be doing one or other of two sharply opposed things, to be called perhaps 'stating' as opposed to 'judging', or 'describing' as opposed to 'evaluating' or 'prescribing'. Austin would obviously, and rightly, object to this, on at least the following two grounds. First, if we are to consider such illocutionary acts as describing and evaluating, we shall need to consider not just those two or any other pair, but some *very* much larger number: his own short list of what he calls 'verdictives', as these presumably are, has twenty-seven members, and no doubt there are a great many more than that to be considered. And second, in what way is it suggested that these illocutionary acts are dichotomously *opposed*? In Austin's text 'describe' and 'value', 'characterize' and 'grade', for example, all appear on the *same* list of illocutionary verbs; they are *alike* in naming certain kinds of illocutionary performance, and moreover the performances named are *alike* in being all susceptible of appraisal for 'satisfactoriness' or acceptability, and at least to a large extent in just the same terms. Thus there is no question here of a neatly contrasted *pair*; there is in the first place no pair (but a very much larger number), and there is no obvious 'contrast'.

That is surely so. But I think that, curiously enough, we can see in Austin's own text that that would not be the end of the matter – that, when all of that is said and accepted, in a way the 'fetish' still holds the field. 'Describe', 'value', 'characterize', and 'grade', for example, are indeed all alike verbs of illocutionary force, and moreover, he says, are in his view actually verbs of just the same illocutionary kind: they are all what he calls 'verdictives', they are alike in that respect. But what is that class? What, in general, is a verdictive? Austin answers this question twice, in very nearly the same terms, and in a way highly relevant to the point at issue: 'It is essentially giving a finding as to something – fact, or value';[63] 'Verdictives consist in the delivering of a finding, official or unofficial, upon evidence or reasons as to value or fact, so far as these are distinguishable.'[64] And if so, of course, the whole trouble breaks out all over again. How far *are* they distinguishable? What is the distinction? Is it a mere 'fetish' to suppose that there *is* a distinction? Does not Austin himself appear, disconcertingly, to be saying here that, numerous and various though 'verdictive' illocutionary performances may be, they nevertheless *are* in a way divisible into two classes – some giving findings as to fact, others as to value? I am not saying for a moment that Austin seriously meant to maintain any such thing, or would have given it any countenance if the point had been seriously put to him. But I do suggest that, rather as in my submission the doctrine of illocutionary forces did not help in 'playing Old Harry' with the true/false 'fetish', it does not help in administering that treatment to the fact/value 'fetish' either. For it seems to emerge quite clearly that, after we have fully conceded that there are many *different* ways of 'verdicting' upon 'evidence or reasons', an apparent general distinction between findings 'as to fact' and 'as to

142

value' is still there, emerges again quite naturally, neither illuminated nor eliminated, and – in a phrase of Austin's own in another context – 'grinning residually up at us like the frog at the bottom of the beer mug'.[65] If it *is* somehow wrong, and it very probably is, to try to operate with a supposed fact/value antithesis, Austin has not only not told us why it is wrong; he has evidently been at least temporarily content, even if not happy, to operate at this very point with just that antithesis, for his own purposes.

Perhaps we can now see what it is that has been giving us so much trouble. The fact is, I would submit, that worries about 'the true/false fetish' *and* about 'the value/fact fetish', however well justified they may be, are *out of place* at this point in the proceedings, where illocutionary acts and forces are the matter at issue. That is simply not where the worries really arise. And in fact I think it can be seen that they have actually been lurking, or latent, as far back as the paper 'Truth', and could perfectly well and appropriately have been explored, perhaps exploded, in *that* context, in which the doctrine of illocutionary forces was not brought into play at all.

In that earlier paper, we remember, Austin raised the question what it is of which 'true' and 'false' are – centrally, typically, 'at bottom' – predicated; and he gave, unferventtly, the answer 'statements'. It is perfectly clear that, in that context, we were not to understand 'stating', or 'making a statement', as a specific kind of illocutionary act, the specific kind which he later says could be 'put absolutely on a level with arguing, betting, and warning'. There, 'statement' is merely used as a convenient label, if not an altogether happy or ideal one, for 'what is said' when a person says, or could or would or might say, that p; it is a name for the 'content' of a possible locutionary act (to use the later terminology) of the '. . . says that . . .' kind. But if so, the question may at once be raised at that level – and of course Austin actually raises it: given that we are to say that 'statements' are true and false, may we say further that *every* 'statement' must be either one or the other? Presumably a victim of the true/false fetish wishes to answer 'Yes' to that question; and Austin gives at that level, or at any rate mentions, a number of reasons for holding that the correct answer is 'No' – that is, for 'playing Old Harry' with the fetish at least to some extent, without making any reference at all to illocutionary forces or illocutionary acts.[66]

The reasons given are of two interestingly different kinds. Take first the case of 'sayings that', of 'statements', which at least purport, or aspire, to 'correspond to the facts'. The point Austin makes there is that it will sometimes be the case that the question whether they do or do not so correspond will have no definite, or no useful, or perhaps even no possible answer. It may be that the question would have an answer only if some condition were satisfied which actually is not: his car would either be in the garage or not, *if* he had a car. Or it may be that 'what is said' – the 'type' of situation which is said to obtain – neither wholly satisfactorily 'fits' the 'historic' situation in question, nor yet completely fails to. (It is here that in my submission Austin both earlier and later enormously exaggerates: 'the statements fit the facts *always* more or less loosely'. Sometimes indeed, but surely not *always*; but no more of that now.) This is to say that, in Austin's own terms, when a certain 'type' of situation is said to obtain, it will in fact not necessarily, not always be sharply decidable whether the actual 'historic' situation is or is not of that 'type'; and if so, 'true or false?' will not always have an answer.

The second kind of reason is quite different. It is that some 'sayings that', some 'statements', do not really purport or aspire or profess to 'correspond to the facts' at all; it is, as Austin puts it, not their 'business' to do so.[67] Earlier we considered mainly the case of 'necessary' statements, sayings, roughly, of the nature of 'formulae in a calculus'; these do not represent any 'historic situation' as being a certain 'type', and therefore also, Austin holds, are not properly classifiable as either true of false. But now let us bring in 'the fact/value fetish'. *Another* kind of 'statement' which, Austin says in 'Truth', is not really a statement, or at any rate could plausibly be held to be not really a statement, is a 'value-judgment'. Now such a judgment – as, for example, that Stiggins's last novel was atrociously bad – presumably is, in a way, 'about' a historic state of affairs, namely the quality of Stiggins's last novel; so, if we are to say that the judgment nevertheless is neither true nor false, the contention must be, I suppose, in Austin's terms that an atrociously bad novel is not a 'type' of novel; to say of a novel that it is atrociously bad is not to assign it to a descriptive 'type'. But if so, it is at *this* point that the 'fetish', if it is so pejorative a thing, comes into play and calls urgently for examination. If there are some non-necessary 'statements' which, in spite of being incontestably 'sayings that', are to be held not 'really' to be statements, not true or false – which do not, in spite of grammatical appearances, represent a situation as being of a certain 'type' and so are non-starters in the matter of correspondence to the facts – we need to be told what they are and how they are to be recognized. And the question that urgently arises is: what is a 'type'?[68] If a cricketer is a type of sportsman, and a first-class cricketer is (perhaps) a type of cricketer, is a very *good* cricketer a type of cricketer? If not, why not? Is a wicked deed a 'type' of deed? Again, if not, why not? There is plenty of reason to suppose that 'fact/value' is an untenable fetish, *if* it is the belief that in natural languages there is a clear dividing line to be drawn between fact-stating, non-evaluative, true-or-false, 'type'-assigning sayings-that on the one hand, and non-factual, evaluative, neither-true-nor-false, *not*-'type'-assigning sayings-that on the other: it looks extremely unlikely that any such line could be drawn, and completely unclear how or where it could be. By my point is not that there is a serious defence to be made for the fetish, but that the question of its credentials is not just bogus, and above all that it arises *at this level.* If there are these sayings-that which, despite grammatical appearances, are not to be appraised as corresponding or not corresponding to 'the facts', it must be something about 'what is said', about the *locutions*, about the words as used in saying-that and their relation to 'the facts', which makes that the case. If we are to excoriate the fetish, we must excoriate it here. I do not particularly reproach Austin for not pursuing this matter in his paper 'Truth' (where he barely mentions it); one is not obliged to pursue every hare that could be pursued; my point is only that he *could* have pursued it there, that it arose at that point and at that level, and that, when he mentions the topic again in close juxtaposition to his examination and catalogue of illocutionary forces, it is, so to speak, in the wrong place. The taxonomy of illocutionary acts throws no light on the matter. At any rate, I have been unable to see that it does.

Austin ends his lecture with an attempt to make lists of, and to distinguish into different species, the illocutionary forces that our utterances may have. I shall not say much about this, as indeed he does not; it is a matter, as he says, of 'prolonged fieldwork' (for example in the pages of dictionaries) and he offers here only examples of what might be done, amounting, as he himself puts it, to 'a run around, or rather a flounder around'.[69]

What, then, in looking through the dictionary (if that is how we go about it – 'a concise one should do'), are we looking for? How are we to identify those verbs that name specific illocutionary acts? Austin seems to have in mind two tests; and one thing that I think should be noted is that these do not quite always give the same result. One test is this: using (with due caution) the notion of 'In saying . . .', we look for the verbs that fit into the Y-place in the schema 'In saying X, I was Y-ing': 'In saying he ought to resign, I was giving him my advice', 'In saying it was unfair, I was protesting', and so on. Here we take it that the Y-verb names the illocutionary act performed 'in saying' what I said, and thus specifies the illocutionary force of my utterance. The other test (also to be used with caution) is that of 'the first-person singular present indicative active form', the form of the explicit performative; if to say 'I Y' is explicity to Y, then Y is the right sort of verb: to say 'I protest' is to protest, 'I promise' to promise, 'I warn' to warn, and so on. But these two tests, clearly enough, will come to the same thing only if it is in general true that the (or even a) way of explicitly Y-ing is to say 'I Y'; and we have already seen reason, I believe, for qualifying that a little. In cases, notably, where the act Y in question really is a 'conventional' act, it simply may or may not be the case that the (or a) way of Y-ing is to say 'I Y'; thus, in legal proceedings, while 'In saying "Not guilty", I was acquitting the accused person' is in order, to say 'I acquit the accused person' is not: that is just not the thing to say in formally bringing in a verdict of acquittal. Perhaps, however, that does not really matter very much; for acquitting is not always a formal, conventional affair, and where it is not the two tests seem to yield the same answer: 'In saying he meant no harm, I was acquitting him of meaning any harm', and 'I acquit him of meaning any harm'. Similarly, while I do not (cannot?) appeal *in cricket* by saying 'I appeal', I can of course non-conventionally appeal to the experts by saying 'I appeal to the experts'. So, in general, 'acquit' and 'appeal' do come out, by either test, as verbs of illocutionary force.

It is a more serious matter that in compiling his lists Austin has clearly misled himself in a few cases by relying injudiciously on 'the first-person singular present indicative active form'. In the list of what he calls 'commissives', for example, we find the verbs 'am determined to', 'mean to', 'intend', 'plan', and (most oddly) 'shall';[70] but whereas of course these all occur in the 'I mean to . . .', 'I intend . . .', 'I plan . . .' construction, it is obviously not the case that to say 'I mean to . . .' or 'I intend . . .' or 'I plan . . .' *is* to mean to or intend or plan. To mean to, or intend, or plan, in fact, is not essentially to *say* anything at all, so that these verbs clearly cannot be names of illocutionary acts. And there is certainly no such illocutionary act as 'shalling'. Again, we find in the list of 'expositives' the verbs 'doubt', 'know', and 'believe';[71] and although Austin indicates with question-marks his own suspicion that these may be interlopers, he surely should have deleted them altogether; for doubting, knowing, and believing are of course not speech-acts of any sort at all. Whatever it may be to *say* 'I doubt', 'I know', 'I believe', it certainly is not to doubt, or to know, or to believe; and to doubt, or to know, or to believe is, again, not necessarily to *say* anything at all. This is simply to say, as of course Austin very well knew, that the construction in question very often is *not* of the explicit performative variety, in which case, from the fact that a verb occurs in that construction, we cannot straight off infer that it is a verb of illocutionary force.

Let us look back, then, over the way the argument has gone. It would be fair to say – well, it would clearly be correct to say – that the way the enterprise begins is as an attempt to distinguish and contrast 'the performative' and 'the constative'. This goes rather badly (though with tremendous fun on the way) – not exactly because there is (as it turns out) no clear and tenable distinction to be drawn, but principally because, as I put it at an earlier stage (p. 117), it is never really clear just what is to be distinguished from what. *One* notion which appears in the early

146

stages is that of utterances which are 'performative' in the sense that they play an operative role in the carrying through of conventional, ritual, ceremonial procedures, such as 'Snap!' in playing snap, or 'I pronounce that they be man and wife together' in the marriage service, or 'How's that?' in playing cricket. This is actually, I believe, a perfectly viable and useful notion; there are all sorts of drills, rituals, ceremonies, conventional procedures to be used in doing this or that – notably in games and in the law, but in many other cases too – and there is indeed a distinguishable class of prescribed utterances which have their operative, effective place in such drills (etc.). But the distinction of *this* class of utterances from others is 'abandoned' by Austin – is never taken really seriously – partly because he seems at times to have embraced the mistaken idea that somehow *all* utterance is *in this sense* conventional, but more importantly, I think, because this (in fact) quite properly distinguishable class would not include quite a lot of the cases he wanted to deal with (and *would* include, come to that, a lot of cases in which he was not much interested). He wanted to bring in, for one thing, utterances in which a speaker does something when (in fact) there is no conventional procedure involved – such as 'Shut the door' said just ordinarily in giving an instruction or making a request; and he wanted to bring in, for another thing, utterances such as 'I advise you to resign', which have the special feature that they may look like assertions by the speaker about himself but are really something else, in this case the giving of advice. But on what basis are *these* to be distinguished from 'the constative'? We do not want the distinction to collapse into a dull bit of grammar about indicative and non-indicative sentences; and if we say that the distinguishing mark of 'the performative' is to be that it is either in, or could in principle readily be put into, the *explicit* performative form, we find (to our embarrassment?) that one who makes a statement could in principle always do so in the form 'I state that . . .', 'I assert that . . .', or something of that sort.

What gradually emerges, I think, in those early chapters is that what Austin is really in pursuit of is not what it was at first presented as being, a distinguishable *special case*. In his first lecture he embarks on what he there calls 'preliminary *isolation* of the performative'; the evident, if only provisional, suggestion at that stage is that there is a special sub-class of utterances – 'the type of utterances we are to consider'[72] – which is to be distinguished from, 'isolated' within, contrasted with, others. What then actually happens is not exactly that this project of 'isolation' 'breaks down', cannot be made to work, but rather that we are gradually drawn to the conclusion that even its success would not be particularly interesting. One *could* 'isolate' performatives in at least two (quite different) ways – first, pick out, and rope off as a 'special case', those utterances which have a conventional, 'operative' role to play in the carrying through of drills, rituals, ceremonies, conventional procedures; or second, pick out, and rope off as a special case, those utterances which distinctively make explicit something that the speaker does in issuing them – in which, namely, the *word for* what he does puts in an overt and characteristic appearance in the sentence he utters. It is not that those recipes for 'picking out' do not work: they pick out, indeed, quite different things, but each, in its own way, works perfectly well as a way of roping off a certain 'type' of utterance from others, and either type we could call 'the performative' if we chose to do so. The trouble is that neither – however clear the class that it picks out – will succeed in picking out the case that Austin is really after: the general case in which a speaker, in *saying* something, *does* something. For of course there are cases in which the speaker's utterance is 'a deed' – ordinary imperatives, for example – which are neither cases of utterance in any ritual, conventional procedure or drill, nor cases of utterance in the explicit performative form. But then we may ask: what *would* pick out the right special case? And now it seems clear that the answer must be: nothing would. For what Austin is really after is not a special case at all; the case of a speaker who, in saying something, does something, is simply that of any speaker at all, on any occasion. It is not so much that, in the early stages, he *fails* in the project of 'isolating' the performative, but rather that his thinking and his strategy move away from the whole idea of trying to do that. It is not a 'type of utterance' in which he is really interested at all – a type which he *could* have distinguished, if he had wanted to, in various ways; he is interested in a certain feature of *every* utterance – the feature that, in saying, something is *done*.

As I mentioned right at the beginning, it is not perfectly clear to me how fully Austin himself grasped what had really happened, or even how far he was interested in that question. Where he decides that it is necessary to 'make a fresh start on the problem', he does rather give the impression that he felt his earlier efforts had somehow failed, and that it is one and the same 'problem' on which a fresh start is to be made. To my eye that is not really the position. The position is that the question 'How are we to distinguish the performative utterance from others?' is thereafter just *abandoned*, and *replaced* by the quite different question: in what senses and ways is every (normal) utterance performative?

The solid, central core of Austin's contribution here is his identification and taxonomy of the levels and types of 'speech-acts' performed by any speaker in normal circumstances. Obviously he does not say the last word on that, nor would he have dreamed of making any such extravagant claim; but at least he got the topic started on very much the right lines. One or two questions arise about the technical terminology he introduces here, and I had better mention some of them, though none, I think, raises issues of very much substance. One is that, so far at least as I have been able to make out, we are provided with more technical terms that we really need. We have the 'phonetic' act, the act of uttering certain noises; we have the 'phatic' act, the 'act of uttering certain vocables or words, i.e. noises of certain types belonging to *and as* belonging to a certain vocabulary, in a certain construction, i.e. conforming to and as conforming to a certain grammar'; and we have the 'rhetic' act, the act of using the sentence 'or its constituents' with a certain (more or less) definite sense and reference. Austin goes on to say that 'the act of "saying something" in this full normal sense I call, i.e. dub, the performance of a locutionary act'.[73] My question is: has he not already called it a *rhetic* act? Austin cites as the specification of a locutionary act 'He said to me "Shoot her!" meaning by "shoot" shoot and referring by "her" to *her*.'[74] But is that not exactly to specify the rhetic act he performed, in performing the phatic act of saying 'Shoot her'? It specifies both sense and reference, which is the business of the 'rheme'. It looks to me as if 'locutionary act' is a Latin-based, and 'rhetic act' a Greek-based, name for exactly the same thing. But that redundancy, if that is what it is, is presumably not harmful (except perhaps in so far as it may mislead readers into cudgelling their brains unnecessarily in search of a distinction); and it is not inexplicable. If we start with the Greek term 'phonetic', and go on to 'phatic', it is natural to round off, so to speak, that particular triad with another Greek-based label, 'rhetic'. If we work backwards from the Latinate 'perlocutionary act' to the Latinate 'illocutionary act', it is natural to fill out *that* triad with an appropriate Latin-based label, 'locutionary'. Austin may just not have noticed – certainly he nowhere says explicitly – what I take to be the case, that in fact we have a sort of overlap here, with one Greek and one Latin label for just the same thing – the Greek label looking backwards, so to speak, to 'phatic' and 'phonetic', and the Latin label forwards, to 'illocution' and 'perlocution'.

It has been made a complaint against Austin's taxonomy that locutionary and illocutionary acts are not always *different* – as, it is implied, Austin must have wanted to hold that they always are. I think that in this case, while the point made is correct, there is no good reason to suppose that Austin did not accept it. There is one clear case anyway, and one perhaps debatable one. The clear case, of course, is that of the explicit performative. It is the special feature – in a way the whole point – of this case that the illocutionary 'force' of the utterance is made fully explicit in what the speaker says - that is, is overtly taken into his actual locution. If so, his illocutionary act is fully determined, as it were, by his locutionary act – the force of his utterance is in this case not 'detachable' from its meaning, as a separate question. That is so; but is there any reason why Austin should have wished to deny it? He wished to 'distinguish force and meaning' on the basis that these are often, even standardly, separable and different: to establish 'what was meant' by what a speaker said is usually *not* to establish what he meant it *as*, how it was to be 'taken'; he said that inflation was likely to rise, but was he objecting to my argument or supporting it? To say that force and meaning are in general different is not to deny that – sometimes – the one may include the other.

The perhaps more arguable issue is this. I said earlier that, as Austin sets the matter out, there appear to be (at least) three different 'kinds' of locutionary act, namely 'say that', 'tell to', and 'ask'. But what is it that distinguishes each 'kind' from the others? Is it not its (very general, unspecific) illocutionary force? In saying 'They've arrived' he said that they had arrived; and so on. But if so, it seems that we shall have to say not only that a speaker's locutionary act may *sometimes* by itself determine his illocutionary act, but that to a certain rather minimal extent it *always* does: we can always say, given the locutionary act alone, at least that the speaker 'said that . . .', or 'told to . . .', or 'asked . . .'; and if so, the locutionary act will never be *completely* detachable from issues of illocutionary force, every locutionary act must already (so to speak) be of some very broadly identifiable illocutionary kind. I am not sure how Austin would have reacted to this point – which he never, I think, quite explicitly put to himself. He might have said: 'Yes – why not?' Given his main point – that the locutionary act of issuing an utterance rather seldom *completely* determines its illocutionary force – may we not just concede that it always does so in some very general, minimal, basic, uninformative way? We know that, in saying 'p', he said that p; but perhaps that is neither informative nor alarming. Alternatively, if he had really wished to hold that the locutionary act often, even typically, leaves *completely* unanswered *any* questions about illocutionary force, he would have to maintain, I suppose, that 'say that', 'tell to', and 'ask' are not (even very broad and general) names of illocutionary performances. But I do not see how one could make that line look very persuasive. My feeling is that it would be better simply to concede that while the locutionary act of saying 'p' is 'detachable', so to speak, from the illocutionary act of, for example, objecting that p or admitting that p or even stating that p, it is *not* detachable from the highly unspecific illocutionary act of 'saying' that p. That does not look to me like a *damaging* concession – if, indeed, for Austin it would really constitute a concession at all.

One final comment, which in a way is very obvious but which nevertheless deserves, I think, to be explicitly made: if one were asked to assign Austin's book to its appropriate department, field, or branch of philosophy, one would have to place it, no doubt, on the shelf marked 'philosophy of language'. I do not say that there would be anything wrong with that. But it is the case nevertheless, and ought to be quite explicitly noted, that about *language* it has almost nothing at all to say. Austin is interested, to use his own phrase, in 'the total speech-act in the total speech-situation'; but he simply takes it for granted that, as a basic resource for his performance of speech-acts, a speaker has a language at his command, a vocabulary and a grammar, enabling him to produce sentences which express 'what he means' and which will (he hopes) be appropriately understood by his audience. His emphasis – and this is of course *the* novelty of his contribution – is on the point that there is a very great deal *more* to 'the use' of language than (just) saying something which has a certain meaning; but the question what it is to do even that much – what it is for certain sounds or marks to 'mean', in a language, this or that, or indeed for them to 'mean' anything at all – is not a question that he even raises. Of course he would not have denied that there are such questions; the fact is, I suppose, simply that they were not questions which he wished to take up for his particular purposes. He was willing simply to assume that we have 'got' a language, with a view to getting on to the question: what do we *do* with it? No doubt it is true that the question had been much neglected, and it was an important service to philosophy to put it firmly into play – where it firmly remains.

Bibliographical Note

As was mentioned in the Introduction, only seven of Austin's papers were published in his own lifetime. After his death these were collected, with three others, in the first edition of his *Philosophical Papers* (Oxford, Clarendon Press, 1961). Two further papers, the manuscripts of which required more than minor editorial work, were added in the second edition (1970). And one additional paper, reconstructed by J. O. Urmson from notes, was included in the third edition (1979).

Sense and Sensibilia, a text constructed by me from Austin's lecture notes, was published in 1962 (Oxford, Clarendon Press).

How to Do Things with Words, edited by J. O. Urmson, was published in 1962 (also by the Clarendon Press). A second edition, revised and supplemented by J. O. Urmson and Marina Sbisa, was published in 1975; and for a new impression of that edition in 1980 a new index was added, compiled by P. H. Nidditch.

There are translations of Austin's works into French, Spanish, Italian, and German.

A most useful collection of twenty-six papers about Austin and his philosophy was put together by K. T. Fann under the title *Symposium on J. L. Austin* in 1969 (London, Routledge & Kegan Paul). That book includes an admirably full bibliography up to that date. *Essays on J. L. Austin* (Oxford, Clarendon Press, 1973), by Sir Isaiah Berlin and others, is a collection of eight papers by seven authors, six of whom were fortunate enough to have known Austin personally and to have seen and heard him at work.

Of many books more or less relevant to Austin's major concerns, I shall mention five: G. W. Pitcher (ed.) *Truth* (Englewood Cliffs, NJ, Prentice Hall, 1964); J. R. Searle, *Speech Acts* (Cambridge, Cambridge University Press, 1969); S. R. Schiffer, *Meaning* (Oxford, Clarendon Press, 1972); C. Travis, *Saying and Understanding* (Oxford, Blackwell, 1975); D. Holdcroft, *Words and Deeds* (Oxford, Clarendon Press, 1978).

Notes

In the notes that follow page references to Austin's writings are to the following editions:

Sense and Sensibilia (Oxford, Clarendon Press, 1962), cited as *S and S*;

Philosophical Papers (Oxford, Oxford University Press, 1979, 3rd edn), cited as *Papers*;

How to Do Things with Words (Oxford, Clarendon Press, Oxford, 1975, 2nd edn), cited as *HDTW*.

I shall also have occasion to refer quite often to *Symposium on J. L. Austin*, edited by K. T. Fann (London, Routledge & Kegan Paul, 1969). I shall refer to this as 'Fann'.

I   Introduction

1   Oxford, Clarendon Press, 1949.
2   G. Frege, *The Foundations of Arithmetic* (Oxford, Blackwell, 1950).
3   I have written more fully about Austin's life and personality in an obituary article for the British Academy (*Proceedings*, 1963) which is reprinted in Fann, pp. 3–21. See also papers by Sir Isaiah Berlin and G. W. Pitcher in *Essays on J. L. Austin* (Oxford, Clarendon Press, 1973); and by Sir Stuart Hampshire in Fann, pp. 33–46.
4   Gilbert Ryle, 'Systematically misleading expressions', *Proceedings of the Aristotelian Society*, 1932; also in Gilbert Ryle, *Collected Papers* 2 (London, Hutchinson, 1971).
5   Quoted from my *English Philosophy since 1900* (Oxford, Oxford University Press, 1969, 2nd edn).
6   *Papers*, p. 232.
7   *Papers*, p. 181.
8   *Papers*, pp. 181–2.
9   *Papers*, p. 185.
10 *Papers*, p. 183.
11 *Papers*, p. 188.
12 Reported by J. O. Urmson in Fann, p. 25.
13 *Papers*, p. 271.
14 *Papers*, p. 183.

15 *Papers*, p. 183.
16 *Papers*, p. 205.
17 I have discussed this rather more fully in my paper 'Saturday mornings', in *Essays on J. L. Austin*, pp. 31–45.
18 *Papers*, p. 175.

II Perception and Other Matters

1 A. J. Ayer, *The Foundations of Empirical Knowledge* (London, Macmillan, 1940).
2 Ayer, not surprisingly, was somewhat wounded when *Sense and Sensibilia* appeared; it treated his own book, he later said, 'in a rather scornful way'. It is possible that this is chiefly my fault, and I think Ayer believes that it is; at any rate he has expressed the view that Austin would surely not himself have published the 'harsh version' which I issued after Austin's death. It is indeed possible that, as I have mentioned, Austin might never have chosen to publish his text at all, and also that, if he had ever got round to publishing it, he might for all I know have felt it decent and proper to soften some of its sharper polemical edges. But it would clearly have been a dubious business for me to presume to do that for him; and I certainly did not put into the text any 'scorn' or scratches that were not in Austin's notes and in the lectures he based on them. My feeling is that Ayer may perhaps underestimate the degree to which Austin was genuinely shocked by what appeared to his eye to be recklessness, hurry, unrealism, and inadequate attention to truth. It has been noted by others (e.g. by Stanley Cavell in Fann, pp. 70–1) that an air of almost moral outrage is discernible in some of his comments on what philosophers get up to.
3 For example by Jonathan Bennett, in Fann, pp. 267–83.
4 Fann, p. 56.
5 Ayer, *Foundations*, p. 14.
6 Ayer, *Foundations*, p. 18.
7 See particularly Ayer, *Foundations*, pp. 243 ff.
8 Ayer, *Foundations*, p. 20. Remember that 'empirical facts' here means 'facts about phenomena'.
9 Ayer, *Foundations*, p. 21.
10 Ayer, *Foundations*, p. 24.
11 *S and S*, p. 96, n.l.
12 Fann, p. 297. Ayer's article is reprinted there from *Synthese* (1967).
13 In *S and S* Austin refers occasionally to H. H. Price's *Perception* (London, Methuen, 1932).
14 *Berkeley* (Pelican Books, 1953; revised edition, Oxford, Blackwell, 1982).
15 *S and S*, p. 130.
16 *S and S*, p. 124.
17 Fann, pp. 285 ff.
18 *S and S*, p. 5.
19 *Papers*, p. 116.
20 *S and S*, p. 46, n.2.
21 H. H. Price, *Perception* (London, Methuen, 1932), p. 66.
22 See, for instance, H. P. Grice, 'The causal theory of perception', in *Aristotelian Society Supplement* 35 (1961).

III   Knowledge and Other Minds

1   *Papers*, p. 32.
2   *Papers*, p. 76.
3   *Papers*, p. 82.
4   *Papers*, p. 84.
5   *Papers*, p. 98.
6   John Wisdom, 'Other minds VII', *Mind* 52 (n.s. 207).
7   *Papers*, p. 90.
8   *Papers*, p. 92.
9   *Papers*, p. 95.
10 See *HDTW*, p. vi.
11 *Papers*, p. 98.
12 *Papers*, p. 99.
13 *Papers*, p. 100.
14 *Papers*, p. 101.
15 *Papers*, p. 103.
16 *Papers*, p. 103.
17 *Papers*, p. 98.
18 *Papers*, p. 99.
19 *Papers*, p. 80, n.l.
20 *Papers*, p. 103.
21 *Papers*, p. 103.
22 *Papers*, p. 104.
23 *Papers*, p. 105.
24 Cp. *S and S*, p. 115.
25 *Papers*, p. 109.
26 *Papers*, p. 110.
27 *Papers*, p. 113.
28 *Papers*, p. 113.
29 *Papers*, p. 115.
30 *Papers*, p. 115.

IV   Truth

1   *Papers*, p. 133.
2   P. F. Strawson, 'Truth', *Proceedings of the Aristotelian Society* supp. vol. XXIV (1950): reprinted – as is Austin's paper also – in G. W. Pitcher (ed.) *Truth* (Englewood Cliffs, NJ, Prentice Hall, 1964).
3   *Papers*, pp. 154–74.
4   *Papers*, p. 122.
5   *Papers*, p. 121.
6   R. M. Chisholm mentioned the same idea in his review (in *Mind* (1963)) of *Philosophical Papers*: 'in proposing his definition, Austin must have been thinking of the simplified world and language which he was to envisage in "How to talk".' But Chisholm does not expand that hint, nor am I sure how he would have done so. He judges 'Truth', in that review, to be 'one of the least satisfactory of Austin's papers', but 'How to talk' to be 'of very first importance to philosophy'. I have not been able to make out what his grounds were for the latter very striking assessment, and it is certain, for what it is worth, that Austin did not share it.
7   *Papers*, p. 137.

8 *Papers*, p. 135.

9 *Papers*, p. 140.

10 *Papers*, p. 141.

11 That the term 'statement' tends to suggest, for present purposes undesirably, something that has been actually stated is no doubt partly why many philosophers prefer the term of art 'proposition'. But Austin notes, correctly, that there is another philosophical use of 'proposition' to mean 'what a sentence means'; and 'we never say "The meaning (or sense) of this sentence (or of these words) is true".' He finds 'statement' *less* objectionable than 'proposition'.

12 *Papers*, pp. 121–2. An important question is lurking here which Austin does not discuss: what is a *type*? This was unproblematic in the imaginary world of S₀, where being 'of a type' could be stipulated to mean simply, for example, 'having a certain geometrical shape' or 'being of a certain shade of colour'. But in a natural language, of course, it is not really clear at all what strings of words can be taken to 'describe' a 'type' of 'situation, thing, event, etc.' We shall have to go a little further into this later (in Chapter VIII). Let us note for the present that, while Austin evidently takes the notion of 'type' to be intelligible enough for his present purposes, he certainly envisages that *some* ordinary indicative sentences do *not* 'describe types' of situation, etc., so that 'statements' employing them do not even aspire to 'correspond to the facts' and are not (had better not be called) either true or false. But how such 'masqueraders', as he later calls them, are to be identified as such remains rather conspicuously under-explained.

13 Remember, however, the lurking problems about 'type'.

14 This must be right, surely, whatever we make of 'type' itself.

15 Is 'Sheep are unintelligent' affirmative or negative?

16 It is, however, a matter of some controversy how important the point is. I shall suggest in due course (pp. 138–9) that Austin is inclined to make more of it than it deserves.

17 I have to note once again that, while this must surely be true, we are somewhat at sea until told rather more about 'types'.

18 I return to this issue at rather greater length discussing the later stages of *How to Do Things with Words* (pp. 138–41).

19 *Papers*, p. 130.

20 *Papers*, p. 123, n. 4.

21 *Papers*, p. 131. He also says here 'When it is a value-judgment'. I return to that topic also in my final chapter.

22 *Papers*, p. 131.

23 It is fair to say here that while Austin himself was clearly sympathetic to some such idea as this, he does not say anything that would clarify or explain it. Among the 'troubles' that arise, as he says, from use of the expression 'fact', it is notable that he does not mention the 'trouble' that it is actually pretty unclear what is, and what is not, a statement 'of fact'. I return to this also at a later stage (pp. 144–5).

24 It is remarkable that Austin never did, either here or elsewhere, go at length into the question what 'meaning' means – though he certainly did not suppose the answer to be obvious and ready to hand. He held no 'theory' of meaning.

25 Strawson in Pitcher (ed.) *Truth*, p. 44.

26 Strawson in Pitcher (ed.) *Truth*, p. 43.

27 Strawson in Pitcher (ed.) *Truth*, p. 42.

28 Strawson in Pitcher (ed.) *Truth*, p. 53.
29 *Mind* (1950); also in P. F. Strawson, *Logico-Linguistic Papers* (London, Methuen, 1970), pp. 1–27.
30 Strawson 'A Problem about truth – a reply to Mr. Warnock', in Pitcher (ed.) *Truth*, p. 84.

V Excuses and Accusations

1 *Papers*, pp. 272–87.
2 *Papers*, p. 175.
3 *Papers*, p. 177.
4 *Papers*, p. 178.
5 *Papers*, p. 179.
6 *Papers*, pp. 175–6.
7 *Papers*, p. 176.
8 *Papers*, p. 178.
9 *Papers*, p. 180.
10 *Papers*, p. 271.
11 *Papers*, p. 180.
12 *Papers*, p. 190. This topic has been vigorously, and adversarially, debated by J. R. Searle ('Assertions and aberrations', Fann, pp. 205–18) and A. R. White ('Mentioning the unmentionable', Fann, pp. 219–25). Both, I think, are partly right and partly wrong.
13 *Papers*, p. 190.
14 *Papers*, p. 190.
15 *Papers*, p. 177.
16 *Papers*, p. 275.
17 *Papers*, p. 274–5.
18 *Papers*, p. 196.
19 See particularly, on this, the elegant and economical footnote 1, at *Papers*, p. 185.
20 *Papers*, p. 283.
21 *Papers*, p. 179.
22 *Papers*, p. 194.

VI Ifs and Cans

1 This is, of course, because of the supposition that a person merits credit or discredit for some action of his only if he 'could have acted othewise' – that he rates neither one nor the other for an action which he could not *not* have done. This is actually not quite such plain sailing as it is often taken for. What about, say, the resistance hero who is highly commended for withstanding extreme pressures to betray his friends? May he not say 'I couldn't have done anything else' without thereby ceasing to be commendable? (Cp. Luther's 'I can no other'.) In such a case there seems to be a sense in which he can truly say that he could not have acted otherwise, *and* a sense in which, of course, he could have – he could have betrayed his friends, as a lesser man might very probably have done. Perhaps we need to distinguish: (a) whether any other course of action was actually available to him, and (b) whether some other course, which was available, was one that *he* could have taken. But in any case, acceptance of 'He could not have done

otherwise' does not necessarily, always and in every sense, lead to the conclusion that his acting as he did was not creditable to him; that he could not have done otherwise *may* be exactly what we admire him for.

2   Oxford, Oxford University Press, 1912.

3   *Papers*, p. 208.

4   *Papers*, p. 209. This topic is thoroughly and most acutely discussed in D. F. Pears, 'Ifs and cans', *Essays on J. L. Austin* (Oxford, Clarendon Press, 1973), pp. 90–140.

5   *Papers*, p. 211.

6   *Papers*, p. 215.

7   *Papers*, p. 212.

8   *Papers*, pp. 214–15.

9   *Papers*, p. 218.

10 *Papers*, p. 218, n.l.

11 P. H. Nowell-Smith, *Ethics* (Harmondsworth, Pelican Books, 1954), p. 274.

12 Nowell-Smith *Ethics*, pp. 275–6.

13 It is only fair to note here that Nowell-Smith himself concedes that his reading *Persuasion* is 'relevant' to the question whether he could have read *Emma*, and is even 'almost conclusive evidence' that he could have. But why 'almost'?

14 *Papers*, p. 223.

15 Nowell-Smith, *Ethics*, p. 278.

16 *Papers*, p. 227.

17 *Papers*, p. 229, n.l.

18 An alternative line sometimes taken for the same reason – namely, that cases greatly differ – is simply to say that 'can' has 'different senses'. Or is that just another way of saying the same thing?

19 That is, Moore and Nowell-Smith.

20 *Papers*, p. 231.

VII   Some Other Papers

1   *Papers*, pp. 288–303.

2   *Papers*, pp. 1–31.

3   H. A. Prichard in *Philosophy* X: also in H. A. Prichard, *Moral Obligation* (Oxford, Clarendon Press, 1949), pp. 40–53.

4   It is not quite true that, elsewhere, he regularly abstained from the use of this notion. For example, in 'Ifs and cans' he distinguished, as we have seen, 'the view that an *if* is required to *complete* a can-sentence' from 'the view that an *if* is required in the *analysis* of a can-sentence'. But he appears to have been neither very fond of the notion of 'analysis' nor particularly alarmed by it. An analysis in his usage, when he uses the expression at all, appears simply to be a clarificatory statement of what some sentence or expression means. There is no hint of the elaborate metaphysical-ontological baggage that went along, at the time, with some theories of what 'philosophical' analysis was.

5   *Papers*, p. 14.

6   *Papers*, p. 13.

7   *Papers*, p. 15.

8   For critical discussion of this literature, see J. O. Urmson, *Philosophical Analysis* (Oxford, Clarendon Press, 1956).

9 *Papers*, p. 14.
10 Prichard, *Philosophy*, p. 33.
11 *Papers*, p. 22.
12 *Papers*, p. 22.
13 R. M. Hare has called particular attention to this, in the Appendix, pp. 115–16, to his collection *Practical Inferences* (London, Macmillan, 1971).
14 *Papers*, pp. 55–75.
15 *Papers*, p. 57.
16 *Papers*, p. 63. The sentence is italicized for emphasis in Austin's text.
17 *Papers*, p. 75.
18 *Papers*, pp. 253–71.
19 'Clarity is not enough' was the title of a discussion, by H. H. Price and others, in *Aristotelian Society Supplement* 19 (1945).
20 *Papers*, p. 189.

VIII Words and Deeds

1 *HDTW*, p. 91.
2 *HDTW*, p. 4, n.1.
3 *HDTW*, p. 3. We remember that this idea surfaced briefly in his paper 'Truth' (*Papers*).
4 The verb 'constate' is not Austin's own invention; it is classified in dictionaries as 'rare'. I think he chose it for use as a sort of technical term – 'constative' to be contrasted with 'performative' – with the advantage of leaving 'state' free for more down-to-earth employment.
5 *HDTW*, p. 6. I have argued, in *Essays on J. L. Austin* (Oxford, Clarendon Press, 1973), pp. 80 ff., that Austin's assertion here is *not* all that 'obvious', but it would be a distraction to pursue that particular issue here. It is interesting that H. A. Prichard (*Moral Obligation* (Oxford, Clarendon Press, 1979), p. 171) writes:

> While everyone would allow that a promise may be either in good or in bad faith, no one would allow that it could be either true or false. Rather, they would insist that promising resembles asking a question or issuing an order, in that it consists not in making a statement but in doing something, in the sense in which we oppose doing to mere talking.

6 *HDTW*, p. 5, n.1.
7 *HDTW*, p. 33.
8 *HDTW*, p. 16.
9 *HDTW*, p. 14.
10 *HDTW*, p. 14.
11 *HDTW*, p. 27. See also 'Performative utterances', in *Papers*, p. 238.
12 *HDTW*, p. 47.
13 *HDTW*, p. 48.
14 *HDTW*, p. 51.
15 'The total speech-act in the total speech-situation is the *only actual* phenomenon which, in the last resort, we are engaged in elucidating' (*HDTW*, p. 148).
16 *HDTW*, p. 54.
17 *HDTW*, p. 55.
18 *HDTW*, p. 58.
19 *HDTW*, pp. 61–2.

20 *HDTW*, p. 91.
21 *HDTW*, p. 59.
22 *HDTW*, p. 94.
23 *HDTW*, p. 92.
24 *HDTW*, p. 97.
25 *HDTW*, p. 93.
26 *HDTW*, p. 97.
27 *HDTW*, p. 94.
28 Perhaps we have here an instance of Austin's rather curious lack of much interest in the notion of *meaning*, which I have remarked on elsewhere.
29 *HDTW*, p. 94.
30 See the examples set out on p. 95 of *HDTW*.
31 A line taken by, for example, S. R. Schiffer in his *Meaning* (Oxford, Oxford University Press, 1972).
32 Several of the Ten Commandments are in the future tense, as also are most written orders, in military usage.
33 *HDTW*, p. 101.
34 *HDTW*, p. 98.
35 *HDTW*, pp. 131–2.
36 *HDTW*, p. 100.
37 *HDTW*, p. 117.
38 *HDTW*, p. 121.
39 *HDTW*, p. 119.
40 *HDTW*, p. 103.
41 *HDTW*, p. 105.
42 *HDTW*, p. 109.
43 *HDTW*, p. 121.
44 *HDTW*, p. 122.
45 *HDTW*, p. 98.
46 *HDTW*, p. 31; 'Performative utterances', *Papers*, p. 245.
47 *HDTW*, p. 134.
48 *HDTW*, p. 140.
49 *HDTW*, p. 141.
50 *HDTW*, p. 141.
51 We remember that Austin himself made this 'suggestion', in 'Truth', *Papers*, p. 131.
52 There is also the case, for example, in which a declaration - 'Here is your new leader' – while not explicitly performative, 'makes' him our new leader, rather than simply saying that he is.
53 *HDTW*, p. 55.
54 *HDTW*, pp. 145–6.
55 *HDTW*, p. 146.
56 *HDTW*, p. 145.
57 *HDTW*, p. 145.
58 We remember that, in 'Truth', *Papers*, p. 130, he had remarked that it is 'jejune to suppose that all a statement aims to be is true.'
59 *HDTW*, p. 146.
60 *HDTW*, p. 149.
61 *HDTW*, p. 151. I am conscious in what follows of trampling rather ponderously on what was very much an *en passant* remark of Austin's. But the topic is an important one, as he would have agreed.
62 *Papers*, p. 130.

63 *HDTW*, p. 151.
64 *HDTW*, p. 153.
65 *Papers*, p. 231.
66 *Papers*, pp. 130–1.
67 *Papers*, p. 131.
68 I noted earlier that, in 'Truth', Austin uses the notion of 'type' without examination. One could also say that there, in deploying his notions of 'demonstrative' and 'descriptive' conventions, he tacitly puts more weight on the term 'descriptive' than, without special measures, it will really bear. He surely did not himself believe that every 'description' is purely factual – or even that that, itself, is a perspicuous remark.
69 *HDTW*, p. 151.
70 *HDTW*, p. 158.
71 *HDTW*, p. 162.
72 *HDTW*, p. 4.
73 *HDTW*, p. 94.
74 *HDTW*, p. 101.

Index

'aberration' (in acting) 70–6
ability 86, 88, 90–1, 93–4
'abuses' 109, 112
accident 68, 72–3, 77, 78
'act', 'action' 66, 67, 69, 78, 103
'agathon' (in Aristotle) 98–101
ambiguity: alleged in verbs of
    perception 19–21; in natural
    languages, 50; of 'phatic acts' 120–1
analysis 85, 87, 92–5, 99, 100, 158
'analytic' 102
Aristotle 98–101
asserting 48, 49, 50
attention 76
Austin, J. L.: appointments in Oxford
    2; election as White's Professor,
    Oxford 1; and 'linguistic
    philosophy' 2–6, 101; and
    philosophy of language 150–1;
    'theory' of philosophy 3–10;
    William James Lecturer, Harvard 1,
    105
authority 33, 36, 38, 39, 43
awareness, 'direct' 14, 15, 16, 21, 22
Ayer, Sir Alfred 2, 11–14, 16–24,
    27–9, 154

believing 32–3, 43–4
Bennett, Jonathan 154
Berkeley, George 24, 131
Berlin, Sir Isaiah 152, 153
'bill-filling' 49

'cap-fitting' 48
'casting' 49
Cavell, Stanley 154
certainty 23, 24, 25
Chisholm, R. M. 155
clarity 104
'commissives' 146
communication 43, 51
conditionals 81–5, 92
conventions: 'descriptive' and
    'demonstrative' 51–5, 161; in
    illocutionary acts 127–33; in
    performative utterance 110–11,
    114–15, 117–19, 128–9, 147, 148; of
    sense and reference 48, 49
co-operation, as philosophical
    'method' 9–10
correspondence (theory of truth) 46–7

definition 100, 104
'deliberately' 73–4
'descriptive' 161; conventions, 51, 52;
    'fallacy' 37, 39; terms 161
determinism 81, 96, 97

emotions 40, 42
entailment 112–13
'eudaimonia' (in Aristotle) 99–100
evidence 23, 25, 26, 27, 41
excuses 65, 67–9, 72–3
'expositives' 146

fact 46; questions of 17–18, 48, 61, 144–5, 156
fallibility 34, 36, 42
Fann, K. T. 152, 153
feelings 40, 41, 42
'force' (of utterances) 126–9, 149–50
Forster, E. M. 79
freedom 69–70
Frege, G. 1, 153

grammar 114–15, 120, 151
Grice, H. P. 154

hallucination 16, 17, 19, 20
Hampshire, Sir Stuart 153
Hare, R. M. 159
Hart, H. L. A. 76
Holdcroft, D. 152
hypotheticals 58–9

'illocution' 125–33, 134, 135, 136, 145–6, 149–50
illusion, 'argument' from 13–22, 27, 30
imperative mood 109, 118
implication 32, 36, 51, 112–13
incorrigibility 23, 24, 25, 42
induction 43, 91
'infelicities' 110, 112
'instancing' 49
intention 66, 76, 78; in speaking 129–32
'intentionally' 74–5, 78

Joseph, H. W. B. 1
justification 34, 38, 43, 44; of actions 67–8

knowledge 32–5; of sensations 34–5; theory of 22–7, 30; and truth 35–40

language: minimal requirements for 47, 51; 'natural economy' of 70, 71, 75–6; philosophy of 150
law: as relevant in philosophy 6; and 'responsibility' 69
'locution' 122–3, 124, 126, 135, 136, 149–50

luck ('bad luck' and 'bad form') 88–9

Magee, Bryan 2
meaning 62, 64, 93, 94, 99–102, 121–2, 126, 149, 151, 156, 160
'mistake' (in acting) 76–7, 78, 79
Moore, G. E. 80–5, 92, 99, 158
motive 92, 93
movements (and 'actions') 66–7

'naming' 48, 49, 52
negation 56–7, 58
Nidditch, P. H. 152
Nowell-Smith, P. H. 89–93, 158

obligation 105–6
opportunity 92, 93–4, 95
optatives 122

Pears, D. F. 14, 158
performatives 35–7, 45, 107–19, 128–9, 133, 146–8, 149; and 'ritual phrases' 37–9, 147, 148
'perlocution' 123–9, 130
'phatic' (acts) 120–1, 122, 149
philosophy, 'linguistic' 2–6
'phonetic' (acts) 119–20, 122, 149
Pitcher, G. W. 152
'placing' 48
Plato 98
Positivism, Logical 3
'precise' 23–5
prediction 34, 83
presupposition 113
pretending 68, 102–4
Price, H. H. 22, 30, 154, 159
Prichard, H. A. 98–100, 105, 106, 158, 159
promising 36, 37, 109–10

questions 122, 150

'real' 69
'reference' 48, 50, 51–3, 121
referring 48, 49, 51, 52
responsibility 68, 69
'rhetic' (acts) 121–2, 149
Ross, Sir David 98

Russell, Bertrand 63
Ryle, Gilbert 2–3, 153

Sbisa, Marina 152
Schiffer, S. R. 152, 160
science 4, 88–9, 96–7
Searle, J. R. 152, 157
self-deception 42
'sense' 52, 121; of words 19–21, 158
sense-data 14, 21–5, 27–9, 30, 31
sentences 49–51, 107, 120;
   hypothetical 58–9
'shall' 83, 146
signs 41
speech acts 47, 48, 148, 151;
   'illocutionary' 125–33, 149;
   'locutionary' 122–3, 124, 125, 149;
   'perlocutionary' 123, 149; 'phatic'
   120–1, 149; 'phonetic' 119–20, 149;
   'rhetic' 121–2, 149
statements 50, 51, 59–61, 107, 143,
   144, 156; categorical 89–92
'stating' 49, 50, 116, 134, 143, 159
Strawson, Sir Peter 46, 62–4, 155, 156,
   157
symbols 51

'synthetic' 102

Travis, C. 152
truth 45–7, 49–51, 53–64, 135–41,
   143–5; contingent and necessary
   59–61; 'fetish' 140–1, 142, 143; not
   always determinable 57–8, 137,
   138–9, 140, 143–4
trying 85–7
'type' 47, 48, 51, 52, 55–9, 144, 156,
   161

'uptake' 127, 132
Urmson, J. O. 152, 153, 158

'vague' 23, 25
value-fact 'fetish' 140–5
value-judgments 61, 144
'verdictives' 142
verdicts 133
verification 22–5; 'direct' 90–1

White, A. R. 157
will, freedom of 69–70
Wisdom, John 34, 155
Wittgenstein, L. 3